History and Cultural Theory

History and Cultural Theory

Simon Gunn

PEARSON
Longman

Harlow, England • London • New York • Boston • San Francisco • Toronto
Sydney • Tokyo • Singapore • Hong Kong • Seoul • Taipei • New Delhi
Cape Town • Madrid • Mexico City • Amsterdam • Munich • Paris • Milan

PEARSON EDUCATION LIMITED

Edinburgh Gate
Harlow CM20 2JE
United Kingdom
Tel: +44 (0)1279 623623
Fax: +44 (0)1279 431059
Website: www.pearsoned.co.uk

First edition published in Great Britain in 2006

© Pearson Education Limited 2006

The right of Simon Gunn to be identified as author of this work has been asserted
by him in accordance with the Copyright, Designs and Patents Act 1988.

ISBN 978-0-582-78408-6

British Library Cataloguing in Publication Data
A CIP catalogue record for this book can be obtained from the British Library

Library of Congress Cataloging in Publication Data
A CIP catalog record for this book can be obtained from the Library of Congress

10 9 8 7 6 5 4 3 2
10 09 08 07

Set by 35 in 10/13.5pt Sabon
Printed and bound in Malaysia

The Publisher's policy is to use paper manufactured from sustainable forests.

For Gabriele

Contents

Preface

The origins of this book go back a long way in my own history. I remember the excitement as a teenager of reading Edmund Wilson's *To the Finland Station* (1972), an intellectual history of European Marxist and radical thought culminating, as the title implies, in Lenin's return from exile to Petrograd and the Russian revolution of 1917. Although in many ways a conventional history of ideas, Wilson's account was exhilarating because it demonstrated how history could be combined with political theory in a mutually illuminating manner. At university in the late 1970s social and labour history were in the ascendancy, and historiographical debates were often presented as set-piece confrontations between Marxists and non-Marxists, an intellectual battle waged over a highly detailed and rapidly growing body of historical scholarship. Through studying European literature and intellectual history, however, I was made aware of new ideas filtering in to the human sciences from diverse theoretical sources, including anthropology, philosophy and psychoanalysis. By the mid-1980s, when I was undertaking my doctorate in modern history it was clear that the intellectual ground was shifting; economistic forms of Marxism had given way to more culturally-inflected versions under the influence of Gramsci and, still more controversial, the ideas of Saussurean linguistics were beginning to be registered in social historical analysis, soon to become christened the 'linguistic turn'. As a historian in a multi-disciplinary school of cultural studies during the 1990s, there was indeed no escaping from cultural theory and what had been designated more generally as the 'cultural turn': literary theory, queer theory, postcolonialism and Lacanian psychoanalysis became part of the fabric of intellectual life.

Autobiography is always both individual and social; it combines in varying proportions the unique and the representative. There is also a tendency, not least among academics, to universalise one's experience and to 'speak the structures' by projecting one's own educational background as a norm. I am aware how much my own intellectual trajectory has been particular, a matter of people, places and times. But having interviewed theoretically-inclined historians of different generations about their entry into the profession and their own intellectual formation, I also recognise how much of the experience we often assume to be individual is in fact shared. Time and again these historians spoke of the importance for their own ideas of mixing in a multi-disciplinary environment, often as research students. In some cases this had fuelled a subsequent sense of disillusion and isolation, resulting from taking up posts in single discipline depart-ments. History, many of them suggested, has become a more insular, inward-looking subject over the last decade or so (Gunn and Rawnsley 2006). At the same time, they also shared a common background in the intellectual changes of the last quarter century, changes which were as often as not marked out by particular theoretical debates within history – Marxism and the labour aristocracy thesis, Gramsci and 'bourgeois he-gemony', the linguistic turn, postmodernism, Subaltern Studies and so on. Intellectually, the careers of many historians, including my own, have been lived out in relation not so much to new empirical findings as to a series of theoretical moments, or, more clumsily if accurately, conjunc-tions of history and theory.

This book is the product, then, of the series of theoretical moments which have marked historical writing in Britain and elsewhere since the 1980s, and which are defined collectively by reference to cultural theory and the cultural turn. It starts from a number of basic questions. In what ways has 'history' been configured in recent cultural theory? How has cul-tural theory impacted on historical practice? How have historians applied cultural theory in their own work? And how is history placed in the wake of the cultural turn? What exactly has changed? Although these questions might seem obvious enough to the outsider, they are not those that have generally been asked within the discipline. The reception of cultural the-ory – more often introduced under the heading of 'postmodernism' – has been highly contentious in the discipline of history and as a result discus-sion of the subject has been polemicised rather than properly debated, especially in Britain and the United States. The polemical tone, in turn, has tended to obscure the particular ways in which theory itself has been adopted in historical circles. There has been a tendency, for instance, to elide cultural theory with a set of epistemological concerns about the sta-tus of historical knowledge and the relationship between 'representation' and the 'real', which relate primarily to American debates of the 1960s in philosophy of history and only correspond in part with the wider concerns of cultural theory. Thus historians could be forgiven for imagining that the topic begins and ends with the question of whether knowledge of the past is possible or not and if so on what terms. But if cultural theorists do demonstrate a concern with knowledge, especially the politics of knowledge, they also have much to say about other topics of historical importance, including those examined in this book: power, identity, modernity, culture and so on. Alternatively, some historians have tended to take inspiration from one specific theorist, such as Michel Foucault or Hayden White, while ignoring the larger field of cultural theory of which such figures are a part. As a result there is often little awareness among historians of what implications this larger body of thought might have for their researches and what opportunities it might offer for the process of historical interpretation.

Indeed, the polemical and largely negative reception that cultural theory has been accorded among historians runs counter to the latter's impulse towards dissolving oppositions and refusing closure. Partly for this reason I have sought in this book to follow the example of Peter Burke in his earlier work *History and Social Theory*, who declared his intention to tread a line between 'the uncritical zeal for new approaches and the blind devotion to traditional practice' (Burke 1999, 164). In effect, I have sought to apply a critical perspective to both histories and theories while allowing readers space to develop their own viewpoint without being rushed to judgement. Arguments are developed within each of the chapters and across the book as a whole. In the latter case, the first chapter, 'Historicising Theory', and the final chapter, 'Theorising History', can be read as a unity, providing respectively a historical framework in which to comprehend the emergence of cultural theory and a summing up through which its multiple effects on historiography can be grasped. As a whole the book seeks to show not only the varied forms that cultural theory takes but also the very different ways it has been appropriated and set to work by historians.

In writing I have also sought to avoid too close an identification with any particular theorist or position for the reasons just stated. Nevertheless, the reader will detect a particular interest in and sympathy for the ideas of Pierre Bourdieu, whose own work consistently strove to move beyond the dualities of contemporary thought, including the division between subjective experience and objective science. Bourdieu (who was the most cited theorist in British sociology journals in 2000) remains relatively unknown in Anglo-American history (Halsey 2004, 173). Given his long-term dialogue with historians of France, such as Roger Chartier, Alain

Corbin and Robert Darnton, and his insistence on the necessity of inter-linking historical with cultural and sociological studies, however, Bour-dieu's work represents an important resource for the creation of reflexive histories in the aftermath of the cultural turn.

It is impossible, of course, to undertake a study of theory without incurring the problems of definition. 'Cultural theory' is a term widely (and loosely) used in the humanities. It overlaps but is not synonymous with 'critical theory' (more strongly identified with Frankfurt School Marxism) and 'social theory' (more directly wedded to the social and political sciences). As I explain in Chapter One, it is used here to designate a number of broad, interconnected currents in contemporary thought, from elements of structuralism and post-structuralism to cultural anthro-pology and postcolonial criticism. The purpose of this book is to examine how these modes of thought have interacted with historical practice – that is to say, scholarly research and writing – over the last twenty years or so. While the aim is to be wide-ranging, the study is inevitably not compre-hensive. There is little of substance, for example, on the influence of Freudian or Lacanian psychoanalysis (an important strand within some cultural theory) on historical thought or, conversely, on the history of *mentalités* (the mental structures of past societies); readers in search of these will need to look elsewhere (e.g. Alexander 1994; Damousi and Reynolds 2003; Burke 1986). In selecting histories that exemplify the rela-tionship with aspects of cultural theory in the chapters that follow, more-over, I am aware how much the examples given reflect the extent of the scope and limitations of my own historical knowledge and expertise, despite efforts to draw on a spread of subjects, regions and periods. As a result, much of the focus is on the social, cultural and political histories of eigh-teenth- and nineteenth-century Britain and northern Europe, with some attention also to parts of what became known for a period as the British Empire. However, the judgement has been made that it is better to argue from those domains in which some expertise or familiarity can be claimed than from those where they cannot. It is to be hoped that readers will find the historical examples instructive when thinking about applying the theo-retical approaches discussed here to their own historical field and questions.

In researching and writing this book I have been very aware of those who have trod a similar path before me, notably Peter Burke, who has written extensively on historiography, culture and theory, and Peter Novick, whose magnificent study of American historiography, *That Noble Dream*, still towers over the field. Nevertheless, so far as I am aware this is the first study which sets out to examine systematically the impact on historical writing of the range of cultural theory produced since the 1960s. In formulating the ideas and in writing I have incurred a substantial debt to friends, colleagues and family which I am pleased to be able to acknowledge. Patrick Joyce and John Seed have provoked and greatly widened my interest in history and theory at crucial points over the last two decades and I remain very grateful for their friendship. Geoffrey Crossick was helpful at the outset in suggesting that this might be a book worth writing and Heather MacCallum at Pearson proved a patient critic of ideas in their early stages. Within the specialist field of modern urban history Bob Morris and Richard Rodger have been generous in tolerating my own enthusiasms for cultural theory and cultural history, and I have learned much from the annual Urban History Group meetings we have organised together since the late 1990s. I was fortunate to have a stay as a Visiting Scholar at the Department of History at the University of Melbourne, Australia in summer 2003, and would like to thank historians there for their hospitality and enthusiasm for intellectual engagement, especially Joy Damousi, Antonia Finucane and Stephen Brown; Alan Mayne was an excellent host, sharing his knowledge of cultural archaeology and the Australian goldfields; Anne Gunn showed me something of my own family history in Melbourne; and Graeme Davison at Monash University was generous in giving his time to discuss Australian history.

Parts of this book have been given at seminars and conferences in Britain and abroad. In particular, I would like to thank Peter Stearns at George Mason University, Washington D.C., for his invitation to contribute to a symposium on 'The Future of Social History' in October 2004, and to the participants for their comments, especially James Cronin, Prasannan Parthasarathi and Daniel Walkowitz; and Jonathan Rose and his colleagues at the History department seminar at Drew University, New Jersey. I was fortunate also to benefit from contributing to an ESRC-funded symposium on 'Bourdieu and Cultural Capital' at St. Hugh's College, Oxford in January 2004; my thanks go to the organisers at the Centre for Research on Socio-Cultural Change (CRESC), Tony Bennett, Elizabeth Silva, Mike Savage and Alan Warde. With Alastair Owens at Queen Mary, University of London, I co-organised a strand at the European Social Science History Conference in Berlin in March 2004 entitled 'Theorising the Modern City' and I am grateful to all the contributors, particularly Matthew Gandy, Leif Jerram and Chris Otter, for what proved an illuminating series on the relationship between urban history and cultural theory. The book has also benefited indirectly from a project, funded by the Higher Education Academy Subject Centre for History,

Classics and Archaeology, on the place of theory in university history, conducted with my colleague at Leeds Metropolitan University, Stuart Rawnsley. For their support and encouragement on this project I am especially indebted to Alan Booth and Alun Munslow.

Closer to home the School of Cultural Studies at Leeds Metropolitan has been a productive environment in which to engage in the study of both history and theory. I have learned – and continue to learn – much from colleagues there. On this occasion I would like to thank especially Krista Cowman, Janet Douglas, Mary Eagleton, Max Farrar, Louise Jackson (now of Edinburgh University), Gordon Johnston, Christer Petley and Fiona Russell. Many of them have offered valuable comments or criticisms on the chapters, though I alone remain responsible for any errors of fact or judgement. The university has also been generous in providing a period of leave and financial support, which has considerably eased the research and writing. Students, too, have played a significant part in the making of this book, not least students of English and History at Leeds Met who will recognise much of what follows from their own studies on my *Reading the Past* course over the last few years. Students on the Masters and PhD programmes have likewise been a continual stimulus to critical thought about how history and theory might profitably be configured in specific research projects; in particular I have benefited from discussions with Gordon Williams, Anne Wilkinson, Ian Macdonald, Lee Edwards, Janet Parr and Susan Cottam. In helping with production of the book I would like to give special thanks to Pat Cook in the School of Cultural Studies and Hetty Reid and Christina Wipf Perry at Pearson.

My greatest debt by far, though, is to my wife, Gabriele Griffin, who not only tolerated me borrowing her books but also shared with me her own wide knowledge of culture and theory. At every stage I have benefited from her enthusiasm, perspicacity and humour. It is to Gabriele that I dedicate this book with love.

Leeds
December 2005

CHAPTER ONE

Historicising Theory

On a freezing November night in 1979 a large audience gathered in a dilapidated church in north Oxford. The occasion was the annual conference of the History Workshop movement and the crowd had assembled to hear a debate between three speakers: E.P. Thompson, the celebrated author of *The Making of the English Working Class*; Stuart Hall, Professor of Sociology and one of the founding figures of the British New Left; and Richard Johnson of the Birmingham Centre for Contemporary Cultural Studies, a centre renowned for its openness to new theoretical currents. What occurred that evening was an electrifying piece of intellectual theatre but one that also disturbed many who witnessed it. The subject of debate was the impact of the French Marxist theoretician, Louis Althusser, on historical thought and socialist politics. Thompson was then at the height of his fame as an historian, and fresh from his lengthy denunciation of Althusser, published as *The Poverty of Theory* (1978). On the stage at Oxford Thompson set out also to demolish Hall and Johnson, who were more receptive to, if not uncritical of, Althusser's brand of structuralist Marxism. While Hall and Johnson protested against the 'absolutist' tone and substance of Thompson's critique, Thompson himself thundered against a theory which he found antihistorical, determinist and inimical to socialist political practice. The result, in the words of an observer, was akin to a 'gladiatorial combat' enacted with 'maximum theatrical force' (Samuel 1981, 376–8).

What was at stake in this now legendary encounter? And why was it so bitter? Revisiting the debate after an interval of some twenty-five years it is possible to peel back successive layers of significance. At the first, most obvious level, the debate concerned the influence of Althusserian ideas on British intellectual life, Thompson warning that this abstract form of 'scientific' Marxism had already permeated philosophy, art history and English studies, and was 'now massing on the frontiers of history itself' (Samuel 1981, 378). Such was Thompson's prestige in left-wing historical circles at the period that he contributed largely to stemming this particular invasion: the impact of Althusserianism on British (and North American) historiography was minimal, although the influence of structuralism – sardonically termed 'French flu' by Thompson – was to return within a matter of years, as we shall see later in the chapter. Secondly, the debate raised the issue of the status of history as a form of knowledge and as a guide to political practice. Thompson's appeal to 'history' as a court in which to judge 'theory' raised the suspicions of Stuart Hall, who saw lurking in it the idea of history as a knowledge in which the evidence merely 'speaks for itself'. From this perspective, Hall argued, 'Thompson's "History", like Althusser's "Theory" is erected into an absolute' (Samuel 1981, 383). Finally, Hall and Johnson both drew attention to the relationship between empirical method and theoretical reflection, questioning where Thompson's model of historical interpretation derived from and how the categories it relied upon, such as 'experience', might be justified philosophically.

Such were the specific intellectual issues that engaged the participants at Oxford. Yet the debate also raised some of the oldest and most vexed questions regarding history and philosophy. In it was reflected the idea that they represent two different orders of knowledge, one local and particular, the other general and abstract. Just as 'history' is often understood by historians to inhabit a sphere outside or in opposition to 'theory', so philosophy is often depicted as occupying a realm of ideas beyond the pressures of historical circumstance. In the encounter with sociology and cultural studies we see reflected history's difficult relations with other disciplines, which the French historian Fernand Braudel famously referred to as a 'dialogue of the deaf' (Burke 1999, 2). Implicit also is the problem of the definition of 'history' itself, whether as a global process – the march of History through time, as the effort to understand the present as the product of the past, or, more modestly, as the attempt to make sense of the patchwork of knowledge about the past. With its plurality of subtly shifting meanings, 'history' itself is a moving target so that it is often unclear in intellectual debate, such as that at Oxford, whether or not the protagonists are talking about the same thing.

Yet history was only one dimension of the History Workshop event. The encounter was also about 'theory', specifically the form of Marxism associated with Louis Althusser, itself seen as representing a larger body of thought identified with French structuralism. 'Theory' can be defined abstractly to mean any model of explanation which seeks to cover more than a single empirical or historical instance. Historians refer to theory in this sense often, distinguishing it from the notion of theory as representing universal laws. Thus one can have a theory of revolutions or of industrialisation that aims to explain in generic terms how these phenomena occur, but is not reducible to a single example, such as the French revolution or Japanese industrialisation. In this book, though, theory refers more specifically to a body of thought known as 'cultural theory', commensurate with a number of major intellectual currents that swept through the human sciences in the second half of the twentieth century. It includes elements of continental (as opposed to Anglo-American analytical) philosophy; structuralism and post-structuralism; cultural anthropology; and postcolonial criticism. Given the eclectic nature of this thought it has impacted differentially across the human sciences, particular ideas and emphases being taken up in anthropology and geography, for example, others in literature and art history. The impact of cultural theory has also been temporally differentiated, new ways of thinking succeeding one another in waves, from structuralism in the 1970s to postcolonialism in the 1990s. This 'theory' has not always come by way of philosophy but from a variety of sources, such as the anthropology of Clifford Geertz and the linguistics of Ferdinand de Saussure. It is 'cultural' in the sense that its practitioners have taken cultural forms – texts, rituals, practices, and, above all, language – as their objects of study. But it is also 'cultural' in its emphasis on hermeneutics, the study of interpretation and the creation of meaning, and its concomitant critique of the positivist or 'scientific' tradition of social science. Cultural theory dovetails here with critical theory, as also in its stress on 'reflexivity', the capacity to reflect critically on the politics of knowledge inherent in any given interpretation or position. Understood in this broad fashion, cultural theory encompasses a range of thinkers from the linguist Mikhail Bakhtin to the sociologist Pierre Bourdieu, from the anthropologist Mary Douglas to the proponent of literary 'deconstruction', Jacques Derrida.

'Culture', of course, has itself become a suspect concept, especially in anthropology where it has come under critical fire for the assumption of depth and coherence that attends its analytical usage, no less than for its historical association with European colonialism (Sewell 1999). But it remains an indispensable part of contemporary theorising as the anthropologist James Clifford, who has done more than anyone to interrogate the term, has acknowledged: culture, Clifford has written, is a 'deeply compromised concept that I cannot yet do without' (Clifford 1988, 10).

Cultural theory likewise has been accused of its own sins of omission, amongst which the assumed absence of an historical dimension looms large. Yet the opposite can also be maintained. Critics like Robert Young have argued that an idea of history haunts contemporary Western theory, including the post-structuralism of Derrida and Jean-François Lyotard. It is thus not 'history' that has been rejected but particular versions of it, those predicated on the grand narratives of progress and Western domin-ance. 'The reproach that post-structuralism has neglected history really consists of the complaint that it questioned History' (Young, R. 1990, 25). More concretely, the biography of an intellectual such as Michel Foucault reveals him as closely linked to the networks of historical thought in postwar France. At the Ecole Normale Supérieure in Paris, where Foucault studied in the late 1940s, he was a contemporary of Jacques le Goff and Emmanuel Le Roy Ladurie, subsequently to become leading figures in the *Annales* school of history. The publication of his sec-ond book, *Madness and Civilization* (1967[1961]), was facilitated by the pioneer of the history of *mentalités*, Philippe Ariés, series editor at the Paris publisher Plon. And Foucault's election to the prestigious Collége de France was sponsored by Fernand Braudel, then the doyen of *Annales* his-torians, where Foucault took the title Professor of History of Systems of Thought (Eribon 1993). The extent of intellectual connections revealed in biographies like that of Foucault belies the idea of disciplinary isolation and a rigid division between 'history' and 'theory'. Not only Foucault, but theorists such as Pierre Bourdieu, Michel de Certeau and Gayatri Chakravorty Spivak have had a long-term interest in or engagement with historical practice.

'History' and 'theory', then, do not exist in a simple state of separation or antithesis. They are complex terms whose genealogies are intimately bound up with each other: there are theories of history just as there are histories of theory. The purpose of this chapter is to explain some of these connections as a precursor to the more detailed examples of history and theory that make up the rest of this book. What is cultural theory? Where does it come from? And what does it mean for historical studies? One of the ways of answering these questions is historically, that is to say by sketching the history of structuralism and post-structuralism as they have impacted on the human sciences over the last half century or so. Before we can do this, however, we need to look briefly at its obverse, the theory of history – how 'history' itself has been constituted as a discipline and an object of knowledge.

The legacy of Rankean empiricism

Far from being innocent of theory, as is often assumed, orthodox professional historiography is in fact replete with it. 'Theory' here takes the form of a series of overlapping '-isms' which have shaped history as a disciplinary practice since the nineteenth century. They include positivism, the belief that the historical process is subject to laws or generalisations akin to the natural sciences; historicism, the notion that each historical period is unique and must be studied on its own terms; humanism, the idea that history is the study of 'man' (and his essentially unchanging nature) across time. Spanning all these is empiricism, the theory that knowledge is derived inductively from sensory experience or visible evidence and that it corresponds to reality. 'History', Richard Evans has asserted, 'is an empirical discipline' and the hard-won knowledge that derives from it can 'approach a reconstruction of past reality that may be partial and provisional . . . but is nevertheless true' (Evans 1997, 249). Not all historians subscribe to these theoretical assumptions. Positivism no longer attracts many adherents as it did in the early twentieth century, for instance, and it is common for professional historians to combine empirical methods with theoretical models drawn from other disciplinary fields, such as economics and social science. Moreover, the theories of history themselves are often complex and ambiguous. Historicism, for example, is both past- and present-centred. For while it affirms the separate integrity of each historical period, it carries a further meaning in which periods may be understood as linked in succession, leading up to and producing the present. Nevertheless, taken as a whole the series of theoretical positions outlined here serve to underpin most if not all modern historical research.

These theories have their own histories, of course, which tend to converge on the figure of the early nineteenth-century German historian, Leopold von Ranke, as the originator of historical empiricism. It is Ranke, as Peter Novick has observed, who stands as the 'imaginary origin' of modern historical method and of its 'founding myth' (Novick 1988, 3). Ranke's empirical method was forged in the 1830s in opposition to the influential philosophical historicism of his contemporary, G.W.F. Hegel, for whom history was understood in idealist fashion as the gradual unfolding of a transcendent Idea or Spirit embodied in an historical community. For Hegel every historian was the product of his own times and modes of thought: he 'brings his categories with him and sees the data through them' (Hegel 1956, 11). By contrast, Ranke proposed a concept of historical knowledge predicated on analysis of the documentary record, scrupulous ascertaining of the historical facts about any events ('what actually happened') and an understanding that every period possessed its own unique essence or character. At the same time, each period was sequentially linked to that which succeeded it, so that history could be understood as a whole, an intelligible linear process connecting the past with the present. History was categorically distinct from philosophy, according to Ranke; it was concerned with the concrete and particular not the general and abstract. But Ranke also warned against a view of history based on specifics or facts alone. From detailed scrutiny of the facts of particular events the historian should move towards a 'universal view', identifying their unity and larger significance, ultimately contributing to the construction of a world history embodied in the progress of what Ranke termed the 'leading nations' (Ranke in Stern 1970, 54–63).

Ranke's legacy has clearly been of great importance for historical scholarship but it has also been an ambiguous one. His emphasis on careful study of documentary sources as the mainstay of historical scholarship and his respect for historical difference – the alterity of the past – continue to serve as fundamental tenets of the discipline. However, recent studies have been cautious about exaggerating the modernity of Ranke's views and lionising him as the 'founding father' of historiography. His famous dictum that the historian should represent the past 'as it actually was' has been mistranslated, according to Georg Iggers; its proper translation is 'how, essentially, things happened' (Iggers 1973, xli–xlii). The error is significant since by emphasising the 'essence' of the past Ranke partook of the tradition of German idealism as well as that of empiricism, and his thought also shared other features of early nineteenth-century German romanticism, its nationalism, conservatism and reverence for the state (Novick 1988, 26–31). Furthermore, while eschewing the idea of divine guidance in human history, Ranke held back from a strictly secular interpretation of the past, arguing that in certain instances it was possible to discern the 'finger of God' at work. However significant a part Ranke may have played in the creation of modern historical method, in short, he too requires historical contextualisation within the beliefs of his time.

The influence of Ranke's thought on the growth of historical scholarship also varied between nation states. In Germany, where twenty-eight university chairs in history had been established by 1850, his role may have been more limited than was once thought since the prestige of the Humboldtian ideal of the university meant that various models of scientific historical research were early in circulation (Breisach 1983,

228–38; Lambert 2003, 45). History was institutionalised later in French universities, though a scientistic, fact-driven model of research spread rapidly under the Third Republic in the last quarter of the nineteenth century; the first PhD programme was established at the Ecole Pratique des Hautes Etudes in 1868 (Nora 1996, 5; Iggers 2005, 27). In France, though, the influence of the German example of historical scholarship was qualified by a native positivism deriving from the thought of Auguste Comte and Henri Saint-Simon (Bentley 2002, 424–5). Oddly, it was therefore in the United States and Britain that the impact of Ranke appears to have been greatest. In North American universities from the later nineteenth century, according to Peter Novick, Ranke was adopted as the architect of a new type of scholarly history, marked by a 'fanaticism for veracity' modelled on the natural sciences (Novick 1988, 23). Yet as we have seen, this adoption of Ranke was predicated on a misreading of what was in fact a more complex body of thought. In Britain Ranke's ideas were likewise taken up with alacrity; the first article published in the *English Historical Review* on its establishment in 1886 was Lord Acton on 'German schools of history'. Here they were yoked to a native tradition of empiricism, seen as stretching back to Bacon and the sixteenth-century origins of the scientific revolution (Joyce 1998, 217–18). Consequently, the establishment of history as an academic discipline under Stubbs at Oxford from the 1860s and Tout at Manchester at the turn of the twentieth century was marked by an unwavering commitment to empirical method, focused on a scrupulous evaluation of primary sources aimed at reconstructing the past on its own terms. While the methods attributed to Ranke were received more cautiously at Cambridge, the study of history had come to form an integral component in the education of the English élite by the early twentieth century. According to Reba Soffer, the historical education provided at Oxford and Cambridge rested on firm empirical foundations: 'every sound student was expected to yield to the force of the evidence which would lead him to the truth . . . Most historians assumed that the unequivocally given and objectively true past yielded truth discernible to any interested student' (Soffer 1994, 12, 210).

As in the United States, therefore, it was a selective version of Rankean thought that was adopted in Britain (Bentley 2002, 436–7). While Ranke could usefully be drawn upon to justify an emphasis on the pre-eminence of political and constitutional history, and national history itself, more conspicuously statist elements in his writings were ignored in the British context where laissez-faire remained the prevailing ideology. Later the same tradition was to be used by historians of parliament like Lewis

Namier to uphold the primacy of political history and defend it against the threats of Marxism and the contaminating influence of other disciplines, such as sociology, when these began to be registered under the auspices of R.H. Tawney and Eileen Power at the London School of Economics in the interwar years (Berg 1996; Colley 1989, 21–45; Warren 2003, 35–6). In the present day Rankeanism continues to serve as an important reference point for the epistemological justification of historical knowledge. In the celebrated libel case on the charge of 'Holocaust denial', brought by David Irving against the American academic Deborah Lipstadt in 2000, it was noteworthy that all parties, including witnesses such as the social historian Richard Evans, appealed to the Rankean model of objective, evidence-based archival research (Evans 2002a).

Not all historians have approved this model, however. In a famous essay, 'That Noble Dream', published in 1935, the American historian Charles Beard dismissed the possibility of objective history and stressed instead the partial nature of all interpretations. Beard deliberately set out to encourage critical reflection on the grounds of historical knowledge by asking the question, 'What do we think we are doing when we write history?' (Stern 1970, 414–28). Nevertheless, the Rankean model functions, especially in Anglo-American historiography, as a disciplinary commonsense. Peter Novick has termed this commonsense 'historical objectivity'. According to Novick it encompasses a 'sprawling collection of assumptions' including:

a commitment to the reality of the past and truth, and to truth as correspondence to that reality; a sharp separation between knower and known, between fact and value, and, above all, between history and fiction. Historical facts are seen as prior to and independent of interpretation; the value of an interpretation is judged by how well it accounts for the facts; if contradicted by the facts it must be abandoned. Truth is one, not perspectival. Whatever patterns exist in history are 'found', not 'made'. Though successive generations of historians might, as their perspectives shifted, attribute different significance to events in the past, the meaning of those events was unchanging (Novick 1988, 1–2).

For Novick, it is these various assumptions which constitute the 'founding myth' of the American historical profession, whose patron saint is Ranke. But they represent, of course, only one way of doing history. Professional history does not have a monopoly of knowledge of the past; memory, biography and archaeology, to name but a few, are other significant ways of knowing about it. It can be argued, indeed, that Rankean empiricism produces a rather narrow version of reality, dependent on a hierarchy of sources which prioritises institutionally-derived documentary records (and thus a particular top-down version of politics, for instance) while denigrating other types of evidence about the past. The distrust of many historians for oral testimony, which requires that every practitioner defend its truth against the alleged vagaries of memory, is one example of the normative regulation of historical enquiry. As this suggests, the ideology of objectivism within which Rankean history operates rests on a number of covert assumptions and orientations. It is Eurocentric to the extent that it views Europe or the West as the originating source of certain historical models – of democracy, capitalism, progress – which the rest of the world is then seen as necessarily following at a later date. Within this perspective history comes to be represented as a unified process with a single direction ('development' or 'modernisation'), an historicism itself predicated on the definition of historical time as linear and homogeneous, rather than as cyclical, multiple or rhythmic (Chakrabarty 2000, 6–11; Ermath 1992). Moreover, for postcolonial historians such as Dipesh Chakrabarty, Eurocentrism and historicism are not merely an unfortunate by-product of certain types of colonialist history which can be avoided by a greater degree of self-consciousness. Rather, they are built into the construction of Rankean historiography as it is deployed within the academy (Chakrabarty 2000). Indeed, Ranke himself maintained that the history of the 'racially kindred nations either of Germanic or Germanic-Latin descent' was 'the core of all modern history' and historicism permeated his thought: 'If we picture [the] sequence of centuries, each with its unique essence, all linked together, then we shall have attained universal history, from the very beginning to the present day' (Stern 1970, 56, 61).

One way of understanding cultural theory, then, is to see it as a critique not of history as such but of historical objectivity or Rankean empiricism – that is to say, of a particular model or construction of history. The concern with history which we have noted in figures like Michel Foucault and Gayatri Spivak derives importantly from the attempt to escape this model with its assumptions of neutral objectivity and linear temporality, and thus to create qualitatively different histories. But the critique of empiricism and historicism stems also from a larger tradition of thought of which Foucault and others are part, whose roots lay in the intellectual movement known as structuralism, centred on France after the Second World War. To understand the history of modern cultural theory, and its relationship with historical thought, we need to look back to the ideas of structuralism.

Structuralism and its impact

The origins of structuralism lie in developments in linguistics around the First World War, associated with the Swiss linguist Ferdinand de Saussure and the Russian literary critic Roman Jakobson. Fundamental to their thought was the idea that meaning was independent of the individual (or in the case of Jakobson, of a particular literary form) and inhered instead in the system or structure of language itself, the principles of which they claimed to illuminate. Structuralism was therefore concerned with the linguistic system which made meaning possible. After 1945 these ideas were taken up in France especially and extended to diverse fields, including anthropology and Marxist political theory. Structuralism in this broader context was concerned with identifying the objective conditions that could be said to underpin and generate the phenomena observed, whether these be cultures, literary texts or social systems (Edgar and Sedgwick 2002, 381–4). In its postwar French form, structuralism came to represent a reaction to certain prevailing modes of thought, notably Sartrean phenomenology, which started from the experience of the embodied individual in practical engagement with the world, and Hegelian Marxism, in which classes rather than individuals were the bearers of history and reason. For structuralists, by contrast, individuals and classes were understood to be the products of systemic or structural processes, not the subjects or agents of history. More strongly than any previous post-Enlightenment philosophy, structuralism sought to move beyond the subject and humanism as the basis of knowledge. Consequently – and controversially – structuralist critics viewed earlier components of Enlightenment thought, notably historicism and humanism, not as antithetical to the fascism, war and genocide that devastated Europe in the first half of the twentieth century, but as at least partly responsible for them (West 1997, 154ff.; Young, R. 1990, 8).

Three key figures shaped and exemplified the development of structuralist thought. The first, as we have seen, was Saussure, whose *Course in General Linguistics* (1916) is regarded as the founding text of semiotics, the science of signs. Saussure's analysis extended to all sign systems, understood as forms of communication, not just to spoken language. His famous distinction between *langue* (language as a system) and *parole* (speech) had a number of important implications for the study of culture. First, meaning was seen not to inhere in words themselves, but was generated by the structural system of relations which underscored language and which he sought to analyse. Consequently, there was no necessary relation between signs (e.g. words) and their referents – objects and people in the 'real' world. Meaning was established within the linguistic system, not in relation to a domain of reality or experience beyond it. As Russian linguists like Jakobson and Mikhail Bakhtin emphasised, one of the key ways in which meaning was constructed in language was through binary opposition, so that the meaning of 'night' was only comprehensible in relation to that of 'day', 'heat' in relation to 'cold', and so on. The variety of languages – English, Russian, Japanese – though organised differently, were viewed by structuralists as operating according to broadly similar principles, so that it was possible to uncover the universal mechanisms by which meaning is linguistically generated.

These insights were taken up by the French anthropologist Claude Lévi-Strauss and applied to the study of culture in works such as *Structural Anthropology* (1958) and *The Savage Mind* (1962). Cultures according to Lévi-Strauss worked like language and could indeed be conceived as such. The meaning attributed to any activity in a given society thus derived from its place within an overall system or structure, so that myths, rituals and kinship relations could all be analysed according to specific principles of organisation. Binary oppositions, especially that between the human and the natural worlds, were also given special importance in explaining the ordering of relationships within a culture. And like Saussure, Lévi-Strauss proposed a universal dimension to culture, so that it would ultimately be possible to find a unifying set of structures which underlay and generated all cultural systems, according to a common logic inherent in the human mind (Sturrock 1993, 41).

By the 1960s structuralism in France had become pervasive, encompassing domains such as Marxist theory, whose chief luminary, as we have already observed, was Louis Althusser. Althusser's Marxism, outlined in a series of works such as *For Marx* (1959) and *Lenin and Philosophy* (1971), both reflected and significantly modified French structuralist thought. It extended the linguistic analogy to the study of society, so that economic relations could be understood as structured like a language, while social systems were seen to work according to a 'logic of arrangement', of 'articulation of parts within a structure', rather than in a hierarchal, causal relationship of pre-eminently economic determination (Hall, S. 1983, 28). As this suggests, Althusser's theory involved a significant downplaying of the economic sphere, which was seen as determining only in the 'last instance', and a concomitant expansion of the 'relative autonomy' of politics and culture. But this did not imply a greater role for human agency. Following structuralist principles, Althusser maintained that culture and ideology produced forms of human consciousness and action, not the other way round. Thus ideology was simultaneously an imaginary relation of individuals to their conditions of existence and what constituted them as individuals in the first place. Through the mechanism of 'interpellation' the individual subject was literally called into existence by ideology, itself operating across the spheres of organised religion, education, the family, the mass media and so on, which collectively Althusser defined as the 'ideological State apparatuses' (Althusser 1971, 136–65).

What, then, did these various sets of ideas have in common and what implications do they have for historical study? First, it is notable that they all took language as the model for the organisation of a wide range of phenomena, from communication to cultural and social organisation. Whether as metaphor or object of study, language was seen to hold the key to how all kinds of cultural, economic and social systems work. Secondly, the mechanisms by which these systems or structures operate were viewed as functioning unconsciously, without the knowledge – or with only the partial knowledge – of the individuals and groups subjected to them. Human agency was therefore greatly reduced; structures operated behind the backs of the subjects who registered and enacted them. In this sense, structuralism represented a form of anti-humanism – hence Lévi-Strauss's famous assertion in the last chapter of *The Savage Mind* that anthropology should start by dissolving the category of 'man'. Finally, the framework of explanation in structuralism was synchronic rather than diachronic; that is to say, the component parts of any system, whether linguistic, cultural or societal, tended to be understood relationally, by reference to their relationship with other parts at any given point, rather than dynamically, in terms of their development over time. Consequently, ideas of historical depth and agency were downplayed or rejected altogether. For Lévi-Strauss, for instance, the commonsense view of history as a chronological progression was predicated on a false notion of continuity, itself rooted in a Western – that is to say, culturally specific – conception of historical time as linear and sequential (Lévi-Strauss 1966, 259–60).

However, history was not banished altogether from structuralism. A later generation of French cultural theorists, including Foucault and Pierre Bourdieu, learned much from a structuralist-inflected history of science, whose luminaries between the 1930s and the 1960s were Gaston Bachelard and Georges Canguilhelm – the latter was the supervisor of Foucault's thesis on the history of madness. What Bachelard and Canguihelm proposed was a history that went beyond the positivist account of the sciences as progressing through a cumulative sequence of 'discoveries', each of which rendered the knowledge that had gone before null and void. Rather than focusing on the products of science, in the form of new discoveries and truths, they directed attention to their epistemological conditions, the particular conditions of truth or the framing of scientific problems – what Bachelard termed the *problèmatique* – operating at a given historical period. Taking the cue from Lévi-Strauss, they also emphasised the differential historical time of the sciences, both in relation to one another and to wider historical developments in the economic and political spheres. The sciences proceeded according to logics and temporalities that did not automatically apply in other areas of historical development. Likewise, the history of scientific knowledge was marked by sharp ruptures and discontinuities that were simply erased or smoothed over in positivistic accounts. Bachelard and Canguilhelm therefore opposed versions of the history of science that saw it as an exemplary illustration of the onward march of reason. Instead they sought to reintegrate what was suppressed in such accounts: science's own failed and discarded past, together with those external 'non-scientific' pressures that helped to define what constituted, historically, the discourses of scientific proof and truth (Bachelard 2002; Canguilhem 1994).

In notions such as 'epistemic break' and 'veridical discourses', first elaborated in French history of science, it is easy to hear the echoes of many of the ideas that were later to be taken up by theorists such as Michel de Certeau and Foucault. Indeed, the ripples from structuralist thought were widely felt in the 1960s, and not just in France. The influence of Lévi-Strauss was implicit in the rise of Anglo-American cultural anthropology (or what was termed 'social anthropology' in the British case) at the period. Although recent critics have suggested that structuralism had only a limited impact in Britain and the United States in the 1960s and 1970s, its impress is nevertheless apparent, especially in the championing by anthropologists such as Clifford Geertz and Mary Douglas of Lévi-Strauss's proposition that what had hitherto been designated 'primitive' cultures were not fundamentally different from those of the modern West (Novick 1988, 549–50; Ortner 1995, 379–82). Douglas in particular was vocal in interrogating ethnocentric assumptions: 'It is part of our culture to recognise at last our cognitive precariousness . . . It is part of our culture to be forced to take on board the idea that other cultures are rational in the same way as ours' (Douglas 1978, xviii). Integral to Douglas' argument was the notion that the historical (and ethnographic) distinction between the traditional and the modern was flawed by its present- as well as its Western-centredness, that is to say, the assumption of the superiority of current knowledge over that of the past. Such arguments were to prove important for historiography precisely because of the influence of cultural anthropology on historical writing in the 1970s, as we shall see in Chapter Three. Through Lévi-Strauss and anthropologists, therefore, structuralist ideas were seeping into history at exactly the point that Edward Thompson was repudiating their provenance from another direction, that of Althusserian theory.

How far was the influence of structuralism apparent more generally in historiography before the later decades of the twentieth century? The question is difficult to answer not only because evidence of any direct transfer is limited but also because similar ideas do not necessarily have a single point of origin and may in any case be inflected differently across various fields. Thus the French *Annales* school of historical research was contemporaneous with the spread of structuralism. The journal from which it took its name was founded in 1929 and *Annales* history reached the zenith of its influence after the mid-twentieth century, following its institutional location in the Ecole Pratique des Hautes Etudes in 1946 and the publication of Fernand Braudel's magisterial *The Mediterranean and the Mediterranean World in the Age of Philip II* in 1949, though in Britain and the United States this was only achieved after the translation of Braudel's work in 1972–3 (Burke 1990). Analogies between structuralism and the *Annales* are observable most obviously – and perhaps most superficially – in the latter's well known desire to break with the dominance of the event in historical writing and to foreground deep historical structures, to move from political and diplomatic history to the ideal of 'total history' embracing society, environment and culture. This implied an openness to other disciplines, such as geography, sociology and anthropology that was indeed promoted by the school's founders, March Bloch and Lucien Febvre, and ensured cross-fertilisation of ideas.

Yet from the structuralist point of view perhaps the most significant development of *Annales* lay in Braudel's approach to historical time. Braudel took as the organising principle of his two-volume study of the Mediterranean a conception of historical temporality as working on three different planes. The first and most fundamental was the *longue durée*, 'man in his relationship to the environment', an 'almost timeless history' of 'constant repetition, ever-recurring cycles' occurring over hundreds of years. The second plane was the medium *durée*, the history of trade cycles, demographic and economic changes taking place within decades rather than centuries. Finally, there was *histoire événementielle*, 'traditional history' chronicling the lives of individuals and the passage of political events. Braudel left no doubt about which of these planes he deemed the most important. In his geological model, the deeper and less perceptible the level, the more powerful were its historical effects. Thus the political events normally taken as the stuff of history were no more than the epiphenomena of deep-lying environmental, demographic and economic shifts: 'Resounding events are often only momentary outbursts, surface manifestations of these larger movements and explicable only in terms of them' (Braudel 1972, 20–1). In Braudel's histories, then, it is possible to see reflected the recognition of differential temporalities demanded by structuralists such as Bachelard and Lévi-Strauss.

If the influence of structuralism on the French *Annales* historians tended to be indirect, its impress on Anglo-American historiography in the 1950s and 1960s was still fainter. It is true that the most important new historical school of these years, the British Marxist historians and 'history from below' – a term coined by E.P. Thompson in 1966 – was self-consciously international in outlook and practice (Thompson 1966). In part this was a product of the socialist commitments of historians such as Christopher Hill, Eric Hobsbawm and Thompson, but it was a function also of their intellectual interests. Hobsbawm described history at Cambridge in the 1930s as 'insular' and 'culturally provincial', and he and others looked outwards to the *Annales* school in the 1950s (Lambert 2003, 44). Hill, Hilton and Hobsbawm were instrumental in setting up the historical journal *Past and Present* in 1952, subtitled a 'Journal of Scientific History', with a strong emphasis on histories of culture and society and on *Annales*-style dialogue with disciplines such as sociology and anthropology (Eley 2003, 73).

The channels therefore existed for the encounter with contemporary French structuralism, but such engagement was rarely more than fleeting in the work of this generation of historians. Philip Abrams, the historical sociologist who was an early assistant editor of *Past and Present*, made a virtue of theoretical history, but the theory was generally derived from the sociological classics – Marx, Weber, Durkheim – or from the American structural-functionalist, Talcott Parsons (Abrams 1982). Edward Thompson, who attacked the sociological functionalism of Parsons in the 1960s in ways similar to those he used to denounce Althusserianism in the 1970s, defined his own approach as 'theoretically-informed empiricism', but again the theory largely took the form of a dialogue with Marxism, together with sporadic references to the ethnographic work of figures such as Pierre Bourdieu (Green and Troup 1999, 40). Outside the relatively small group of Marxists, a figure such as Sir Lewis Namier, the historian of parliament, was known in the 1960s as a 'structural' historian for his emphasis on the deep networks of kinship and interest that underlay parliamentary behaviour, but the reference here was to behavioural psychology rather than to French structuralism (though Namier himself was more interested in the pyschoanalytic ideas of Freud and the theory of political élites of the Italian Vilfredo Pareto). Indeed, it was this form of psychologism, a belief in the 'hidden springs of human behaviour', which Miles Taylor has seen as informing the origins of social history in the 1950s and 1960s, preceding the influence of Edward Thompson rather than following it (Taylor, M. 1997, 156, 169).

Consequently, it was only with a later of generation of historians in the 1970s that structuralist ideas began to filter into Anglo-American historiography, via cultural anthropology in the case of early modern historians such as Natalie Zemon Davis and Alan Macfarlane, and via cultural studies in that of the 'structuralist Marxism' proposed by Richard Johnson (Davis 1975; Johnson 1978; Macfarlane 1977). Overall, though, historiography was relatively untouched in the main period of structuralist influence between 1945 and 1970. In the world of Anglo-American history at least, the verities of the Rankean legacy – empiricism, humanism, historicism – remained intact. They would only really begin to be shaken with the advent of post-structuralism.

The challenge of post-structuralism

Post-structuralism is the movement in thought that comes closest to defining cultural theory. It is also the body of ideas that has had the most profound effect on the human sciences, including history, in the last quarter century. Robert Young views French post-structuralism as sharing with Frankfurt School Marxism 'a critique of reason as a system of domination'. But whereas Frankfurt School theorists such as Jürgen Habermas have maintained the possibility of purging reason of its dominating impulses through democratising the processes of communication, post-structuralism concentrates 'on the possibility of other logics being imbricated within reason which might serve to undo its own tendency to domination' (Young, R. 1990, 8). In undertaking an analysis of the operations of reason, in other words, post-structuralism proposes that discourses of domination contain within themselves the principles of their own dissolution, which can be identified if never finally 'mastered' by the analyst.

As the term itself implies, post-structuralism is seen as both a product of and a move beyond structuralism; it is 'critique of structuralism from within' (Sturrock 1993, 137). Two aspects of this critique are especially significant for its relationship with history as well as with other areas of the human sciences. The first is the rejection of the totalising implications of the notion of 'system', whether applied to language, culture or society. Such systems are seen as the product of the observer, not of the object itself; language and cultures are therefore never closed and determinate in the manner suggested by the theories of Saussure and Lévi-Strauss. Implicit here is a rejection also of the notion that structures are necessarily 'deep' and that they can account fully for all forms of practice or meaning. Hence Foucault was suspicious of *Annales*-style 'total history' for its attempt to encompass the diversity of societies and periods within a single frame of reference, despite his admiration for many other aspects of its methods (Foucault 2004, 10–11).

Secondly, post-structuralism emphasises the instability and, ultimately, the undecidability of meaning. Whereas Saussure explained meaning as linguistically produced through binary oppositions, post-structuralists like Jacques Derrida argued that meaning was never fixed as Saussure had assumed. Meanings produced through language (*langue*) – and Derrida did not consider there were any other kind – are multiple and not merely binary; words acquire meaning from a variety of other words, not just their nominal opposites, and meanings are constantly shifting according to the linguistic context. Consequently, language resembles a kaleidoscope rather than a stable structure. Derrida coined the neologism *différance* to express the mobile and uncertain status of representation. The concept draws its own sense from the play between two terms: 'differ', expressing the idea that all meaning is produced through difference; and 'defer', indicating that meaning is never closed, finally settled, but always open to new interpretations (Derrida 1982, 1–27). On this basis, and focusing on the written rather than the spoken word, Derrida argued for 'deconstruction' as a strategy of reading that searches the margins and silences of texts for their significant blind spots and absences (*aporias*). Indeed, the past for Derrida was only ever present in textual form: 'The age already in the *past* is in fact already constituted in every respect as a *text* . . . (Derrida 1976, lxxxix, italics original). There is by extension no 'context', historical or otherwise, outside themselves to which texts can be referred to verify their meaning, and 'history', as the body of texts which represent the past, remains resistant to the efforts of historians to impose truth statements upon it.

As this brief resumé suggests, post-structuralism borrowed from structuralism a number of features. They included the distrust of historicism as presenting a unified, linear past and of reason as a transcendent value. They encompassed also an attention to language as the source of meaning, or 'discourse' in Foucault's terms, defined as 'the group of statements that belong to a single system of formation' so that one 'can speak of clinical discourse, economic discourse, the discourse of natural history, psychiatric discourse' (Foucault 2004, 121). Structuralism and post-structuralism are indeed loose terms of convenience and the boundaries between them were never clearcut. Foucault has been identified with both camps, though he refused the label 'structuralist' in the 1960s, and the term 'post-structuralism' itself has an Anglo-American rather than a French origin. It is also the case that the term post-structuralism brings together an intellectually heterogeneous assemblage of theorists, including Foucault, Derrida and Certeau as well as figures outside France such as Gayatri Spivak and Judith Butler.

Yet there are good reasons for maintaining the term post-structuralist as a descriptor of a specific group of critics and theorists. In France especially, this group possessed a significant degree of cultural unity. It represented a distinct generation, succeeding that of Canguilhelm, Sartre and Lévi-Strauss, and coming into its own in the 1960s. Its members were all formed within the same French élite educational institutions in the late 1940s and 1950s, above all the Ecole Normale Supérieure, and took their place in the most prestigious sites of French higher education – the Collège de France, the Ecole des Hautes Etudes en Sciences Sociales, the Ecole Normale Supérieure, and so on in the 1960s and 1970s. Their intellectual biographies make it clear that they were aware of each others' work and in most cases knew each other personally in the tight-knit world of the Parisian radical intelligentsia (e.g. Eribon 1993; Bourdieu 1990). Moreover, as a generation they were shaped not only by a shared intellectual inheritance but by a common set of traumatic political events. Robert Young has gone so far as to claim that French post-structuralism was a product of the Algerian War of Independence (1954–61), noting the numbers of theorists – Derrida, Lyotard, Bourdieu, Hélène Cixous, Frantz Fanon – who grew up in Algeria or became personally involved with the struggle (Young, R. 1990, 1). For others, such as the Catholic Michel de Certeau, the events of May 1968 in Paris acted as an equivalent catalyst to criticism, a cultural revolution that called into question, in Certeau's words, 'our entire system of representation' (Ward 2000, 5).

Post-structuralism differed also from structuralism in the extent of its influence. Whereas the latter, as we have observed, had limited impact outside linguistics, anthropology and political theory, the challenge of post-structuralism was registered across the humanities and social sciences, including historical studies, from the 1970s onwards. In France it found complex resonance in the work of the major sociologist Pierre Bourdieu, who acknowledged his debt to the structuralism of Lévi-Strauss while at the same time seeking to move beyond it by developing an idea of agency rooted in bodily practices, defined by concepts such as 'habitus' and 'hexis' (Bourdieu 1977). With his longstanding interest in historiography, Bourdieu represented a vector for the transmission of post-structuralist ideas into French historiography while simultaneously offering a vantage point from which to critique them (Corbin *et al.* 1999; Vincent 2004). The influence of the thought of Derrida and, especially, Foucault in French historiography was still more marked, however. Thus the historian of antiquity, Paul Veyne, a close friend of Foucault in the 1970s and 1980s, could write of the need to expose the 'hidden grammar' underlying discourse, 'to relate the so-called natural objects [of historical enquiry] to the dated and rare practices that objectivate them and to explain these practices, not on the basis of a single moving force, but on the basis of all the neighbouring practices in which they are anchored' (Veyne 1984, 236). The cultural historian Roger Chartier argued in similar terms: 'There are no historical objects outside the ever-changing practices that constitute them, thus there is no field of discourse, no sort of reality that is defined once and for all, shaped definitively and traceable in all historical situations' (Chartier 1993, 60). In both instances the influence of post-structuralism was manifest in the critique of historicism, the apprehension of meaning as fundamentally relational and the understanding of history as an intrinsically open-ended, undetermined process.

Post-structuralism requires to be differentiated from 'postmodernism' with which it has often been conflated, especially in Anglo-American circles. As I shall argue in Chapter Five, the latter represents a very broad term that has been used to describe *inter alia* movements in post-1945 art and architecture, the condition of Western knowledge after the demise of the 'grand narratives' and a distinct historical era or phase. In these respects it is a term more properly explored in the works of theorists such as Frederic Jameson, Jean-François Lyotard and Jean Baudrillard (Jameson 1993; Lyotard 1992; Baudrillard 1983). Terms such as postmodernism and post-structuralism, as I have already indicated, are loose and overlapping; Lyotard for instance can be fitted relatively easily into both camps. Yet with its roots in a distinctive tradition of intellectual thought, post-structuralism represents a more specific and rigorous way to approach the field of recent cultural theory than the somewhat amorphous concept of postmodernism.

Post-structuralism entered the historical academy in different ways and via a number of intellectual channels in Britain and the United States. In North America the initial impetus came from within philosophy of history and intellectual history, represented by the figures of Hayden White and Dominick Lacapra respectively. Borrowing from Foucault and Derrida among others, White and Lacapra challenged the boundaries which conventionally set historiography apart from literature and philosophy as well as historians' claim to be representing a past that was obviously and neutrally 'there'. Instead they proposed a version of historical practice that was self-consciously literary and acknowledged history's status as both a rhetorical and ethico-political enterprise (White 1973; LaCapra 1985). It was not until the late 1980s, however, that their arguments began to be addressed in mainstream historiography in ways that were constructive rather than hostile (Novick 1988, 605–7; Kramer 1989).

In Britain, by contrast, debate from the 1970s revolved around structuralism, notably the implications of Althusserian Marxism, which percolated into the mainstream from the emergent 'anti-discipline' of cultural studies and its major institutional locus at the period, the Birmingham Centre for Contemporary Cultural Studies (Dworkin 1997; Hall, S. 1992). But antipathy to Althusser among British Marxist historians, notably E.P. Thompson, was visceral, as we have seen. Following the famous History Workshop debate, the influence of Althusserianism among historians – never more than marginal to start with – was stopped in its tracks; Thompson's 'French flu' did not cross the Channel. Less than four years later, however, structuralism was back, this time in the shape of Saussure's linguistic theory. The context was the publication of an important essay, 'Rethinking Chartism', by the social historian Gareth Stedman Jones, which sought to reverse many of the assumptions that had underpinned Marxist historiography in Britain since the 1950s and earlier. Rather than viewing the politics of Chartism as the consequence of the social conditions of industrialism, as orthodoxy would have it, Stedman Jones took politics as an independent variable, the medium through which Chartist 'interests' – and even 'social conditions' themselves – were defined. In so doing he directed attention to the study of political language understood in terms drawn from Saussurean linguistics: 'Concretely, this meant exploring the systematic relationship between terms and propositions within the language rather than setting particular propositions into direct relation to a putative experiential reality of which they were assumed to be the expression' (Stedman Jones 1983, 21).

More than any other work, Stedman Jones' essay was the catalyst for what became known as the 'linguistic turn' in British historiography. Language, understood in its full sense as a system of communication, was not a product of 'experience' or 'society'; it shaped experience and the meaning of the social. As the ideas of post-structuralism – of Derrida, Foucault, Hayden White and so on – were added to the mix, so the implications were extended, especially in social history where debate generated the most heat (Jenkins, K. 1997, 239–73, 315–83). If categories such as class were only meaningful at the level of language, how was it possible to sustain a materialist account of history? What happened to the grounding of social history once the 'social' itself was revealed as a discursive manoeuvre, a convenient fiction (Eley 1996; Joyce 1995a)? One response to the questions, common to France, Britain and the United States, was a move away from social history towards a 'new' cultural history, in which post-structuralism was at least partly inscribed, and language and discourse became principal objects of analysis (Burke 1991; Chartier 1993; Hunt, L. 1989).

Other channels were no less important as conduits for post-structuralist ideas in the 1980s and 1990s. One such was feminist thought, itself operating as a disruptive agent in established fields of knowledge and contributing directly to post-structuralism through theorists such as Hélène Cixous and Judith Butler. In Britain and North America post-structuralism was implicated in the transition from women's to gender history, though as in other areas, not without considerable tensions (Downs 2004, 88–105). What post-structuralism brought was ways of understanding – and subverting – gender identity and relations without resorting to essentialised ideas of women's 'nature' or transhistorical categories of patriarchy. These new ways of understanding were exemplified most dramatically in the queer theory of the early 1990s and Judith Butler's depiction of both femininity and heterosexuality as 'regulatory fictions', which we shall examine in Chapter Six (Butler 1990). But they were also argued out in the work of feminist historians, such as Joan Scott and Catherine Hall, whose own intellectual trajectory took them in the direction of a history of gender as constructed in language and representation, and in which gender itself figured as a central discursive component of all kinds of historical categories, from class to monarchy and the nation (Scott 1988; Hall, C. 1992). From a different direction, post-structuralist

ideas also entered history by way of postcolonialism, associated with literary studies and the historiographies of imperialism emerging in former
colonies such as India (Said 1985a; Guha 1982). Here the emphasis was
less on language *per se* than on Derridean deconstruction, reading the
texts of empire as evidence of the complex power relations between
coloniser and colonised. As part of this project, postcolonialism also
necessitated a critical examination of 'history' itself as a colonial discipline, a form of knowledge in which European domination is seen to be
unmistakably inscribed.

By the 1990s, then, ideas derived from post-structuralism, and cultural
theory in general, had begun to impact on history in Britain and North
America, though the precise character of the encounter varied in scope
and intensity. The impact was probably greatest in social history, where
post-structuralism appeared to challenge the existence of the discipline,
and least in economic history, where it was generally ignored. Somewhat
apart from either of these stood intellectual history, where ideas emanat-
ing from structuralism and post-structuralism had been discussed much
earlier and absorbed less problematically. Yet as the examples of feminism
and postcolonialism indicate, post-structuralism swept across the humanities and the social sciences as a whole in the last two decades of the twentieth century, with significant consequences from discipline to discipline.
English studies witnessed the ascendancy of literary theory, art history the
move from narrow connoisseurship to the study of visual culture, sociology the impress of the 'cultural turn' and postmodernism, and so on (e.g.
Eagleton 1983; Lash 1990; Tagg 1988). By comparison, its impact on history has been tardy and contested. Even so, history too has undergone its
own crisis of disciplinary identity, with effects on the way the subject is
researched and taught. The crisis itself is not our immediate concern here;
it has in any case been described and debated elsewhere (e.g. Appleby,
Hunt and Jacob 1994; Fullbrook 2002). Nevertheless, this book is in large
measure the product of that crisis and its partial resolution in recent years.

Conclusion

How, then, does this preliminary survey further our understanding of history and cultural theory, their meaning and how they might relate to one
another? In the first place, returning to the History Workshop debate in
Oxford with which we started, it helps to explain some of the sound and
fury witnessed on that freezing night in 1979. For what was enacted in the

confrontation between E.P. Thompson, Stuart Hall and Richard Johnson over the ideas of Louis Althusser was simultaneously a very old debate and a very new one. On the one hand, it replayed an enduring division about the different kinds of knowledge produced by history and theory. This was an age-old dispute, a staple subject of philosophy of history stretching back to Hegel and Ranke in the early nineteenth century and beyond. On the other, the debate was new in that it represented the first major public encounter between those who considered themselves professional historians – and radical ones to boot – and the ideas of (post-)structuralism, already in wide circulation on the Continent but which had only recently been made available in translation in Britain and North America. The event thus stood on the cusp between an older Marxist-informed social history and a newer, post-structuralist inflected cultural history. Significantly, less than a year after Thompson's denunciation of Althusser at Oxford, *History Workshop Journal*, the leading mouthpiece of 'history from below', published for the first time an editorial entitled 'History and Language' exploring the implications of structuralism and semiotics for historical work (History Workshop Collective 1980).

Secondly, while emphasising how history as a discipline is itself inherently theoretical, this account has sought to emphasise the plural character of cultural theory, itself in part an effect of its multiple derivations. The contribution of philosophy, strictly defined, to cultural theory has been limited. Instead its practitioners have ranged across the human sciences, including linguistics, literature, anthropology, politics – and history. I have argued that the tradition of structuralism and post-structuralism is central to this body of thought. Yet this tradition does not wholly encompass all the critics identified with cultural theory whose ideas are discussed in this book. Figures associated with the German Frankfurt School Marxism, for instance, such as the critic of capitalist modernity Walter Benjamin and the social theorist Jürgen Habermas, stand apart. Benjamin committed suicide in 1940, before structuralism had fully taken hold, although his antipathy to historicism and positivism meant that his thought was congruent with many of its precepts (Benjamin 1970). As heir to the Frankfurt School, Habermas has been one of the most stringent critics of French post-structuralist theory, but his own work on the origins and transformation of the public sphere have acquired an important place in cultural theory and cultural history (Habermas 1992). While I have emphasised the centrality of the structuralist and post-structuralist tradition, therefore, it is necessary not to overlook the contribution to cultural theory made by figures who stand at a tangent to or outside that tradition.

I have also sought here to define cultural theory historically, by tracing the filiations of ideas and their links to other bodies of thought over time. No doubt this attempt is simplistic, open to accusations of teleological reading and a narrow concentration on the ideas themselves. When they are finally written, I would argue, both the history of theory and the history of history require to be understood not solely in the realm of ideas but also in relation to what Bourdieu might have termed the changing structure of the intellectual field, the cultural position of the 'theorist' and 'historian' themselves, their relationship to the academy and to wider publics, and the hierarchies of intellectual power and esteem in which they operate (Bourdieu 2003). Yet the effort to place ideas about history and theory in some kind of historical perspective, however limited, enables us to view their newness and 'difficulty' from a necessary perspective, to understand them as products of particular intellectual milieux and to set them within larger frames of thought. It encourages us to think beyond the individual theorists in whom we are, perhaps, especially interested and to consider the wider field of cultural theory in a more generic sense. And it requires us also to recognise that the effect of cultural theory has not been achieved in a sudden, once-and-for-all manner, but has occurred serially over the quarter of a century or so in a succession of overlapping waves: structuralism, post-structuralism, postcolonialism, and so on.

Finally, the chapter has also begun to spell out some of the key characteristics of cultural theory as a mode of thought. Most obvious here is its anti-positivism, the objection to the ideas that history is subject to general laws like a natural science and, more controversially, that history can be seen to follow a single logic or line of development over centuries. In this last case, positivism comes close to the way in which some philosophers and historians have defined 'historicism' (Chakrabarty 2000, 22–3). As such it includes as objects of critique both Marx's theory of history as the shift through historical stages linked to modes of production (primitive, feudal, capitalist, etc.) and (non-Marxist) modernisation theory, which constructs history as a record of social, political and economic progress occurring through a series of generic developments – industrialisation, urbanisation, democratisation, and so on. Thus Walter Benjamin could write: 'Overcoming the concept of "progress" and overcoming the concept of "period of decline" are two sides of one and the same thing' – both belonged to the positivist conception of history (Benjamin 1999, 460).

Equally important in cultural theory is the frequently articulated resistance to a dyadic model in which knowledge is seen to revolve around a number of fundamental binary oppositions: subject/object, self/other, cause/effect. Historical reasoning itself often participates in exactly this mode of reasoning when it insists that an interpretation be either true or false rather than entertaining the possibility that the interpretation might be both true *and* false, or that the terms themselves might require critical reflection. Cultural theorists are therefore concerned to examine the operations of power that inhere in the dyadic model of knowledge and to find ways of moving beyond its reductionist logic (either/or) by introducing the values of ambivalence and indeterminacy into analysis. This implies a rejection of interpretations that are totalising in the sense that they refuse to recognise the legitimacy or possibility of other constructions of the subject. Such totalisation, in the eyes of a postcolonial theorist like Gayatri Spivak, amounts in certain situations to a form of epistemic, neo-colonialist violence (Spivak 1993). Cultural theory thus requires of the historian an openness to the act of interpretation and an acknowledgement of its provisionality. It also demands reflexivity, a critical awareness of the situatedness of the historian and of the knowledge s/he produces.

The rest of *History and Cultural Theory* elaborates and expands these ideas in relation to the particular theorists and currents of thought with which they are associated. A consistent focus is the ways that history is configured within different types of cultural theory, a number of which have been introduced in this chapter. At the same time, through the book I continuously seek to demonstrate how historians have taken up and deployed elements of cultural theory in their own work, to make theorised histories. At present this relationship appears more one-way than reciprocal: most historians are not sufficiently well versed or confident to intervene in theoretical debates, while theory itself often appears somewhat naively ahistorical, as if echoing an older view of philosophy as timeless. In order to keep the spotlight on history as a practice and form of knowledge the book is divided into chapters each of which focuses on a conceptual domain of demonstrable importance in recent historiography – culture, identity, power and so on. We start with what is perhaps the most primordial of these categories, the idea of history as narrative.

CHAPTER TWO

Narrative

What is history? One of the simplest ways to define history is to say that it is a narrative about real events that happened in the past. By narrative is meant the arrangement of events in a sequential order, with characters and a plot, in the manner of a story. Thinking of history in this way connects it with earlier literary forms, such as the epic and the saga, a connection that was made in an important philosophical debate from the 1960s about history and narrative, mainly carried out in the American journal *History and Theory*. According to W.B. Gallie, a leading figure in the debate, 'history is a species of the genus Story' (Gallie 1964, 66). Other philosophers of history, such as Louis Mink and Maurice Mandelbaum, took issue with Gallie, but not so far as to dispute that narrative was a central component of historical writing (Mandelbaum 1977; Mink 1987; see also Roberts 2001). In this latter, limited sense, many practising historians would concur. Writing in 1979, a leading advocate of the new social history, Lawrence Stone, spoke of a 'revival of narrative'. By this, Stone meant a return to description and biography in historical writing, in reaction to the 'scientific' (predominantly quantitative) and social structural history prevalent at the period (Stone 1981, 74–96). But Stone's argument was very different from the claim of Gallie, Mink and their radical successors, such as Frank Ankersmit and Hayden White, that *all* historiography, however quantitative or scientific, takes the form of narrative. It was thus unsurprising to find Stone protesting some twelve years later that the idea that the past should be understood as a text would make history 'an endangered species' (Stone 1991). For many historians the idea that history is, at root, a narrative, text or story appears to equate it with literary fiction and to undermine historians' claims to achieve substantive knowledge of the past. Consequently, the issue of narrative has played a significant part in debates about history, language and post-structuralism (Brown 2005; Munslow 2003).

For the most part, the philosophical debate about history and narrative in the 1960s had little impact on practising historians at that time. Indeed, in Lawrence Stone's 1979 article on the 'revival of narrative' its existence is registered only in passing, in a footnote reference to an article from *History and Theory* and Hayden White's *Metahistory* (1973), to which a colleague had drawn his attention (Stone 1981, 268). Of greater importance in alerting historians to the question of narrative from the mid-1980s onwards were ideas drawn from French cultural theory. Notable here was the philosopher Jean-François Lyotard's argument that the Western world has entered a 'postmodern condition', a condition whose defining feature was 'incredulity towards metanarratives' (Lyotard 1992, xxiv). Seen loosely by some critics as signalling an end to 'grand narratives' of all kinds, Lyotard's thesis had in fact a more restricted meaning, referring to the loss of belief in any overarching legitimation for science or knowledge. This included metanarratives such as progress, human emancipation and the increase of material wealth, which, since the eighteenth-century Enlightenment, Lyotard argued, had justified the creation and diffusion of knowledge. Lyotard only invoked history insofar as it represented a transcendent subject identified with these metanarratives – for example, the Marxist view of history as a movement through specific stages towards a classless society. Nevertheless, the idea of the 'end of grand narratives' has been appropriated by historians to argue variously for the end of 'master narratives' such as class and nation and the break-up of the Enlightenment foundations of modern Western historiography (Jenkins, K. 1991, 59–60; Joyce 1995a, 163–4).

The single most important influence on recent ideas about history as narrative, however, was the French cultural critic Roland Barthes. In an article entitled 'The Discourse of History', first published in 1967, Barthes posed the question of how history as a science, 'placed under the imperious warrant of the "real"', differed in discursive terms from 'imaginary narration as we find it in the epic, the novel, the drama' (Barthes 1986a, 127). History, he argued, borrowed techniques from fiction in order to claim to represent 'what really happened' in the past. Like certain novelists, for instance, the historian tended to absent himself from the narrative, so that 'history seems to *tell itself*' (Barthes 1986a, 131, italics original). This technique, termed by Barthes the 'referential illusion', made it appear that historical works could provide direct, unmediated access to the events described. Collectively, devices such as these, Barthes proposed, contributed to a 'reality effect', in which the fact that the events had happened and that they could seemingly be viewed objectively and transparently lent historical knowledge a heightened authority and prestige. 'Historical discourse is a fake performative discourse in which the apparent constative (descriptive) is in fact only the signifier of the speech-act as an act of authority' (Barthes 1986a, 139). In other words, historians do not passively summon up the reality of the past, but actively constitute it as an effect of their discourse. Paradoxically, Barthes claimed, narrative, originally rooted in fictional sources such as myth and epic, had become 'both sign and proof of reality' (Barthes 1986a, 140). This, in turn, was a product of the movement of nineteenth-century realism, which had given birth to photography, the social documentary and the realist novel, together with Rankean historical method.

Barthes' essay anticipated many of the key themes of subsequent debate about history as narrative, questioning the nature of historical reality, the status of historical knowledge and the relationship between history and imaginative literature. The references to 'fake', 'illusion' and 'reality effect' led many to see the essay as an attack on historical scholarship. In part this was no doubt the case. But Barthes' study was also a serious attempt to analyse how historical discourse operates linguistically and any verdict about his innate hostility to history should be tempered by his complex yet sympathetic treatment of the nineteenth-century historian, Jules Michelet (Barthes 1986b).

Indeed, responses to Barthes' ideas among historians are symptomatic of attitudes to narrative theory as a whole in recent skirmishes between traditionalists and 'postmodernists'. While the former see narrative as a threat to be resisted at all costs, the latter view it as proof that no direct correspondence exists between historiography and the past. Both sides, however, tend to assume that narrative itself can be treated as a unified category, when there is in fact no such agreement within contemporary cultural theory. There are very different viewpoints about how narrative works and what *kind* of narrative history, in particular, represents. In the rest of this chapter we shall look at three approaches to these issues. These are selected for their significance and diversity as well as the fact that they seek to work on the interface of history and cultural theory; there exist, of course, many other important theories of history as narrative (see for example Ankersmit 1983; LaCapra 1983; Veyne 1984). The first, asssociated with Hayden White, views history as a branch of literature, close to poetry and the novel. In the work of Paul Ricoeur, by contrast, history is treated as a form of narrative that is distinct from imaginative literature, albeit sharing certain fundamental links to it. Thirdly, we shall investigate the ideas of Michel de Certeau, who saw history as a form of practice and a species of writing. We shall conclude with a consideration of how ideas about narrative have been deployed in recent historical studies. In this way the chapter will indicate something of the range of possibilities (and problems) confronting historians interested in working with theories of narrative.

History as literature

Whether history is an art or a science has long been debated. In 1903 the Cambridge historian J.B. Bury famously proclaimed that while history 'may supply material for literary art or philosophical speculation, she is herself simply a science, no less and no more'. Bury's view was vigorously contested by his peer, G.M. Trevelyan, who argued that the 'art of history remains always the art of narrative' (Stern 1970, 223, 234). By the 1970s, however, 'scientific history' in the form of demographic and quantitative methods and social structural analysis had become significant components of the field, as Lawrence Stone acknowledged in his 1979 article (Stone 1981, 75–9). This predominance partly explains the relative neglect at the time of the important study of the American philosopher of history, Hayden White, entitled *Metahistory*, first published in 1973. Following on from the earlier ideas of Gallie and Mink, White's thesis, expounded in *Metahistory* and a series of subsequent articles, radically challenged the pretensions of history to scientific knowledge. In structure and form, he argued, historiography was essentially a literary creation, albeit in ways which historians themselves were largely unaware. '[I]n general there has been a reluctance to consider historical narratives as what they most manifestly are: verbal fictions, the contents of which are as much *invented* as *found* and the forms of which have more in common with their counterparts in literature than they have with those in the sciences' (White 1985, 82, italics original). White has modified his ideas since the 1970s, prioritising the role of figurative language in shaping historical narratives over an earlier emphasis on the process of 'emplotment'. Nevertheless, his core arguments have remained remarkably consistent (see White 1999 and 2000). They have also been highly influential: overlooked for much of the 1970s, Hayden White had become effectively synonymous with narrative theory in Anglo-American historical circles some twenty years later and the 'patron saint' of the new cultural history (Eley 1996).

Though complicated in its details, the major components of White's thesis are relatively straightforward. He starts by distinguishing between the basic forms of historical record: annals, chronicle and history. In essence, annals represent the most rudimentary form of historical representation, little more than a list of dates and events with no attempt made to link them into a meaningful sequence or whole. Chronicles like those written by medieval scholars contained fuller information about the past and achieved greater coherence by virtue of their focus on a specific subject, such as a monarch's reign. But the chronicle still depended heavily on chronology, the sequential narration of events: 'typically, it lacks closure, that summing up of the "meaning" of the chain of events with which it deals that we normally expect from the well-made story' (White 1990, 16). Annals and chronicle therefore fall short of what is expected of a history: they lack a clear sense of relationship between the events recounted, an explanation of their causes and consequences and an overall interpretation of their historical significance. In order for a proper history to be created, the story of the events would need to be reconstructed from the evidence of the real events and then subjected to historical interpretation. But this is where White parts company with historical orthodoxy. Echoing Louis Mink's argument that 'stories are not lived but told', White argued that there are no stories in the past for the history to reconstruct and interpret; the past does not come pre-packaged in narrative form (Mink 1970). It is the historian who imposes a narrative order on the past and in this sense 'makes history'.

How is this process of 'making history' effected? White argues that the act of historical interpretation is achieved by predominantly literary means. In the first place, the historian 'emplots' the events studied using a number of archetypal stories: romance, comedy, tragedy, satire. These story types or plots are not arbitrary, according to White. They correspond to deeply embedded cultural archetypes through which the reader is able to recognise and understand the kind of story being told. Romance represents a drama of redemption and transcendence, the triumph of good over evil. Satire is its obverse, a tale of limits based on the recognition that fate or the world will always win out over human endeavour. Comedy and tragedy are located between these two extremes. Comedy is a drama of reconciliation in which the forces and protagonists at play are ultimately brought into some form of accommodation with each other. Tragedy, on the other hand, stresses resignation in the face of fate and the inevitability of the ultimate fall of the protagonists, yet brings an advance in emotional understanding for those who are witness to it (White 1973, 7–11).

Following literary critics like Northrop Frye, White proposes that all stories conform to one or more of these archetypes (certain combinations, like satirical tragedy, are also possible, though not others, such as romantic satire). As a form of story, historiography does the same. The historian configures the events according to one of the archetypal plots, which then necessitates a certain type of interpretation. Hence, the capacity of historians to interpret the same set of events differently is not a function of evidence, method or technique; rather, it is because the historians concerned have chosen to emplot the events differently. White gives the example of nineteenth-century interpretations of the French Revolution. While Jules Michelet depicted the Revolution as a romantic drama of the triumph of the people, his contemporary Alexis de Tocqueville construed it as an ironic tragedy. It was not the selection of different facts that distinguished their interpretations, White argues. 'They sought out different kinds of facts because they had different kinds of story to tell' (White 1985, 85).

In addition to emplotment White outlined two other 'levels of conceptualisation' in *Metahistory* which determined the types of interpretation to be found in historical works. The first level was 'mode of argument', made up of four approaches which he termed formist, organicist, mechanistic and contextualist. Thus in a mechanistic mode of argument historical acts are seen as determined by laws, as in classical Marxism; in formist argument, explanation takes place by identifying the uniqueness of the events or, conversely, their conformity to certain types, as in much narrative political history. The final level described by White is 'mode of ideological implication', in which there are, again, four categories: anarchism, conservatism, radicalism and liberalism. Every history, White asserts, has a particular political or ideological position embedded within it. This is apparent, for example, in fundamental attitudes to social change, time and progress, with conservatives naturally favouring current institutions and piecemeal, evolutionary change, radicals being most predisposed to emphasise rupture and the possibility of revolutionary transformation. Within this model of levels of conceptualisation, White suggests that there are 'elective affinities' between the various possible modes of emplotment, argument and ideological implication. Thus the selection of a comic mode of emplotment, for example, is likely to predispose the historian towards an organicist mode of argument and a conservative ideological stance; the satirical tends towards the contextualist and liberal. *Metahistory* consists of demonstrating the efficacy of this model in relation to what are considered the major historical thinkers of the nineteenth century: Ranke, Burckhardt, Michelet and Marx.

However, this somewhat mechanical schema plays a less important role in White's later writings, post-*Metahistory*, than his theory of tropes or figures of speech. Unlike the natural sciences, White argues, history has no technical language of its own. It is therefore forced to rely on ordinary, educated language, such as that used in imaginative literature, and on the figurative language or tropes intrinsic to it. According to White, there are – by now predictably – four basic tropes: metaphor, in which an object or action is compared to something else with which it is imaginatively but not literally applicable ('the rise of the middle class'); metonymy, when the name of an attribute is substituted for the thing designated ('crown' for 'monarch'); synecdoche, when a part is made to stand for the whole ('reign of terror' for French Revolution); and irony, in which characters or events are treated in such a way as to show inconsistencies between appearance and reality ('friendly fire'). These tropes are crucial to the type of interpretation an historian makes. Before engaging in any other act of interpretation, including modes of emplotment and argument, White contends, the historian will 'prefigure' the series of events under study by selecting the 'dominant tropological mode' in which to cast them. The types of figurative language used to describe variously the events, the relationship between them and their collective 'historical' significance thus determines the history written. 'The implication is that historians *constitute* their subjects as possible objects of narrative representation by the very language they use to *describe* them' (White 1985, 95, italics original). In effect, historians behave in exactly the same way as novelists in carving out the story that they wish to tell from the tangle of other possible narratives in any given situation. This is because in history as in life there are no stories waiting to be told; the historian like the novelist creates them. For White, this makes historical work a poetic act, an act of literary imagination. Thus, history 'is always written as part of a contest between contending poetic figurations of what the past *might* consist of'; history 'is made sense of in the same way that the poet or the novelist tries to make sense of it, i.e., by endowing what originally appears to be problematical and mysterious with the aspect of a recognisable, because it is a familiar, form' (White 1990, 98).

Contrary to what professional historians generally claim, therefore, historical research and writing is essentially a literary enterprise according to Hayden White. Those processes which historians consider as essential to their discipline and its claim to knowledge – the evaluation of sources, the application of methods, the weighing of evidence – are seriously downgraded in his account. Linguistic protocols, such as modes of tropology and emplotment, determine historians' interpretations of the past, not historical evidence or analysis. The very categories which historians use to emplot their narratives, such as romance or tragedy, are themselves drawn from literature. Historical events are not in themselves inherently tragic, comic, romantic or ironic; they have to be constructed as such by an external observer, in this case the historian. Sensitive to the charge of historical relativism, White has acknowledged (albeit somewhat ambiguously) that there may be 'limits to representation' in the sense that evidence will allow catastrophic historical events such as the Holocaust only to be properly emplotted in certain restricted forms, such as epic or tragedy (White 1992). But this acknowledgement is not allowed significantly to alter his general thesis. History is, at the deepest level, a form of narrative whose closest links are to imaginative literature not to science. Modern historiography therefore needs to acknowledge and reconnect with its literary roots if it is to recapture the promise of its nineteenth-century inheritance. The highest ambition of historical writing should be to produce classics, such as the histories of Michelet and Burckhardt, whose status as great works of literature means that they cannot be disconfirmed or surpassed by new research. In the present era this also means breaking with the nineteenth-century tradition of historical realism and adopting new forms of literary expression characteristic of cultural modernism; here White has cited variously the novels of Marcel Proust, Virginia Woolf and Primo Levi as examples of modernist approaches to the representation of the past (e.g. White 1999, 40–2). After all, White urges, acknowledging its links with fiction will not diminish history's status as knowledge; novels, for example, have much to tell us about reality, our world and our relations with others.

Not surprisingly, many practising historians who generally ignored White's work before the 1990s have greeted his arguments with hostility (e.g. Evans 1997; Marwick 2001). On the whole, however, such critics tend to defend conventional historical practice rather than engaging actively with his ideas. In fact, White's thesis can be read in two very different ways. A positive view might suggest that his aim has been to redraw attention to historical style, to history as a form of writing, and thus to re-emphasise its roots in rhetoric. This is a valuable contribution since as White has consistently pointed out, historians prioritise the content of historical work – evidence, data, interpretation – over its form; hence the title of his 1987 collection, *The Content of the Form*, which set out to redress this imbalance. Less charitably, White's thesis could also be seen as a species of linguistic determinism, in which the structures of language

– figures of speech, plot – in historical work invariably predominate over other, knowledge-based, sources of interpretation. In particular, it is unclear in White's account whether in prefiguring the historical field the historian consciously chooses a specific trope and mode of emplotment, or whether this occurs unconsciously as a cultural reflex or psychological tendency. White's own terminology of 'deep structures', 'historical consciousness' and so on contributes to this ambiguity, while appearing to privilege the latter option (Kellner 1980).

There are indeed many justified criticisms that can be made of White's arguments, which do not, however, render his ideas redundant – critique is not a zero-sum game. Here I shall focus on three key sets of issues. In the first place, it has been argued that White conflates narrative and fiction, thus confusing them (Carroll 2001). For White, as we have seen, historians' interpretations of the past are essentially narratives in the sense that they are 'invented' by historians. But the notion of 'invention' does not necessarily mean that they are imaginary or false. White's argument about the status of history can be seen to rest, in fact, on a series of dubious counter-positions. The first such counter-position is between history as the past – everything that has happened – and history as a narrative about the past. Clearly, the latter is not a direct mirror image of the former, but to acknowledge that historical narrative and the past are categorically different does not indicate that the narrative is therefore a fiction. For a philosopher such as David Carr, narrative is a fundamental attribute of human consciousness and as such part of 'reality' itself, not something imposed artificially by the historian or critic (Carr 1986). The second dubious counter-position is between history and science. While the former is located close to the pole of imaginative literature in White's argument, the natural sciences are projected as representing a wholly different form of analytical, objective and fact-based knowledge. White, indeed, presents a very traditional, absolutist version of 'science'. Yet as recent writings have demonstrated, not only is modern science dependent upon imaginative thought, it has also been driven by deep-rooted meta-narratives of human emancipation and dominance of the natural world (e.g. Lyotard 1992; Haraway 1992). Despite his protestations on behalf of imaginative literature, therefore, White tends to overlook the significance of narrative as a mode of understanding across different domains of knowledge, the sciences as well as humanities.

The second area of criticism that has been levelled at White is that he ignores (or perhaps more accurately, dismisses) the technical procedures that historians actually use in studying the past. It is the case that, on the whole, White seems relatively uninterested in present-day historiography – his major study, *Metahistory*, was based on nineteenth-century historians and philosophers of history. Yet even cultural historians favourably disposed to narrative theory find perplexing White's assumption that it is feasible to ignore matters of historical procedure and to evaluate historiography as a whole on the basis of a select group of nineteenth-century authors. Criticising Barthes' similar use of eighteenth- and nineteenth-century authors to illustrate his arguments about the nature of historiography, Michel de Certeau argued that such an approach assumes among other things a false homology or equivalence between the historical writing of different types and periods (Certeau 1988, 41). The cultural historian Roger Chartier likewise deemed the absence of a consideration of the processes by which history constitutes itself as a mode of knowledge a singular weakness in White's argument. 'How indeed can history be thought of', Chartier asks, 'without ever (or hardly ever) referring to the operations proper to the discipline – the construction and treatment of data, the production of hypotheses, the critical verification of results, the validation of the coherence and the plausibility of interpretation?' (Chartier 1997, 35). In effect – and quite apart from questions of the epistemological validity of the knowledge produced – White overlooks the specific operations by which history creates itself as a body of knowledge, a discipline. By contrast, philosophers like C.B. McCullagh continue to insist that history's disciplinary procedures remain valid: narratives can be judged on historical grounds either fair or misleading, and metaphorical statements used by historians can similarly be judged true or false (McCullagh 1998, 126–8; 2004).

At times, indeed, White's arguments appear to come close to collapsing history into fiction. It is true that he frequently claims to acknowledge the distinctive constitution of historical writing. In the quotation that historical narratives are 'verbal fictions, the contents of which are as much *invented* as *found*', for instance, nominal equality appears to be accorded each of the two elements, what is fabricated by the historian and what is found in the historical record. But in practice the whole weight of White's thesis is on the former – the production of history as narrative – not the latter – the traces of the historical past. The reader is told repeatedly that there are no stories in the past and that in the creation of historical works methods and evidence are secondary, if not irrelevant, to the poetic and linguistic act. Nor is Hayden White shy in making his own literary preferences explicit. From *Metahistory* onwards he has consistently affirmed the belief that major historical works, such as those of Michelet and

Burckhardt, are literary 'classics' which as a consequence cannot be 'refuted' or 'disconfirmed' by new research or theoretical models, most recently citing Frank Ankersmit to the same end (White 1973, 4; 1990 180–1; 1999, 7; Ankersmit 1994). Such works have moved beyond the time-bound category of historiography and entered the pantheon of great works of literature, exemplifying the 'timeless fascination of the historio-graphical classic' (White 1990, 181). In espousing this view White seems curiously innocent of the whole critique of the literary canon undertaken by Barthes and a generation of English studies critics, which has high-lighted the invested, ideological and historically changeable nature of the canon of 'great works' (Baldick 1987; Barthes 1977; Gilbert and Gubar 1979). Still more important in the present context, by effectively dissolv-ing history into fiction White ignores them as forms of writing as well as forms of knowledge. We are left, in short, without an understanding of what it is that distinguishes historiography as 'historical' as well as those textual conventions that constitute, in Dorrit Cohn's phrase, the 'distinc-tion of fiction' (Cohn 2000).

White's contribution has been to highlight the literary and linguistic resources which historical writing draws upon and the way these shape the processes of historical interpretation. For those who champion his work, such as Keith Jenkins and Alun Munslow, its value resides precisely in the capacity of White's ideas to open up historiography to other ethical, political and stylistic ways of writing about the past (Jenkins, K. 1995, 134–79; Munslow, 1997, 140–62). His arguments have flaws, some of which I have indicated. But narrative theory does not begin and end with Hayden White. There are other important theories of the relationship between history and narrative, relevant to current historians. Among the most notable of these is the work of the French philosopher, Paul Ricoeur.

History as narrative

As a philosopher Ricoeur has long been interested in history, both as a process and a branch of knowledge. In 1965 he published L'Histoire et la Verité [History and Truth], followed between 1983 and 1985 by a three volume study, Temps et Récit [Time and Narrative]. This last work is a major study of the relationship between time and narrative, concepts which, Ricoeur, argues, are mutually constituting: 'time becomes human time to the extent that it is organised after the manner of a narrative; nar-rative, in turn, is meaningful to the extent that it portrays the features of temporal experience' (Ricoeur 1984, 3). Historical and fictional writing figure strongly in the work as representing specific forms of narrative whose temporal dimension Ricoeur seeks to identify and interpret.

Ricoeur is not an iconoclast in the mould of contemporary French thinkers such as Jean Baudrillard and Jacques Derrida. He does not attempt to destroy received ideas about history, but rather to engage with them constructively and build upon them (Simms 2003, 1). He also approaches the subject of history and narrative in a different way from Hayden White. Ricoeur is respectful of history as a branch of knowledge, inquiring about its procedures and methodology and interested in twentieth-century historiography, including those works most challenging to narrative theory. An important section of volume one of *Time and Narrative* is devoted to an analysis of Fernand Braudel's *The Mediterranean and the Mediterranean World in the Age of Philip II*, originally published in 1949 and the exemplar of the *Annales* school's ambition to create a non-narrative, 'total history' centred on long-term economic and demographic change. Although he considers history to be a form of narrative, Ricoeur disagrees with W.B. Gallie's dictum that it is a 'species of the genus Story' or, following White, that it resembles literary fiction (Ricoeur 1984, 161–8, 177). History differs from fiction in the sense that the events described actually happened and are not the creation solely of the author's imagination. There is likewise such a thing as historical truth, which is distinct from poetic or novelistic truths. Furthermore, where White emphasises the centrality of figurative language – tropes – in the production of historical narrative, most markedly in his later works such as *Figural Realism* (2000), Ricoeur stresses the role of emplotment. In Ricoeur's hermeneutic or interpretative theory, plot is what gathers together the discrete elements or events and makes them into a meaningful whole.

Narrative is important for Ricoeur because he sees it as a fundamental way of human understanding. It is by telling their lives as a story that individuals apprehend themselves, their identity and the meaning of their existence. 'To answer the question "Who?" . . . is to tell the story of a life. The story told tells about the action of the "who". And the identity of this "who" must therefore be a narrative identity' (Ricoeur 1988, 246). The identity not only of individuals but also of collectivities, like societies and nations, is forged by narrative means, a process with which historiography is necessarily bound up. Like White, Ankersmit and other poststructuralist theorists, however, Ricoeur acknowledges that the relationship between history and the past is enigmatic; historical writing, however scholarly, cannot simply reflect what happened in the past since that reality has gone and is beyond reconstruction. Instead, like all narrative forms, history relies upon a principle of mimesis – literally, imitation – to represent events or developments in the past. Ricoeur's theory identifies three different dimensions of mimesis which correspond to different stages in the comprehension of any narrative. What he terms mimesis$_1$, prefiguration, requires that an individual has a practical understanding of the world and of the meaning of human actions, which are necessary for a narrative to be understood. A second stage, mimesis$_2$ or configuration, is concerned with emplotment, the organisation of the elements or events into a comprehensible story form that is recognisable as such. Finally, mimesis$_3$ or refiguration enables the narrative to be referred back to the world and its point or purpose grasped by the listener or reader. All narratives contain these mimetic components, which comprise an important temporal dimension (before, during, after) and a circular movement: through mimesis$_1$ and mimesis$_3$ the world of the text is connected with the world of the reader (Ricoeur 1984, 52–87). The importance of mimesis in this context is that it helps to create an analogical or metaphorical relation between narrative and reality. Historical narratives are able to 'stand for' the past in the same way that in metaphor one term comes to stand for another. They occupy a position of 'as if' with regard to the past.

Narrative and history are therefore profoundly linked. Nevertheless, Ricoeur goes to great lengths to distinguish history from the kinds of narratives associated with imaginative fiction. There is an 'epistemological break between historical knowledge and our ability to follow a story' (Ricoeur 1984, 175). A whole series of reasons are given for this sharp distinction between history and fiction. Not only does history deal with events that really happened, but the historian is also compelled to respect the chronological ordering of events which the novelist can creatively rearrange. Historiography is based on documents and other traces from the past in the present, to which any interpretation must refer. Certain types of scientific history, such as demographic and 'structural' history, do not take narrative form; they deal with long-term developments, not particular events, and with collectivities, not individual characters.

The main point where history and imaginative literature differ, though, is in their mode of procedure. Whereas fiction proceeds by recounting, history is concerned above all to argue and explain.

Poets also create plots that are held together by causal skeletons. But these latter are not the subject of a process of argumentation. Poets restrict themselves to producing the story and explaining by narrating.

In this sense, Northrop Frye is right: poets begin with the form,
historians move towards it. The former produce, the latter argue.
And they argue because they know that we can explain in other
ways *(Ricoeur, 1984, 186, emphasis original).*

Enquiry, argument, explanation: this is the characteristic mode of procedure of scholarly history. It is manifest, first, in the pursuit of objectivity,
an impossible goal but which is pursued nevertheless in the quest for the
complete interpretation, understood as the judgement that cannot be disconfirmed. Still more fundamental, historical argument and explanation
are focused on questions of causality, or what Ricoeur terms 'singular
causal imputation' – the capacity to explain a course of events by indicating why it occurred in one way rather than another and which factors
were decisive in bringing it about. Singular causal imputation, as Ricoeur
defines it, represents a level of explanation that lies between a purely narrative explanation of causality, on the one hand, and a sociological explanation by reference to laws, on the other. Again, this puts the historian in
a quite different position from the novelist or poet. 'Historians are in the
situation of a judge: placed in the real or potential situation of a dispute,
they attempt to prove that one explanation is better than another.'
Moreover, they confront a quite different type of audience. Whereas fiction requires, in Samuel Taylor Coleridge's well-known phrase, the 'will-
ing suspension of disbelief', 'historians address themselves to distrustful
readers [other historians] who expect from them not only that they nar-
rate but that they authenticate their narrative' (Ricoeur 1984, 175–6).

Given his insistence on the uniqueness of history as a form of knowledge, how does Ricoeur maintain the view that it is also a form of narrative? Ricoeur's answer to this question is complex and lengthy, not least
because in the case of scientific history the links to narrative are buried.
The question also returns us to two of the fundamental features of his theory of narrative, mimesis and emplotment. The concept of mimesis points
to the analogous status of narrative, the idea that the elements in a story
'stand for' something else, in the way that the hero and villain in a novel,
for example, are implicitly understood to stand for the moral categories of
good and evil. Ricoeur suggests that these features of mimesis and analogy
apply equally to historical works. He argues that in scholarly history
the objects of analysis (classes, societies, nations) are made to function
as if they were characters – for this reason, Ricoeur terms them 'quasi-
characters'. These collectivities take on a role in historical narratives akin
to individual characters in other types of story: 'historians attribute to

these singular entities the initiative for certain courses of action and the historical responsibility . . . for certain results, even when these were not intentionally aimed at.' It is a legitimate device, according to Ricoeur, because the collectivities are understood to refer back to the individuals who composed them. But it is also inescapably a narrative device: 'it is because the technique of narrative has taught us to dissociate characters from individuals that historical discourse can perform this transfer on the syntactical level' (Ricoeur 1984, 200). In a similar way, the use of causal explanation gives history a 'plot-like' appearance, linking disparate events to one another in a seemingly logical temporal succession. Historical events serve as incidents within the 'quasi-plot'. This applies not only to sudden, dramatic events, like a political assassination, but also to long-term developments, such as gradual economic transformations or demographic shifts: 'all change enters the field of history as a quasi-event' (Ricoeur 1984, 224). Ricoeur acknowledges that the 'quasi' aspect of historical discourse places a strain on its linkage to narrative, most evident in forms of historical writing that are explicitly non- or anti-narrative, like Braudel's *Mediterranean*. But he also maintains that it is these same 'quasi' features that constitute 'historical intentionality' – what is most distinctively historical about history as a form of knowledge. The 'quasi' status of historical discourse emphasises its analogous character; it 'expresses the tenuous and deeply hidden tie that holds history within the sphere of narrative and thereby preserves the historical dimension itself' (Ricoeur 1984, 230).

In volume three of *Time and Narrative* Ricoeur goes further than this and suggests that, though separate forms of narrative, history and fiction are 'interwoven'. This implies not simply that the two narrative forms help to define each other by their very opposition, but that each borrows from the other (Ricoeur 1988, 101). Historiography, like literature, is a work of the imagination, consisting of interpreting the traces of the past in the present in conjunction with the wider historical context that gives them meaning. Such traces take on meaning 'only when we provide ourselves with a figure of the context of life, of the social and cultural environment, in short . . . only when we provide ourselves with a figure of the world surrounding the relic that today is missing, so to speak' (Ricoeur, 1988, 184). This task of 'providing a figure of' is fundamentally an imaginative and literary enterprise. Moreover, in a manner similar to White, Ricoeur suggests that the historical imagination borrows modes of emplotment – tragedy, comedy, horror and so on – from fiction. Horror, for example, draws meaning from its use as a literary category, but it is an essential part of the ethical importance of history that it teaches us to see certain events, such as war and genocide, as horror. The relationship, however, is not one way; fiction too borrows modes of narrative from history. Novels, for instance, frequently imitate historical narratives by using the past tense to tell the story, as if the events described were located in a real past. Fictional narratives in this sense become 'quasi-historical' (Ricoeur 1988, 190). Additionally, in requiring that a plot be probable or convincing, fiction owes a debt to history, since the probable in fiction is measured by its resemblance to what has been historically. The attention to the impact of nineteenth-century realism on both the novel and historiography (as in Barthes' 'reality effect'), Ricoeur argues, has obscured the deeper affinity of history and fiction in this regard (Ricoeur 1988, 191).

The interweaving of fiction and history is important in providing the latter with its ethical dimension, which Ricoeur sees as one of the prime purposes of history. Thus, events which are considered 'epoch-making', such as the French Revolution, become part of the narrative identity of the collective (in this case the French people); defining who 'we' are implies telling 'our' (hi)story. History also calls on the resources of fiction when the events concerned have such ethical intensity that mere historical explanation is insufficient. The Holocaust is one example, giving rise to a literature whose purpose is to preserve the suffering of the victims in the collective memory. Fiction here is 'placed in the service of the unforgettable', enabling 'historiography to live up to the task of memory'. As with epic, in which the deeds of dead heroes are commemorated, so the interweaving of history and fiction can transform narrative into a means to justice: 'there are perhaps crimes that must not be forgotten, victims whose suffering cries less for vengeance than for narration' (Ricoeur 1988, 189).

The simultaneous similarity and distinctiveness of history and fiction within the circle of narrative extends, finally, to their ethical motivation or purposes. Echoing Jules Michelet, Ricoeur argues that historical work has an 'implicit ontology': 'Everything takes place as though historians knew themselves to be bound by a debt to people of earlier times, to the dead' (Ricoeur 1988, 100). This debt can never be adequately repaid; in this sense, historians are always in the position of 'insolvent debtors'. It is the idea of doing justice to the people of the past that drives historians to think of their work as the reconstruction of a real past, instead of what it in fact is, according to Ricoeur, a re-presentation of the traces of the past in the present. Much of social history in the 1960s and 1970s was fired by the idea of unacknowledged debt and restitution, as in E.P. Thompson's memorable statement in the preface to *The Making of the English Working Class*: 'I am seeking to rescue the poor stockinger, the Luddite cropper, the "obsolete" hand-loom weaver, the "utopian" artisan, and even the deluded follower of Joanna Southcott, from the enormous condescension of posterity' (Thompson 1968, 12). Efforts to recuperate groups 'hidden from history' had a broadly similar aim, affording recognition to oppression at the same time as according such groups historical agency (e.g. Rowbotham 1973; Genovese 1975). But Ricoeur is arguing more broadly that the debt to the dead extends to all historical representation and is consequently integral to the entire historical enterprise. 'As soon as the idea of a debt to the dead, to people of flesh and blood to whom something really happened in the past, stops giving documentary research its highest end, history loses its meaning' (Ricoeur 1988, 118). Fiction, by contrast, has no such ethical responsibility. What it does have by way of purpose, however, is an aesthetic duty 'to render as perfectly as possible the vision of the world that inspires the artist', which corresponds 'feature by feature with the debt of the historian and of the reader of history with respect to the dead' (Ricoeur 1988, 177). Despite their difference of purpose, therefore, history and fiction share a homology or equivalence within the realm of narrative.

Ricoeur's view of history as narrative does not in any way diminish its importance as a branch of knowledge. On the contrary, he attributes to history a seriousness of intellectual and moral purpose that some historians might find excessive. Understanding history as narrative does not undermine the necessity for facts or chronology, nor does it lessen the significance of the role of the historian as mediator between present and past, the living and the dead. Ricoeur would differ from some historians in arguing that as a narrative history has a metaphorical rather than a referential relationship to the past, but this is a long way from proposing, in the manner of Hayden White, that history is a verbal fiction produced by figurative and literary means. Indeed, while characteristically acknowledging White's importance for narrative theory, Ricoeur effects an ironic reversal of his ideas by proposing that the historian's debt to the dead 'makes the master of the plot a servant of the memory of past human beings' (Ricoeur 1988, 156). From the literary side too, recent critics have taken up Ricoeur's themes. In *The Distinction of Fiction* (2000) Dorrit Cohn argues that readers fully understand the fictional character of the novel form through conventions inherent in the text. While fiction requires an understanding of the relationship between story and discourse, history adds in the relation between story and the historical record. Novels can – and indeed must – represent the inner thoughts and feelings of characters, while historical writing cannot do so without breaching disciplinary protocols. Finally, the novel allows for 'unreliable narration', a difference of viewpoint between the author and their narrator, which again is not open to the historian, who is bound by codes of ethical responsibility and reliability (Cohn 2000). Following Ricoeur, therefore, it is the distinctiveness of forms of narrative that have preoccupied many recent cultural theorists, rather than the collapsing of all narratives into fiction.

This is not to suggest that *Time and Narrative* is without problems in its account of historiography. Hans Kellner has noted in particular the 'considerable dangers' attending the notion of the 'quasi', and many historians are likely to agree, seeing it as having more to do with the logical requirements of Ricoeur's own thesis than with the actual structure of historical interpretations (Kellner 1993, 54). There is equally the problem, noted by Peter Burke among others, that Ricoeur's conception of narrative is so broadly drawn as to risk blurring into other categories, such as description and analysis (Burke 1991, 234). One could also point out that Ricoeur's analysis of historical procedures is largely concentrated on particular, largely empirical, examples, and that historiography is more methodologically diverse than this allows. But if there are questions about the value of the overall thesis, Ricoeur's ideas provide us with an important insight into how historiography works, illuminating both the integrity of history as an intellectual enterprise as well as its often unacknowledged relationship with other forms of knowledge.

History as practice

Within cultural theory, history is not always considered, primarily or exclusively, as a narrative. There are other ways of thinking about what defines historiography. One of the most compelling in recent cultural theory has been the argument of Michel de Certeau that history is to be understood, at root, as a practice, a set of specific operations or procedures which mark it out from other types of intellectual endeavour. Certeau, who died in 1986, was a French historian of religion. A polymath interested in anthropology, psychoanalysis and linguistics, he oversaw a research project on contemporary culture, resulting in the publication of a two-volume study, *The Practice of Everyday Life*. He also wrote directly on history and historiography, in the form of essays in works such as *Heterologies* and at length in his major work *L'Ecriture de l'Histoire* [*The Writing of History*], first published in 1975. Unlike Ricoeur or

White, Certeau's thought was deliberately unsystematic; termed 'anti-conformist' by his fellow researcher, Luce Giard, he saw the purpose of his writings as disrupting accepted models and systems of thought (Certeau, Giard and Mayol 1998, xiv). Consequently, his ideas about historiography do not amount to a coherent theory of history, nor were they intended to do so. All this can make his arguments difficult to follow, but it does not make them any the less rewarding for those interested in the nature and possibilities of historical writing.

Certeau did not deny the narrative status of history: 'It remains always a narrative. History tells of its own work and, simultaneously, of the work which can be read in a past time' (Certeau 1988, 43). As a practice, history is a matter of texts, both a form of writing in its own right and a study of writings (and textual artefacts) in the past. Because it is centrally concerned with texts, historiography has at best an ambiguous relationship to past reality. Historiography insists on its privileged claim to represent reality by counterposing fiction as its false 'other'. But Certeau himself remained suspicious of the 'institution of the real' carried out in history's name, not least because it suppresses the variety of pressures and influences at play in both the textual documentation of the past and the process of historical interpretation (Certeau 1986, 199–224). At the same time, he was wary of a literary analysis which, through its own construction of 'literariness', detached the critic from the text and the text from the circumstances of its production. Certeau therefore sought to navigate a path between the historical 'real' and the literary 'gaze' in the direction of what has been termed a 'textual historicity' (Ahearne 1995, 20, 121).

While acknowledging the narrative character of history, Certeau also maintained its scientific aspect. Despite his emphasis on historiography as a form of writing, he did not follow his contemporary Hayden White in identifying history predominantly as a literary creation. History, according to Certeau, is always a mixture of science and fiction – neither wholly one nor the other – and is in this sense a 'heterology', combining different knowledges (Certeau 1986, 215). But it is also a practice, something that historians 'make' or 'do' through a series of disciplinary activities. In *The Writing of History*, Certeau termed the ensemble of practices by which the past is turned into history, the 'historiographical operation'. This involved 'envisaging history as an operation between a *place* (a recruitment, a milieu, a profession or business, etc.), analytical *procedures* (a discipline) and the construction of a *text* (a literature)' (Certeau 1988, 57, italics original). The historiographical operation thus encompassed an institutional context, a set of scientific practices and a process of writing.

Certeau's argument that history is the product of a particular place, or social and institutional space, is important, since it is largely neglected by White and Ricoeur as well as by most professional historians. 'Place' here has a series of overlapping meanings. It designates, most obviously, the institutional site – university, academy, archive – where history, as a generic category, is produced. Beyond this, it can represent a school of historiography (e.g. *Annales*, History Workshop) and an academic field, 'at once the law of a group and the law of a field of scientific research' (Certeau 1988, 61). The most immediate and important audience for historians' work, as Ricoeur noted, what makes or breaks professional reputations, is the judgement of peers not of the public at large. Place is also a social location, a site which maintains a relationship with the wider society. All this means, according to Certeau, that historiography requires to be understood as a collective product, not that of an individual historian. 'The historical book or article is together a result and a symptom of the group which functions as a laboratory. Akin to a car produced by a factory, the historical study is bound to the complex of a specific and collective fabrication more than it is the effect merely of a personal philosophy or the resurgence of a past "reality". It is the *product* of a *place*' (Certeau 1988, 64, italics original). This social and institutional location remains the invisible condition of historical work, one of the essential conditions that must be suppressed in order for the knowledge produced to be deemed 'scientific'. For these reasons, 'it is impossible to analyse historical discourse independently of the institution in respect to which its silence is organised' (Certeau 1988, 62).

In addition to place, the historiographical operation does not so much represent the past as produce or fabricate it through a set of analytical procedures. As we saw in Chapter One, the establishment of modern scholarly history is usually associated with the development of Rankean historical method in the nineteenth century. Certeau, however, viewed modern historiography as having a much longer gestation, dating from as far back as the fifteenth century with the formation of libraries and circles of the erudite, the spread of printing and practices of collecting, copying and classifying, and, from the eighteenth century, the creation of national archives in Europe. Through these processes, artefacts, correspondence, institutional papers and personal ephemera were turned into a documentary record, the objects of research, which historians then subjected to analytic scrutiny, to verification, evaluation and interpretation, according to protocols that were themselves established over time. Historical study, Certeau stressed, 'means changing something which has its own definite status and role into *something else* which functions differently'. It is precisely this change that marks out the scientific status of history or any body of knowledge: 'What is "scientific" in history and in other disciplines is the operation that changes the "milieu" – or what makes an organisation (social, literary, etc.) the condition of a transformation' (Certeau 1988, 73–4, italics original). Absorbed as historians tend to be in practical or technical questions (How much weight can be put on a particular source? Does the evidence bear out this or that interpretation?), they tend to ignore the transformation in the order of knowledge which their researches effect.

Most fundamental of all in this context, is the process by which historiography creates the past by severing itself from it: 'History is played [out] along the margins which join a society with its past and with the very act of separating itself from that past'. Characteristically, though, Certeau insisted that this is an artificial separation which the practice of history persistently subverts: 'Founded on the rupture between a past that is its object, and a present that is the place of its practice, history endlessly finds the present in its object and the past in its practice' (Certeau 1988, 36–7). In the argument of Michel de Certeau, then, histories are not the product of individual historians – this is the 'illusion of mastery' to which White and Ricoeur as well as many historians succumb. Rather, history is the product of the historiographical operation understood as a combination of place, procedure and writing.

On the basis of this analysis, Certeau outlined the purposes and limits of history as practice and the role of the historian within it. While the historiographical operation created a certain scientificity for history, he himself was agnostic with regard to such claims. Towards computer-based quantitative history, for instance, in vogue at the time that Certeau was writing, he was neither approving nor hostile. What interested him about the computer was its capacity to combine processes – the creation of objects of historical research (serial data) and their analysis – which had previously been separate, and the fantasy of interpretative mastery which the computer fostered. Certeau, however, did not indulge this fantasy; against it, in fact, he proposed an identity for the historian as *rôdeur*, a 'prowler' who 'no longer envisages the paradise of a global history', but 'works in the margins', 'comes to circulate *around* acquired rationalisations' (Certeau 1988, 79, italics original). Rather than reconstructing the past, he proposed using historical knowledge critically, against received 'models' and current systems of thought. Borrowing from Foucault, Certeau proposed that the historian's strategy should be to turn thought towards that which it cannot explain, 'to place discursivity in its relation to an eliminated other, to measure results in relation to the objects that escape its grasp' (Certeau 1988, 40).

Thus it was no coincidence for Certeau that at the same moment the computer was holding out the possibility of a new scientific mastery of the past, historians began to explore 'pre-' or 'counter-rational' subjects of enquiry: histories of madness, sorcery, festival, 'all these zones of silence' (Certeau 1988, 79). He himself undertook research on the possession of the nuns of Loudun and on seventeenth-century mystics, topics that posed extreme challenges as regards questions of agency, subjectivity and interpretation. In the case of Loudun in 1632, the problems were inherent in the evidence itself. They derived from the statements of the possessed to the authorities, whose purpose was to extract from the nuns' testimony the identity of what it was that possessed them, an identity which, in the nuns' speech, was shifting and opaque – 'I am Leviathan, Asmodeus, Behemoth', etc. Precisely who this 'I' referred to was a problem that the nuns' confessors found near impossible to resolve; they were confronted by the conundrum posed by the poet Arthur Rimbaud: *Je est un autre* ('I is another') (Certeau 1988, 255). Rather than seeking to solve the exorcists' puzzle, Certeau was interested in the way the nuns' speech disturbed a socio-linguistic order, invoking a 'crisis of nomination' which only the nuns' confession, and the subsequent re-stabilising of the identity of possessor and possessed, could bring to an end (Certeau 1990). Similarly, in his study of seventeenth-century Christian mysticism Certeau sought to show how mystic speech disrupted the contemporary religious order, together with an increasingly powerful order of writing (or 'scriptural economy') with which organised religion was associated (Certeau 1992). In each case, the subjects concerned – mystics, the possessed – were perceived to effect an 'alteration' in the existing order, to represent something which that order could not account for and which affected it in ways it was unable to control. This is precisely what Certeau himself saw as the purpose of historical work: to put in question existing interpretative models by confronting them with modes of thought which lay at or beyond the limits of explanation.

For Michel de Certeau, therefore, history, properly conceived, is a 'heterology', a discourse on the other, an 'other' which enables the discourse itself to be established as a mode of knowledge. 'A structure belonging to modern Western culture can doubtless be seen in this historiography: *intelligibility is established through a relation with the other*; it moves (or "progresses") by changing what it makes of its "other" – the Indian, the past, the people, the mad, the child, the Third World' (Certeau 1988, 3, italics original). But just as the other of historiography is elusive, ungraspable in its alterity, so history is confronted with a past it can alter but never fully contain. The past comes back to haunt historiography in ungovernable ways; akin to the psychoanalytic concept of the return of the repressed, the past will not stay in its place. Whatever a form of historiography 'holds to be irrelevant – shards created by the selection of materials, remainders left aside by an explication – comes back, despite everything, on the edges of discourse or in its rifts and crannies: "resistances", "survivals" or delays discreetly perturb the pretty order of a line of "progress" or a system of interpretation' (Certeau 1988, 4). A historiography that aims at mastery inevitably fails to recapture the strangeness and alterity of the past; every interpretation is marked by its incompleteness, its lack. Yet in acknowledging the limitations of historical knowledge, its flawed and tenuous relationship to past reality, Certeau nevertheless concluded by affirming the mysterious sovereignty of historical practice. 'Thus historians can write only by combining within their practice the "other" that moves and misleads them and the real they can represent only through fiction. They are historiographers. Indebted to the experience I have had of the field, I should like to render homage to this writing of history' (Certeau 1988, 14).

Certeau's vision of history, then, was of a critical discipline that works at and on the limits of understanding, that seeks out whatever eludes effective interpretation and uses it to disrupt and alter dominant orders of knowledge. Far from being the master of the past, the historian becomes its servant or accomplice against totalising systems of rationality which claim to explain its nature. Such a view of historiography has its critics, even within the field of cultural theory. Paul Ricoeur, for example, sees Certeau's arguments as providing a 'negative ontology of the past' and an 'apology for difference'. The excessive validation of the 'other' risks becoming a species of 'temporal exoticism'. Furthermore, the 'notion of difference does not do justice to what seems to be positive in the persistence of the past in the present' (Ricoeur 1988, 147–51). It ignores, for instance, the importance of inter-generational continuity and cultural tradition in the construction of individual and collective identity. By extension, it has been argued that Certeau tends to valorise resistance for its own sake, independent of any relationship to democracy. There is a danger that the radical gesture becomes a substitute for a more durable, if less dramatic, politics of change (Ahearne 1995, 186). These criticisms are not without substance: it is easy to idealise or aestheticise 'difference' in the past, a risk of which Certeau himself was aware, as in his potent critique of the historiography of popular culture with its ironic title 'The beauty of the dead' (Certeau 1986, 119–36). But it was his belief in the radical potential of historical study, in a discipline often identified with a conservative emphasis on continuity, the empirical and the established order, that ultimately distinguished Michel de Certeau's work. As the historian Roger Chartier concluded, his emphasis was on the 'discontinuities of history, on the tensions between the discourses of authority and rebel wills, tensions that permeate our present just as they did societies now dead. History is a place of experimentation, a way of bringing out differences. It is a knowledge of the other, hence of the self' (Chartier 1997, 47).

Evaluation

While the idea of narrative has been central to the 'cultural turn' (Bruner 1991), narrative theory does not offer a uniform or singular view of historical knowledge. The differences between the theorists examined in this chapter illustrate the point. While all of them understand history to be a form of narrative, they each articulate that formation very differently. For Hayden White, history works in similar ways to other narrative forms, such as epic or fiction. It therefore requires to be understood in essentially linguistic terms as a branch of literature. Paul Ricoeur, however, emphasises the distance between historiography and imaginative literature. If history remains with the definable boundaries of narrative, it has its own distinctive mode of proceeding which mirrors but does not replicate literary fiction. In the case of Michel de Certeau, history is narrative but not only this; it also has an epistemological dimension, which requires investigation of the grounds of knowledge at the same time as it tells the story. Historians, however, generally overlook these significant theoretical differences between cultural theorists in discussing discursive approaches to the past. 'Narrative' tends to be invoked in opposition to 'empirical' history as if each was a monolithic entity.

But if a comparison of these writers must be weighted towards their differences, they also share, between themselves and with other cultural theorists, certain perspectives on history. To begin with, they all envisage an epistemological break between present and past. For some, such as Ricoeur, this is inherent in the philosophical problem of time; for others, like White and Certeau, it is pre-eminently a problem of epistemology or knowledge. But in either case, the present cannot be viewed in linear terms as an extension of the past. The past has gone, it cannot be resurrected, and our knowledge of it is necessarily fragmentary and partial. The corollary of the rupture between past and present is that historiography creates rather than reflects the past; in the terms of Ricoeur and Certeau, the work of history is both to demarcate the past as a separate and analysable entity while simultaneously affirming its continuities with the present. Secondly, and by extension, cultural theory renders problematic the representation of the past. Whereas historians normatively assume that the documents and artefacts of the past point to a reality beyond them, for cultural theorists the reality of the past cannot be represented in unmediated fashion in historiography. In Ricoeur's theory, narrative plays the mediating role by 'standing for' the past in a relation of analogy. For Certeau, the past is represented in the form of 'textual historicity', but the question of the relationship of primary sources (or texts) to what lies outside them remains open. Thirdly, for each of the theorists, history has affinities with fiction, however much this association may be denied by professional historians. Even Michel de Certeau, the most insistent in proposing a scientific dimension to historiography, observed that fiction 'haunts the field of historiography', a ghostly presence which must be continuously repressed for history to lay claim to a 'discourse that is legitimated as scientific' (Certeau 1986, 219).

How, then, have recent historians sought to utilise these understandings in their own studies? 'Narrative' has indeed been a prevalent concept in British, French and North American historiography since the 1980s as a cursory examination of a number of recent histories reveal. An early and influential example was Judith Walkowitz's, *City of Dreadful Delight: Narratives of Sexual Danger in Late Victorian London* (1992), a study in urban cultural history. The narratives referred to in the title were those concerning identities of gender, sexuality and the metropolis, circulated through Victorian scandal journalism and melodrama, together with the historical narratives through which these topics have conventionally been depicted. An awareness of narrative is also seen to have shaped research and writing in specific ways. Thus Walkowitz resisted 'providing narrative closure to some chapters, or organising its historical account in terms of fixed gender and class polarities', while acknowledging that the conceptual and interpretative strategy adopted in the book owed its conditions of possibility to the very discourses of social and sexual relations under investigation (Walkowitz, J. 1992, 10). Equally, in *Re-Reading the Constitution: New Narratives in the Political History of England's Long Nineteenth Century* (1996), edited by James Vernon, the narratives described were those which contemporaries deployed about the English constitution (whose existence was itself a matter of debate) between 1780 and 1930, along with the related frameworks of interpretation subsequently applied to them in English political historiography. Vernon sought to extend these concerns further in an essay entitled 'Narrating the constitution: the discourse of "the real" and the fantasies of nineteenth-century constitutional history'. Here Barthes, White, Certeau and others are invoked in an essay which argues that late nineteenth-century histories of the English constitution by historians such as Stubbs and Maitland were attempts to establish history as a discipline of knowledge, distinct from rhetoric and literature with which earlier historians, like Macaulay, were identified. In so doing these historians appealed to a discourse of 'the real' as a ground both for the construction of proper historical knowledge and for securing the constitution, deemed vulnerable by its unwritten character, against the various challenges of lawyers, reformers and suffragettes (Vernon 1996, 204–29).

More recently, the idea of narrative has figured largely in Callum Brown's *The Death of Christian Britain* (2001), an account of the process of secularisation between 1800 and the present which draws extensively on cultural theory. Brown's history deploys the notion of narrative in two main senses. First, 'secularisation' is itself seen as a narrative, an influential sociological framework of interpretation in which the alleged waning of religious – and specifically Christian – belief is seen as a 'prolonged, unilinear and inevitable consequence of modernity' (Brown 2001, 11). The purpose of the book is precisely to challenge this narrative, to link secularisation not to overarching processes such as industrialisation, or even church attendance *per se*, but to the decline of what he terms 'discursive Christianity', a specific culture of religiosity which was understood to shape the identity of both society and individual at a powerful level. This occurred in Britain, Brown claims, not until the 1960s, long after the onset of urban, industrial and other forms of modernity, and largely separate from them. Secondly, the concept of narrative is applied to the changing ways women and men shaped their personal identities between the early nineteenth and the mid-twentieth century. Narrative here is related in particular to the story-forms, such as melodrama, which permeated novels, the press and other domains of public discourse. Within the framework of evangelical narratives in particular, the identity and life course of the individual could be imagined. While this culture of religiosity remained stronger for women than for men throughout this period, it was only after the mid-twentieth century that Christianity effectively dissolved as an effective cultural matrix in which identities and lives were forged.

Understanding secularisation, according to Brown, is therefore less a matter of abstract social processes than of the cultural meanings that shaped religious beliefs by narrative means.

Even in this brief description it is not difficult to see how these works, like those of many other recent historians, have been shaped by an encounter with narrative and cultural theory. Vernon's essay is notable in this regard, with its questioning of a problematic 'real', its treatment of histories as texts and its invocation of the literary theorist Jacques Derrida in support of the argument that contexts – social, political, historical – are themselves always textualised. My purpose here is not to engage in a critique of these historical works, which indeed point to many of the productive possibilities in the links between historiography and contemporary cultural theory. Rather, I am concerned with them as exemplifying a number of more general issues that have arisen from historians' attempts to employ aspects of narrative theory.

First, historians such as Walkowitz, Vernon and Brown tend to apply notions of narrative to discourses located in the past – narratives of sexual danger in Victorian London, of constitutionalism and evangelical belief in nineteenth-century England – and, additionally, to other (usually earlier) historians' efforts to construct histories about these discourses. Thus it is possible to find a small number of studies of how specific bodies of historiography, such as those concerned with the French Revolution and English working-class formation, have themselves been shaped by particular narrative forms and literary tropes (Halttunen 1999; Maza 1996; Somers 1992). This implies, at the very least, different categories of narrative – historical and historiographical – which points to a larger, unanswered question: what is meant by 'narrative' in historians' accounts? Vernon and Walkowitz are not alone among recent historians in providing little or no definition of the concepts of narrative with which they work; Brown is somewhat more forthcoming, though even he tends to conflate the categories of narrative, discourse and story (Brown 2001, 69–72). Clarification is evidently necessary, however, given the different narrative theories discussed in this chapter.

Secondly, and related, historians tend to assume that 'narrative' belongs to others (rather in the manner of a previous use of the concept of 'ideology') and exempt their own work from the description. Consequently, they do not generally engage reflexively with their own construction of history as narrative. By ignoring this dimension, though, they neglect the argument of White, Ricoeur and others, that historiography *as a whole* requires to be understood as a species of narrative. Indeed, historians tend to avoid reflecting on their own body of work as writing; even the most theoretically aware are prone to deem such reflection self-indulgent and contrary to what other historians will find of most interest in their work, its substantive content of findings and argument. Yet attention to the stylistics of historical writing is important insofar as it points beyond simple questions of style (whether or not the writing is clear, concise, etc.) to the whole manner of proceeding, of conceptualising and articulating a particular set of events or developments. As we shall see in Chapter Eight, where a very small number of historians have begun to experiment critically with the narrative form of their own historical work, the results can be intellectually productive as well as historically provoking.

At the same time, the reluctance of historians to move beyond a partial application of narrative theory in the direction of the experimental forms of literary modernism advocated by Hayden White may itself be instructive. As White himself observes in his appreciation of Ricoeur, 'the very notion of a modernist historiography, modelled on the modernist, anti-narrativist novel, would be in Ricoeur's estimation, a contradiction in terms' (White 1987, 173). Historians, then, may have good grounds for resisting certain claims to set historiography free from the chains of an outmoded and unreflexive narrativity. For following Ricoeur, to cut historiography loose from its moorings in a form of narrative defined by specific rhetorical and ethical features would be not to liberate it, but to risk sacrificing its very intentionality – what makes historiography uniquely 'historical' in the first place. Nevertheless, in rejecting White's extreme identification of history with fiction, the theories of Ricoeur and Certeau still offer historians much scope for exploring the creative possibilities of narrative form in framing their own accounts as well as in analysing the histories of others. For what an engagement with the concept of narrative demonstrates among other things is that in cultural theory the forms of historical knowledge are indissoluble from their manifest content.

CHAPTER THREE

Culture

If a concern with narrative has been one of the defining features of historical writing over the last twenty years, it has been part of a much wider movement, the 'cultural turn', registered across the human sciences and involving culture in all its forms, from the construction of meaning to the consumption of goods. Consequently the concept of culture stands at the centre of the relationship between new kinds of theory and new types of history. It is built into the definition of cultural theory as a distinctive way of thinking and it was likewise both inspiration and object of the 'new cultural history' that took shape from the later 1980s (Burke 2004).

Yet the term 'culture' creates immediate difficulties. It is notoriously vague and slippery, possessing several different meanings. In *Keywords* (1976) the literary theorist Raymond Williams called culture 'one of the two or three most complicated words in the English language'. By studying the usage of the word over a long historical time-span Williams sought to unpick its various intersecting meanings. From its application to the tending of crops or animals in early modern England, 'culture' was extended during the sixteenth century to describe the intellectual and spiritual development of humans. By the eighteenth century it had broadened to encompass matters of taste, as in the term 'cultivated'. But 'culture' and its associated terms were less commonly used in this period than 'civilisation' and 'civility'. Consequently, 'culture' only took on its modern importance in the nineteenth century, according to Williams, partly in response to changes in the meaning of the term elsewhere in Europe, especially the powerful German notion of *Kultur* which was used to denote cultures in the plural, referring to different peoples and societies. Alongside the idea of intellectual and spiritual development 'culture' replaced 'civilisation' in Britain as indicating a particular way of life of a people or group; it was used in this sense in the new discipline of anthropology after 1870. From the late nineteenth century, too, 'culture' came to serve as a cover-all term for the arts. These three distinct meanings of 'culture' – referring to intellectual development, to way of life and to the arts – were further complicated in the twentieth century by differences in usage between academic disciplines. Williams noted, for example, how in archaeology 'culture' was used to refer to material production ('material culture'), whereas in cultural studies it generally denoted symbolic systems (Williams 1976, 87–93).

Despite these semantic complexities, the concept of culture enjoyed a renewed ascendancy in Western intellectual life after 1945. From the 1950s it occupied a central place in the structural anthropology of Lévi-Strauss in France and in the classic works of Raymond Williams, Richard Hoggart and Edward Thompson in Britain, which were to become the foundational texts of the emergent field of cultural studies (Lévi-Strauss 1955; Hoggart 1957; Williams 1958; Thompson 1968). When the new cultural history developed in the 1980s, however, it did not merely borrow the meanings and approaches to culture developed by this earlier generation of studies: instead, it critically questioned them (Hunt 1989). Historians looked to new trends in anthropology, in which culture was treated primarily as a semiotic process, a matter of meaning rather than of behaviour. In this light, the conventional division between 'structure' and 'culture', characteristic of the work of Williams and Thompson, appeared rigid and unconvincing (Hall, S. 1983). In *The Making of the English Working Class*, for instance, originally published in 1963, E.P. Thompson had depicted culture as the means by which individual and collective 'experience' was given historical form, mediating between economic and social structures on the one hand, and politics and class consciousness on the other. But this separation now seemed artificial. Were the social and the political themselves, or significant elements of them, not culturally produced? At the same time, the new cultural history also attacked the pretensions of history to scientific status, to provide a 'macro-history' of society that was objective, value-free and all encompassing. This was an attack not only on Marxist histories that insisted on the primacy of economic conditions, but also on the French *Annales* tradition with its insistence on the determinacy of long-term demographic and environmental factors in historical development (Chartier 1993, 19–52). In both cases, culture had been given, at best, a marginal and dependent status, seen as an epiphenomenon of deeper, more fundamental historical processes

(Darnton 1985, 110–11). The new cultural history was thus an attempt to put 'culture' at the beginning rather than the end of historical analysis.

The aim of this chapter is to examine the consequences of this attempt, and specifically some of the more important theoretical influences that have informed the cultural turn in historical studies since the 1980s. For purposes of clarity, the chapter is divided into four parts. The first looks at the influence of cultural anthropology, exemplified by the thought of Mary Douglas and Clifford Geertz, conventionally cited as the leading inspiration behind the new cultural history, especially in the United States. In the second part, I shall examine the Russian theorist Mikhail Bakhtin whose ideas of carnival and of language have had a significant impact on the study of popular culture. Thirdly, I shall analyse the ideas of French sociologist Pierre Bourdieu, whose sociology of culture offers historians an important set of conceptual and theoretical tools. In the light of these various perspectives, the chapter will conclude by examining recent critiques of the cultural turn in historiography together with some of the neglected aspects of cultural theory that historians might productively utilise in their own writings.

Cultural anthropology

One of the most significant intellectual developments of the later 1960s and 1970s was the rise of cultural anthropology, whose impact was registered across the social sciences. Two of the leading figures in this intellectual movement were the British anthropologist Mary Douglas and the American Clifford Geertz. Their major works, *Purity and Danger* (1966) and *The Interpretation of Cultures* (1973) respectively, were landmarks in the development of cultural anthropology and have continued to influence social and cultural historians ever since. Both Douglas and Geertz followed the French structuralist Claude Lévi-Strauss in understanding culture as a symbolic system whose meanings it was the purpose of the anthropologist to decipher. However, they were critical of Lévi-Strauss's representation of cultures as defined by deep mental structures, seemingly universal and impervious to historical change. Geertz went so far as to claim that Lévi-Strauss had created an 'infernal culture machine' which 'annuls history, reduces sentiment to a shadow of the intellect, and replaces the particular minds of particular savages in particular jungles with the Savage Mind immanent in us all' (Geertz 2000, 355). Though continuing to work within the structuralist paradigm of culture and the symbolic as representing integrated 'systems', Douglas and Geertz emphasised the highly specific and differentiated character of those systems and their capacity for creative innovation.

For Mary Douglas, a culture is a 'series of related structures which comprise social forms, values, cosmology, the whole of knowledge and through which all experience is mediated' (Douglas 1999, 129). In much of her work, however, the focus is not on culture *per se* so much as on the symbolic order and specifically the 'classifying symbols . . . in relation to the total structure of classifications in the culture in question' (Douglas 1999, vii). In *Purity and Danger*, the symbols she was concerned with are those to do with purity and pollution. Codes regarding uncleanness, dirt and defilement are important, she argued, because they are a fundamental way in which cultures organise relations between the sexes, between groups within the society and between the social and the natural world. Studying the symbolic boundaries between what is considered pure and impure, therefore, tells us a great deal about how a particular culture works. This is the case not only for the culture of specific groups, such as individual tribes, but also for larger social and historical entities. Douglas argued, for example, that a major distinction between 'primitive' and 'modern' societies is that in the former codes relating to pollution and uncleanness are applied systematically across the society, whereas in the latter they tend to be separated off from mainstream life, identified with specialised departments such as sanitary hygiene or specific areas in the house, like the kitchen and bathroom.

In analysing purity and pollution in both modern and pre-modern settings, Douglas rejected explanations based on functionalism, psychology and medicine. Attitudes to cleanness and dirt in any given culture are not defined by relation to an unchanging social need, nor are they to be understood as the product of unconscious drives and desires. Most contentiously, she was critical of 'medical materialism', the argument that attitudes to pollution are determined by basic notions of hygiene. Her objection to medical explanation was based importantly on an opposition to the linear idea of progress implicit in the assumption that modern Western societies are inherently more rational in their approach to dirt and cleanness than supposedly primitive cultures. 'The more deeply we go into this [pollution rituals] . . . the more obvious it becomes that we are studying symbolic systems. Is this then really the difference between ritual pollution and our ideas of dirt: are our ideas hygenic where theirs are symbolic? Not a bit of it: I am going to argue that our ideas of dirt also express symbolic systems' (Douglas 1999, 35–6). From the anthropological viewpoint, she argued, dirt is not a fixed category but 'matter out of place', the meaning of which is established by relation to larger symbolic systems of purity and pollution, order and disorder.

Recent historians have made extensive use of Douglas' ideas of pollution. In her study of child sexual abuse in Victorian England, for instance, Louise Jackson argues that the evidence of witnesses in cases of child abuse routinely described abusers in terms associated with dirt and contamination. The effect of this was to cast abusers not only outside the norms of civilised society, but also outside the social circles of family, from which inevitably they so often came. Here, as in matters to do with bodily boundaries and excreta, pollution was seen as much in moral as physical terms and held to threaten the social fabric (Jackson 2000, 32, 88). In a similar fashion, historians of social policy have argued that the sanitary movement in early nineteenth-century Britain was not so much a response to a growing problem of pollution and disease as a pathologising of certain features of urban life in the 1830s and 1840s. What spokesmen for the movement consistently did was to connect sanitation with deep-rooted ideas about the individual and the social body, gender relations and domesticity (Poovey 1995, 115–31; Hamlin 1998). From this perspective, it was fears of pollution, not simply medical evidence, that defined sanitary conditions as a 'problem' in the first place, and they did so according to a particular hierarchical view of what constituted social order.

Douglas extended the principle that dirt is 'matter out of place' to dietary rules about what is and what is not permissible to eat. Taking the example of the instructions in the biblical book of Leviticus as to which animals may and may not be eaten (oxen, sheep and goats, in the former category, for example, winged insects, hares and frogs in the latter), she rejected the view that the categories must either be arbitrary or, alternatively, have a rational medical basis. Instead, she saw the basis of the so-called 'abominations of Leviticus' as a logical extension of the idea that holiness in the Old Testament applies to what is set apart, itself closely linked to the ideal of completeness. As such, 'holiness requires that individuals shall conform to the class to which they belong' (Douglas 1999, 54). Sin or evil in this view is understood as involving the confusion or mixing of classes which should be kept apart; it is this transgression, for example, that defines sexual perversion. The long list of animals abominated in Leviticus imitates the principle of holiness. Those species which humans are prohibited from eating confuse categories of earth, water and air, which Genesis had declared to be distinct. Thus Leviticus explicitly proscribes eating any animal 'that swarms upon the earth', like insects, since they confuse categories of earth and air. The same principle applies to any animal that lives in water, but 'has not fins and scales', like frogs; such species are, literally, neither fish nor fowl. Because of its powerful symbolic associations, food was also directly associated with social order. Thus the medieval historian Caroline Bynum has described how fasting was used by women in particular as a means to exercise control over men in situations of patriarchal and/or religious authority (Bynum 1987).

Douglas was interested, therefore, in the way that fundamental concepts, such as purity and pollution, 'make sense . . . in reference to a total system of thought, whose key-stone boundaries, margins and lines are held in relation by rituals of separation' (Douglas 1999, 42). Her approach involved placing classifying systems at the centre of attention; understanding these becomes a primary task of the anthropologist and the historian of culture. Nor are matters of dirt or of diet of peripheral interest to the student of politics and society. On the contrary, Douglas argued that ideas of pollution and purity are integral to the upholding of social order and the exercise of power. At the most fundamental level, they work to organise relations between the sexes; in many cultures, for example, women are seen by men as potential sources of pollution and danger, through their connection with sex, menstruation and the preparation of food (Douglas 1999, 141–59). As this suggests, the body itself is an important symbol linking pollution and power. While on the one hand, 'there is hardly any pollution which does not have some primary physiological reference', on the other the body frequently acts as a metaphor for the social order. In Hindu India, for instance, the caste system is represented as a human body, characterised by a division of labour in which 'the head does the thinking and praying and the most despised parts carry away waste matter' (Douglas 1999, 124–5, 165). As these examples imply, cultural systems are not free of conflict. They have sources of danger and pollution built into them as a continuously referenced 'other', against which order and purity are defined. Nevertheless, like all symbolic systems, rituals of purity and impurity are essentially unifying; they 'have as their main function to impose system on an inherently untidy experience' (Douglas 1999, 4).

Mary Douglas's contemporary, Clifford Geertz, shared this emphasis on the importance of culture and symbol in ethnographic analysis. As an anthropologist he was interested in explaining cultural variety and difference, and in defining the specific part played by cultural determinants in any larger explanation of an event. In contrast to Douglas, however, Geertz played down the concept of culture as system, preferring to approach it in semiotic vein as a matter of interpretation and meanings. 'Believing, with Max Weber, that man [sic] is an animal suspended in webs of significance he himself has spun, I take culture to be those webs, and the analysis of it to be therefore not an experimental science in search of law but an interpretive one in search of meaning. It is an explication I am after, construing social expressions on their surface enigmatical' (Geertz 2000, 5). Geertz was careful to define what culture is and what it is not. He emphasised that culture is not psychological, located purely in people's heads, but public in the sense of representing a shared, creative understanding. In order to escape the charge of subjectivism, of merely seeing culture as something 'out there' which can be recreated, he depicted cultural analysis as having a 'double task': 'to uncover the conceptual structures that inform our subjects' acts, the "said" of social discourse, and to construct a system of analysis in whose terms what is generic to those structures . . . will stand out against other determinants of human behaviour' (Geertz 2000, 27). Nevertheless, Geertz remained sceptical of the scientific claims of anthropology (or history) to knowledge on the model of the natural sciences. Harking back to the question of narrative, he argued that anthropological writings are 'fictions, in the sense that they are "something made", "something fashioned" – the original meaning of *fictiô*' – not that they are false, unfactual, or merely "as if" experiments' (Geertz 2000, 15). Cultural analysis is not a matter of causal explanation or scientific proof, but of increasing levels of precision in the interpretation and understanding of human events.

How, then, should we go about the business of analysing culture? Borrowing a phrase from the philosopher Gilbert Ryle, Geertz proposed that cultural analysis be understood as 'thick description'. Using Ryle's example of the complex ways in which an observer may interpret the movement of an eyelid – is it a blink, a twitch, a wink? – Geertz saw cultural acts as providing 'piled up structures of inference and implication through which an ethnographer is continually trying to pick his way'. The task of the student of culture is to peel back the layers of meaning in which actions and events are encased, to decipher and redescribe them (Geertz 2000, 7, 9). At this point Geertz introduced a familiar linguistic analogy: a cultural event is an 'acted document', akin to a text that must be read or a language that must be learned. 'Thick description' is therefore interpretive and 'consists in trying to rescue the "said" of [social] discourse from its perishing occasions and to fix it in perusable terms'. It is also 'microscopic' in focus (Geertz 2000, 20–1). Geertz's approach is concerned with the small-scale and the detailed instance rather than with grand concepts such as power or gender. This is not because the latter are irrelevant to cultural analysis, as I shall indicate, but because he was not concerned to construct general theories on the basis of examples, but to use such examples to illuminate the differences within and between cultures – 'not to generalise across cases' as he put it, 'but to generalise within them' (Geertz 2000, 26). It is this sense of the small-scale, the particular and the non-generalisable that Geertz evoked when he spoke of 'local knowledge' and its importance (Geertz 1983).

A classic illustration of Geertz's method is his essay 'Deep play: notes on the Balinese cockfight' (Geertz 2000 [1972], 412–44). The essay provides a description of cockfights Geertz witnessed on the Indonesian island of Bali and an analysis of their meaning and significance in Balinese culture. As such it has provided something of a model for cultural historians studying their own historical episodes. Geertz described cockfighting as an obsession in Bali, though technically illegal. Events were made up of a number of fights, lasting up to five minutes each, between rival cocks matched by their owners and attended by large crowds and gambling. Both cocks were fitted with spurs and the fight was decided by which died first, subject to numerous rules upheld by an umpire. The ideal contest was defined as a 'deep match', defined as one that was as interesting as possible to spectators, in which cocks were evenly matched and the betting was heaviest. For Geertz, the central questions were about why the cockfight was so important a ritual for Balinese men, how it figured within the wider culture and what, precisely, constituted the fascination of the 'deep match'. To begin with, he noted the symbolic centrality of animals in general and cocks in particular, the latter representing not only masculinity but also the Balinese nation. Animals were both a source of symbolic identity and of fear and disgust – demons were given animal form – so that in the cockfight opposites were fused in a 'bloody drama of hatred, cruelty, violence and death' (Geertz 2000, 421). The interest in 'deep matches', which attracted the largest bets, he related to the concept of 'deep play', developed by the early nineteenth-century philosopher Jeremy Bentham in order to describe games in which the stakes are so high that it is irrational for the participants to engage in them. In Balinese cockfighting this was seen to correspond to the 'deep match' on which rival parties placed abnormally large bets – 'they are both in over their heads' (Geertz 2000, 433). According to Geertz, this was not because money was irrelevant to the participants, but because beyond money what was at stake was status and honour. To decipher the meaning of the 'deep match' was to understand its underlying organisation, involving rival kin groups, often from different villages and invariably of near equal status. Cockfighting was therefore sociologically structured in ways that participants and spectators implicitly understood; it represented, literally, a 'status bloodbath' (Geertz 2000, 436).

'Thick description' as exemplified in 'deep play' represents a mode of cultural analysis that is consciously non- (or even anti-) functionalist. Geertz emphasised that events like the Balinese cockfight were examples rather than expressions of a culture (Biersack 1989, 75). Such distinctions may seem fine but they are crucial to grasping Geertz's argument. In social terms, he insisted, the cockfight did not *do* anything: 'its function is neither to assuage social passions nor to heighten them . . . but to display them'. So far from having a social function, Geertz argued, in its aggressiveness and cruelty cockfighting ran counter to the everyday reserve and control of Balinese life (Geertz 2000, 444, 446). What analysis of the cockfight tells us is about the way Balinese men imagined their society to be, about the codes of honour, status and prestige that were understood ideally to order social relationships and the social hierarchy as a whole. In this sense, the cockfight is an event that creatively makes cultural meaning rather than expresses pre-given structures. It is a 'metasocial commentary' on hierarchy or, more simply, 'a story they tell about themselves' (Geertz 2000, 448). The textual analogy is important since it informs the whole concept of 'thick description' as a way of analysing culture. Geertz concluded his meditation on Balinese culture with a statement that referred back to the image of the cockfight and linked it with the idea of text and the larger problem of interpretation itself. 'The culture of a people is an ensemble of texts, themselves ensembles, which the anthropologist strains to read over the shoulders of those to whom they properly belong' (Geertz 2000, 452). It is a statement that applies equally to cultural historians as they struggle to decipher the meanings of a religious rite or a hanging from the medley of contemporary accounts.

The work of Douglas and Geertz has been the object of critique from within and beyond anthropology. Postcolonial critics have accused them of distorting their subjects, feminists of obscuring the dynamics of gender, while historians have noted that the model of analysis – especially that of Geertz – tends to be static, fixing cultures in an eternal present (e.g. Clifford and Marcus, 1986; Moore, 1994; Biersack, 1989). Yet it is clear that cultural anthropology, especially that of Geertz, has had a major influence on certain types of historical writing since the 1970s. It is directly apparent in the growth of 'micro-history', which draws on Geertz's concepts of 'thick description' and 'local knowledge' to develop a microscopic history of a place or person – the everyday life of a medieval village or the world of a sixteenth-century miller – as an entry into understanding the larger culture of which they are a part (Ladurie 1978; Davis 1981 and 1983; Levi 1991; Ginzburg 1992 and 1993). It has also had a more general impact on the development of the new cultural history since the 1980s.

An historical study that exemplifies the impact of cultural anthropology is Robert Darnton's, *The Great Cat Massacre and Other Episodes in French Cultural History*. In the foreword to the book Darnton acknowledges his debt to Geertz, with whom he taught at Princeton University. The kind of cultural history he proposes is consciously anthropological in intent. It 'treats our own civilization in the same way that anthropologists study alien cultures. It is history in the ethnographic grain.' As in Geertz, culture is understood as a text: 'one can read a ritual or a city just as one can read a folktale or a philosophic text' (Darnton 1985, xiii, 3, 5). Through the various chapters, each of which deals with a separate event or theme, the book seeks to apply these perspectives to instances of both 'high' and 'popular' culture – part of the anthropological intent is to ignore the conventional differentiation between them.

In the essay from which the book takes its title, Darnton examines the curious story of a massacre of cats, carried out by the apprentices and journeymen of a Paris printing workshop in the 1730s, in revenge for the injustices suffered at the hands of the bourgeois *patron* and his wife, who is engaged in a secret affair with the local priest. In the 'massacre', the artisans kill not only the cats of the neighbourhood but also the mistress's own pet cat. Thereafter, the episode was regarded as a great joke in the workshop and mimicked on numerous occasions. But as Darnton notes, it does not seem remotely funny to us. This is, in itself, an important signal, since it underlines the 'otherness' of the culture investigated by the historian. 'When you realise that you are not getting something – a joke, a proverb, a ceremony – that is particularly meaningful to the natives, you can see where to grasp a foreign system of meaning to unravel it' (Darnton 1985, 78).

The purpose of Darnton's analysis, therefore, is to reconstruct the world of meaning within which this event could be seen as humorous. To begin with, he locates the episode in the context of the economic pressures affecting the printing trades in early eighteenth-century Paris. Printing workers felt pressures from above, in obstacles preventing journeymen rising into the ranks of the masters, and from below, in the form of unemployment and plentiful cheap hired labour which made the situation of apprentices and journeymen precarious. There were material reasons, in short, why artisans in the printing trades should band together in hostility to their employers. But such factors do not explain why hostility took the particular form of a cat massacre. To shed light on this aspect, Darnton explores the cultural and symbolic dimensions of the event. First, he relates the cat massacre to the popular tradition of carnival, of ceremonies in the early modern period when the conventional social order was temporarily suspended or reversed. It also had affinities with the popular custom of charivari or 'rough music', when husbands cuckolded by their wives were attended by a jeering crowd banging pots, pans and kettles. Cats had a part in these festivities since their howling, purposely provoked, was sometimes used as part of 'rough .music'. Secondly, Darnton pursues the specific symbolic meanings of cats in popular culture of the period – their identification with witchcraft, with bad luck and with the master and mistress of the household, as in the folk tale 'Puss in Boots'. Cats were also identified with women, their sexual parts and with sex in general. Hence the cat massacre, and in particular the killing of the mistress's cat, was a calculated insult to the master and his wife, an insult that was simultaneously social and sexual. It was a means of ridiculing the existing order and extracting revenge through laughter, the traditional weapon of carnival. Because it was symbolic, the workers could get away with it. The episode thus demonstrated that workers were not simply the victims of their situation: 'they could manipulate symbols in their idiom as effectively as poets did in print' (Darnton 1985, 101). In short, artisans no less than artists were makers of cultural meaning.

Darnton's 'Great Cat Massacre' provides an object-lesson in how techniques of analysis drawn from cultural anthropology can be applied in cultural history. As the French cultural historian Roger Chartier noted, the essay 'follows the model of "thick description" to the letter' and it exemplifies the advances in understanding to be gained from applying anthropological techniques to established historical areas such as labour history (Chartier 1993, 98). But such approaches also have critical limitations. In Darnton's case, for instance, the analysis assumes a direct relationship between the story of the 'Great Cat Massacre' and the larger social and cultural context of the period, just as Geertz did in his analysis of the Balinese cockfight. But how far can one assume that a text draws its meanings from a social context or that the former necessarily illuminates the latter? Do not stories (as we saw in Chapter Two) have their own specific conventions that are at least partially distinct from other areas of social practice? And if meaning is itself mobile and unstable, how can we be sure that Darnton's interpretation of the meaning of particular symbols is reliable (see also Chartier 1993, 95–111)? As the chapter continues, we shall begin to see some of the problems of viewing culture as a 'text' and the unspoken ground of knowledge.

Culture, language and carnival

While cultural anthropology has had an indubitable impact on historical writing since the 1970s, the influence of the Russian cultural theorist, Mikhail Bakhtin, has been limited, despite the fact it has a more explicitly historical dimension than is provided by Geertz, Douglas and their followers. Bakhtin has indeed much to offer historians, as commentators like Peter Burke have acknowledged (Burke 1988; Dentith 1995). Born in 1895 Bakhtin lived through the creation and ossification of the Soviet Union. He was little known in the West until after his death in 1975, a situation not aided by uncertainty as to the authorship of particular works in the circle with which he was associated (Bakhtin 1994, 1–4). But since the 1980s Bakhtin's ideas on language as a social or 'dialogic' process, on the polyphonic or 'multi-voiced' character of texts, and on carnival as a dynamic and subversive element of popular culture, have entered the conceptual lexicon of cultural theory and, to a lesser extent, cultural history.

Language or 'discourse' (defined as 'language in its concrete living totality') was fundamental for Bakhtin because it is the basis of social interaction and of culture itself (Bakhtin 1994, 50–72). It is important for historians because the languages of the past, embodied in written, visual and oral forms, are what they study. Bakhtin's particular theory of language was defined in critical opposition to that of Ferdinand de Saussure, the Swiss linguistic philosopher. As we saw in Chapter One, for Saussure language required to be understood as distinct from 'speech' and from the act of individual speaking or 'utterance'. He conceived language as a self-contained system of forms and rules that exists independent of the speaker; this system was his object of study. Language, according to Saussure, is therefore wholly distinct from utterance, which is the product of an 'individual act of will and intelligence' (Saussure 1983, 14).

In developing his own theory of language, Bakhtin opposed both what he termed 'individualistic subjectivism', in which language is seen as the product of individual psychology, and 'abstract objectivism', associated with the theory of language as a system reducible to its phonetic, lexical and grammatical forms (Bakhtin 1994, 26). In the latter case, Bakhtin had as his principal target the structuralist theory of Saussure. First, in contrast to Saussure's structuralist theory of language as a static or synchronic system, Bakhtin argued that language is fundamentally diachronic – historical, changing in line with the 'historical evolution of the speech community'. Secondly, he observed that Saussure's view of language as an abstract system unwittingly privileged the standpoint of the hearer over that of the speaker; 'objectivism' was therefore never properly objective. Finally, and most important, Bakhtin insisted on language as a social process that is always contextual. If individuals do not simply invent language, nor are they merely the subjects of the linguistic system. Verbal communication takes place in a concrete social situation. 'Any utterance – the finished, written utterance not excepted – makes response to something and is calculated to be responded to in turn. It is but one link in a continuous chain of speech performances' (Bakhtin 1994, 27–35). In divorcing utterance from its verbal and social context, therefore, Saussure's theory of language is defined by Bakhtin as 'monologic'. 'Any true understanding of language is dialogic in nature. Understanding is to utterance as one line of dialogue is to the next' (Bakhtin 1994, 35).

Bakhtin's refutation of Saussure and his insistence on language as irremediably social place him in opposition not only to postmodern theorists, such as Jacques Derrida, who argue that 'there is nothing outside the text', but also to historians influential in the 'linguistic turn', whose arguments were based directly on the ideas of Saussure (Derrida 1976; Stedman Jones 1983; see also Spiegel 1997). Language is social for Bakhtin, in the first instance, because people are members of a language community, which is predicated on a shared understanding of linguistic protocols. Language in the sense of utterance or discourse occurs at the boundary between self and others. Its dialogic nature means that language is never static, but a source of 'unceasing creative generation'. It is also social in the sense that language is, in Bakhtin's view, ideologically saturated, permeated by power and those forces – political, cultural and aesthetic – existing at any given historical point. In practice, a language community can be divided into multiple 'socio-ideological' languages, by status, profession, generation, and so on, which contribute to linguistic vitality but also make language a site of social struggle. In particular, a language community is marked by a constant conflict between a centripetal 'unitary language', the product of institutions, such as those of the state, that 'unite and centralise verbal-ideological thought', and centrifugal 'heteroglossia', which work towards fragmentation and subversion of the dominant linguistic order. The division between unitary language and heteroglossia thus incorporates the opposition between 'official' and 'unofficial' discourse and between monologic and dialogic language (Bakhtin 1992, 270–75). As the bearer of truth, unitary language seeks to impose itself on the national culture but in so doing inevitably brings into being its other, represented by heteroglossia; every official discourse calls up unofficial counter-discourses. Furthermore, as products of language, texts may be not only as dialogic but also as 'polyphonic' or multi-voiced, to the extent that they draw on elements of many discourses (Bakhtin 1994, 89–96).

Bakhtin therefore provides historians with a way of thinking about culture through its principal medium – language. But unlike the Saussurean model, which tended to predominate in historians' 'linguistic turn', Bakhtin rejected formalist approaches that effect a radical separation of text and context, language from its specific historical location. So far from being divorced, language (or text) is permeated by its social context, so that the critic or historian must move ceaselessly between the two. Bakhtin, indeed, applied many of his ideas about language to cultural history in a book entitled *Rabelais and His World*, first published in 1965. Though often viewed as such, the book is not primarily a work of literary criticism. It invoked the figure of the French satirical writer François Rabelais (*c.* 1494–1533) in order to explore the larger culture of carnival that fascinated Rabelais and inspired his writings. As an idea, 'carnival' drew its meanings from the community festivals which punctuated the calendar of medieval Europe (and elsewhere), involving feasts and celebrations that could last for days or even weeks. Yet the notion of carnival applies to more than a specific event. In Bakhtin's hands, it stands for a powerful tradition of folk humour and a popular worldview, which, though in decline even in Rabelais' day, was only eclipsed by the romantic movement of the late eighteenth century.

The task that Bakhtin set himself was to recuperate this obsolescent component of popular culture, to analyse its dynamics and to evince its capacity to challenge the authority of the established order. Carnival embodied the spirit of unofficial against official culture, of dialogic imagination against monologic truth. In adopting this viewpoint, Bakhtin looked beyond carnival as ritual spectacle to its intimate relationship with other forms and sites of medieval popular culture. Of particular importance here was the genre of parody, the mimicking of aspects of official culture, notably organised religion, in the form of the scriptures and the liturgy. Mockery of the serious, laughter as a weapon wielded against the holy and highbrow, was thus an essential component of the carnivalesque. Carnival also encompassed the spirit of the marketplace, of curses and street cries, which made town markets a distinctive space of 'freedom, frankness and familiarity' in medieval society. In Bakhtin's account, carnival therefore stood for more than festivity. It represented a fusion of what he saw as the defining features of pre-modern popular culture: scurrilous humour, profane expression and a conviviality that bespoke a utopian desire for a better, more just world.

What forms did the carnivalesque take in early modern Europe according to Bakhtin? In the first place, it offered a temporary suspension and even inversion of normal hierarchies, symbolised by the 'king's uncrowning', the representation of the king as clown, revealed in his true human colours through the mocking laughter of the crowd. It was not the figure of the king alone who was derided, but all institutions of authority, including the church. In carnival everything 'high' became 'low', and everything austere and pious made the subject of comic mimicry. 'This old authority and truth pretend to be absolute . . . they do not recognise their own ridiculous faces or the comic nature of their pretensions to eternity and immutability . . . [In carnival] time has transformed old truth and authority into a Mardi Gras dummy, a comic monster that the laughing crowd rends to pieces in the marketplace' (Bakhtin 1968, 212–13).

Laughter was thus the emotional leitmotif of carnival, the laughter not of the individual but of the people as a whole, an expression of festive gaiety and comic derision. This combination of humour and mockery was also present in its dominant mode of representation, which Bakhtin termed 'grotesque realism', whose 'essential principle is degradation, that is, the lowering of all that is high, spiritual, ideal, abstract; it is a transfer to the material level of earth and body' (Bakhtin 1968, 19–20). Grotesque realism was part of a larger medieval worldview, the world conceived on a vertical up/down axis; it thus designated a 'mighty thrust downward into the bowels of the earth, into the depths of the human body' (Bakhtin 1968, 370). Images of the body inevitably loomed large in the imagery of grotesque realism. The downward thrust drew attention to the belly, the genitals and the buttocks in exaggerated form. It focused on orifices and excrescences, the main points of contact between body and world. 'The main events in the life of the grotesque body, the acts in the bodily drama, take place in this sphere. Eating, drinking, defecation, and other elimination (sweating, blowing of the nose, sneezing) as well as copulation, pregnancy, dismemberment, swallowing up by another body – all these acts are performed on the confines of the body and the outer world' (Bakhtin 1968, 317). Yet the grotesque body was not individual, nor simply a source of laughter and disgust. It represented the body of the people, the preserve of fertility, abundance and creative renewal.

Through his analysis of Rabelais and early modern literature, Bakhtin described carnival as containing an essential utopian element. Laughter unmasked temporal and spiritual authority, and dissolved the cosmic terror of death; in grotesque realism the body of the individual may die but the body of the people is immortal. In Bakhtin's terms, the heteroglossia of carnival had the capacity to subvert official discourse, whether secular or religious, and its claims to a monopoly of truth and virtue. Yet even as Rabelais was writing, the medieval tradition of carnival, together with the popular culture it symbolised, was on the wane. Bakhtin described a change occurring by the sixteenth century in which the vertical axis of the medieval worldview, with its upward/downward movement, was replaced by a horizontal axis. 'A new model was being constructed in which the leading role was transferred to the horizontal lines, to the movement forward in real space and historic time' (Bakhtin 1968, 403). A similar shift was discernible in art and iconography, replacing the grotesque body with a 'new bodily canon' in which excrescences were smoothed over, orifices closed and 'the basis of the image is the individual, strictly limited mass, the impenetrable façade' (Bakhtin 1968, 320). Elements of an earlier folk culture, of symbolism, mockery and laughter, lived on as we saw in Darnton's account of the artisans of eighteenth-century Paris. But it became harder to hear the 'voice of the people' beneath the blare of official ideology. Even so, Bakhtin urges cultural historians to discover that voice. 'All the acts of the drama of world history were performed before the laughing people. Without hearing this chorus we cannot hear the drama as a whole' (Bakhtin 1968, 474).

A number of cultural historians have responded to Bakhtin's appeal. In *Popular Culture in Early Modern Europe* (1978), Peter Burke utilised Bakhtin's notion of carnival to identify and explore its three main ingredients, sex, violence and food. Still more extensively, Thomas Laqueur has drawn on Bakhtin in a detailed analysis of crowd behaviour at executions in England between the seventeenth and mid-nineteenth centuries. The central actor at public executions in London, Laqueur argued, was not the state nor even the condemned person, but 'the people'. 'At the heart of the canonical image of the execution is the crowd: boisterous women, men, and children of all ages and classes engaged in festival' (Laqueur 1989, 332). As such, Laqueur's interpretation places the event squarely within the categories of Bakhtinian carnival, identified with the suspension of normal order, the grotesque body and popular laughter. Not only was an execution an excuse for carnival, contemporaries noting the excesses of drink and revelry among the crowd; it was also, like carnival, a means to demarcate order, 'a classificatory and socially constitutive ritual, defining the boundaries between state and society, between the propertied and the propertyless, between high and low' (Laqueur 1989, 340). The politics of this drama were, Laqueur affirms, essentially conservative, 'the people' being displaced onto the side of the state and social order. Even so, the

politics were not simple: the fact that it was the crowd, not the represent-atives of the law that were the central players in the public execution said much about the weight of popular opinion in relation to the state. It was thus only after 1868, when executions in England were held in private behind prison doors, that the state was able to reclaim full control of the rite of official murder (Laqueur 1989, 354).

Characteristically, however, historians have been as quick to interrog-ate as to investigate ideas such as carnival. Bakhtin has been criticised for his utopian notion of 'the people' as a radical and transcendent historical force. Significantly, Laqueur interprets the tradition of carnival as incor-porating an altogether more conformist aspect and function. Yet his an-alysis of executions has likewise been viewed as exaggerating the power of the crowd and the capacity of the events to represent a 'world turned upside down'. Rather, as V.A.C. Gatrell mordantly puts it, in the public execution 'the harsh realities of worldly power were incontrovertibly affirmed. The state controlled the violence, not the people' (Gatrell 1994, 94). Bakhtin's chronological account of the decline of 'folk laughter' and the rise of 'rational individualism' has also been attacked as deterministic. It is possible to find occasions in modern societies, such as fairs, football and pleasure grounds, which equate in terms of popular behaviour to medieval and early modern carnival (Bennett 1995, 242–5). In the light of this, it is more plausible to argue in the manner of Peter Stallybrass and Allon White that the carnivalesque did not simply disappear in the face of modernity, but rather was 'sublimated' geographically and temporally, continuing to irrupt at specific, marginalised sites and at random moments in urban capitalist culture, from the advertising hoarding to the pop con-cert (Stallybrass and White, 1986). Yet as these examples suggest, if some of the details of Bakhtin's thesis have attracted critical fire, the notion of carnival has continued to be productively deployed in studies of both 'high' and popular culture. While less attention has been paid to his ideas on language – an odd oversight given their potential to serve as a radical alternative to approaches to language based on Saussure – he remains an important theoretical reference point and resource for cultural historians of all periods.

The sociology of culture

Rather like Bakhtin, the work of Pierre Bourdieu has something of a ghostly presence in cultural history. Historians frequently reference Bourdieu, but rarely apply his ideas in any detail. Yet Bourdieu, who died in 2002, was perhaps the most important contemporary sociologist of culture and he wrote widely on epistemology, education and consumption among other subjects. Even more than anthropologists such as Douglas and Geertz he was shaped intellectually in reaction to structuralist ethnography. He had lifelong interests in the operations of language and in literary fiction, which he regularly utilised as both a source and an object of study (e.g. Bourdieu 1993). He had much to say about a variety of subjects of direct historical concern, such as gender, the exercise of power and the effects of domination (e.g. Bourdieu 1996; 2001; Bourdieu *et al.* 2002). And he engaged in dialogue over the years with numerous historians including Roger Chartier, Robert Darnton and Arlette Farge (e.g. Bourdieu, Chartier and Darnton 1985; Corbin *et al.* 1999). Here, however, I shall limit discussion to Bourdieu's ideas about culture and to his principal concepts, field, habitus and capital, which are of value to historical as well as to sociological analysis.

Bourdieu's key ideas about culture are contained in what is probably his best-known work, *Distinction: A Social Critique of the Judgement of Taste*, first published in 1979 and translated into English in 1984. It is a book that is concerned specifically with the ways that the multifarious forms of cultural consumption are socially classified according to ideas about 'taste'. As the title implies, *Distinction* is a critique of the philosopher Kant's concept of the 'pure aesthetic', articulated in his *Critique of Judgement* (1790), which, Bourdieu argued, continues to structure Western attitudes towards art, culture and consumption. The pure aesthetic represents a viewpoint that denies art and culture any link to the social world and any moral purpose; instead, it emphasises a disinterested perspective as essential to a proper appreciation of art and culture. In *Distinction*, Bourdieu sought to show that ideas associated with the Kantian pure aesthetic are false and mystifying. First, he demonstrated that these ideas have come to inform attitudes to all forms of cultural consumption, transmitted through dominant ideas of good and bad taste. Thus the tastes for music or interior decoration of the majority of the population can be dismissed from the Kantian viewpoint as 'inferior' and 'vulgar'. Furthermore, Bourdieu claimed, ideas about taste and cultural value overlap with and reinforce ideas about social hierarchy and class division.

The denial of lower, coarse, vulgar, venal, servile – in a word, natural
– enjoyment, which constitutes the sacred sphere of culture, implies an
affirmation of the superiority of those who can be satisfied with the
sublimated, refined, disinterested, gratuitous, distinguished pleasures

forever closed to the profane. That is why art and cultural consumption are predisposed, consciously and deliberately or not, to fulfil a social function of legitimating social differences (Bourdieu 1992a, 7).

In short, judgements of cultural value derived from Kant's pure aesthetic play an important part in the sustenance and reproduction of an unequal social order.

In pursuing this argument, Bourdieu engaged in two conceptual manoeuvres. First, he anthropologised the concept of culture; that is to say, he transformed Culture (high art, great ideas, etc.) into culture, the domain of everyday life. In *Distinction* attitudes to painting and music, for instance, are conjoined with taste in furniture and food; the aesthetic is correlated with the mundane in an act of demystification. Secondly, Bourdieu aimed to historicise culture as a field in order to negate its effects, which are to turn 'culture' into 'nature', to make what is arbitrary and contingent appear as necessary and permanent. Thus, the predominance of Kant's pure aesthetic in the world of educated opinion, according to Bourdieu, was related to the emergence of art as an autonomous sphere, independent of church, court or any external agency, in modern Europe (Bourdieu 1993, 215–66). Bourdieu's instinct was always to historicise categories such as the 'pure gaze', 'distinction' and 'taste', denaturalising them in the process. However, his purpose was neither to engage in ideology critique for its own sake, nor to pursue a materialist strategy of reducing the cultural to the economic or to an effect of power. On the contrary, he wished to show that culture is a field with its own rules and boundaries, which have to be grasped in order to understand its workings. Thus, Bourdieu described the field of cultural production (i.e. art and creative practice) as an 'economic world in reverse'. In its purest form as art, the field of cultural production works according to 'a systematic inversion of the fundamental principles of all ordinary economies: that of business (it excludes the pursuit of profit and does not guarantee any sort of correspondence between investments and monetary gains), that of power (it condemns honours and temporal greatness), and even that of institutionalised cultural authority (the absence of any academic training or consecration may be considered a virtue)' (Bourdieu 1993, 39). Modern historians (and sociologists) are therefore wrong, according to Bourdieu, to view art and taste either as autonomous creations or, conversely, as the by-product of wider economic structures or power relations. For in so doing they overlook, simultaneously, the subtle way cultural forms interact with the economy and social order as well as the specific 'logic' of the field in which cultural activity occurs.

In *Distinction* Bourdieu undertook a six-hundred-page study of taste and cultural consumption in 1960s and 1970s France, based on a battery of empirical data from questionnaires, surveys and interviews. He divided culture and the tastes derived from it into three types: legitimate, middle-brow and popular. These types were implicitly linked to class and a social order of upper/bourgeois, middle/petit bourgeois, and lower/working class. Yet Bourdieu was insistent that art and taste are not the direct reflection or expression of class; there is no easy match between class and culture of the kind implied by historians when they refer to 'middle-' or 'working-class culture'. Art and taste were seen to refract larger sets of social relations, within as well as between classes, but also, crucially, to naturalise divisions by making them seem at once significant and in-evitable: 'taste classifies, and it classifies the classifier' (Bourdieu 1992a, 6). Class is not produced by culture according to Bourdieu – it is the work of other sorts of pressure and relationship – but culture has a vital part in the sustenance and reproduction of class. In particular, Bourdieu was con-cerned with the 'sense of distinction' itself, the set of cultural competencies that derive from a secure identification with legitimate taste. These com-petencies are associated, in the first instance, with the characteristics of the pure aesthetic: with disinterestedness, the ability to view things neutrally and objectively. Competencies are transferable from the domain of art to that of taste more generally: 'nothing is more distinctive, more distin-guished than . . . the ability to apply the principles of a "pure" aesthetic to the most everyday choices of everyday life, e.g. in cooking, clothing or decoration, completely reversing the popular disposition which annexes aesthetics to ethics' (Bourdieu 1992a, 5). At a certain point, indeed, com-petencies associated with distinction cease altogether to be confined to the sphere of legitimate taste and culture. They become instead social attributes, symbolic of the habit of authority, in which 'distinction' comes to be seen as natural, inhering in the individual rather than a series of learned behaviours. Here among other manifestations Bourdieu noted a certain bodily ease and mental detachment, identified with the freedom from economic necessity on which the whole ideological assemblage of the pure aesthetic is seen ultimately to rest (Bourdieu 1992a, 55).

Culture in this sense represents a form of capital – what Bourdieu termed 'cultural capital' – which can be built up, inherited and exchanged, just like economic capital. The forms of knowledge, perception and behaviour which collectively define distinction are learned, initially through family upbringing and later through education. It is this lengthy gestation, according to Bourdieu, that makes the attitudes and tastes of the dominant class appear so natural and that equally makes it so hard for other individuals and groups, such as the 'new rich', to acquire them: 'true culture is nature – a new mystery of immaculate conception' (Bourdieu 1992a, 68). Distinction is thus a strategy for marking social distance from others; occupying a position of judgement, distinction moves effortlessly between aesthetic categories (beautiful/ugly) and social categories (upper/lower). The exercise of power and authority is never just a matter of wealth, ownership or influence, crucial as these are. For Bourdieu it is fundamentally a matter of cultural prestige, the ability to manipulate the symbolic register, to define 'schemes of perception', to embody 'class' in manner, gesture and physical bearing. It is for this reason that, within the dominant or bourgeois class, so much effort (and money) goes into the transmission of cultural competencies across generations, from training in manners in early childhood to 'character formation' in élite private schools. Consequently, the popular assumption, scorned by most histor- ians and sociologists, that 'class' is immanent in appearance (rather than hidden in the relations of production, for example) is not wrong. For Bourdieu all power is rooted in, and refers back to, the body.

Much of *Distinction* is given over to a critical analysis of the implica- tions of the pure aesthetic as these are manifested in legitimate culture and the dominant class. However, the study is not simple in its treatment of class and culture, nor is its attention confined to 'cultural nobility'. Within the dominant class, for instance, Bourdieu noted persistent divisions between business employers and executives, on the one hand, and profes- sionals, on the other, in attitudes to taste and cultural consumption. Far from composing a unity, the dominant class is an uneasy coalition of groups, the 'site *par excellence* of symbolic struggles' (Bourdieu 1992a, 254). A similar division is observed in the petit bourgeoisie, between shopkeepers and craft employer families, whose taste for the popular approximates to that of manual workers, and the 'avid but anxious' attitude of white-collar groups, such as teachers, who aspire to legitimate culture, but whose cul- tural preferences for light opera or ballet ineluctably stamp their tastes as 'middlebrow' (Bourdieu 1992a, 327). Within the middle classes of mod- ern societies, Bourdieu suggested, economic and cultural capital stand in complex and often inverse relationship to one another – the more a group has of one, the less it is likely to have of the other. On a different axis, the dominant aesthetic is in direct opposition to the dominated aesthetic, strongly identified with the culture of manual workers and their families. Popular taste thus becomes the 'other' of the pure aesthetic of legitimate culture. Whereas the pure aesthetic demands that art should invoke disinterested contemplation, the popular aesthetic demands that it should be 'agreeable' and 'moral'. Yet in depicting working-class tastes sympathetically and in detail Bourdieu – unlike many historians – refused to celebrate the autonomy of popular culture. Instead, he reasserted its dialectical relationship with legitimate culture. 'It must never be forgotten that the working-class "aesthetic" is a dominated "aesthetic" which is constantly obliged to define itself in terms of the dominant aesthetic' (Bourdieu 1992a, 41–3). Bourdieu differed from Bakhtin in his estimation of the subversive power of the popular, but he shared with him the understanding that struggles between classes are also crucially struggles about meaning.

How, then, have historians sought to deploy Bourdieu's theoretical armoury, especially that outlined in *Distinction*? Perhaps unsurprisingly, it has been utilised most extensively in studies of nineteenth- and twentieth-century bourgeois and élite cultures, and most systematically in recent French historiography. Christophe Charle, Director of the *Institut d'Histoire Moderne et Contemporaine*, who was a close associate of Bourdieu in a research group on the history of intellectuals from the mid-1980s, has applied Bourdieu's conceptual framework historically in numerous studies of intellectuals and (with Daniel Roche) of metropolitan cultures (Charle 1994; 1996; Charle and Roche 2002).

In the English-speaking world its usage has been somewhat more tentative if still significant. In *Subjectivities* (1991) Regenia Gagnier draws on Bourdieu's critique of the Kantian aesthetic as a basis for understanding and critiquing the subjectivities depicted in Victorian autobiographies by both middle- and working-class writers. This then allows her to analyse, among other things, Victorian classifications of taste in relation to the form and content of autobiography, and specifically the delineation of the 'modern literary subject' with all its assumptions of autonomy, selfhood and sensibility (Gagnier 1991, 14 ff). Linda Young has similarly deployed Bourdieu's ideas on taste as a social marker to analyse the construction of gentility as a 'transnational cultural system' in the course of the nineteenth century (Young 2003). Echoing Bourdieu's affirmation that all significant social categories refer back to the body, she analyses gentility in particular as a system of bodily regulation and prohibition. The appearance of gentility, and thus of middle-class status, required mastery of bodily movements such as sitting, standing and walking as well as control of bodily substances, including activities such as nose-blowing (Young 2003,

108–17). To be 'middle class', Young insists, was not simply a function of an ascribed or inherited position: 'Believing like the middle class, performing like the middle class, consuming like the middle class, constituted agents *as* the middle class' (Young 2003, 20). Meanwhile, in examining cultures of a more marginal kind, John Lowerson has invoked Bourdieu's evaluation of the uneasy relationship of the lower middle class to dominant cultural norms as a departure point for an investigation of amateur operatics and 'middlebrow' taste in early twentieth-century England (Lowerson 1999).

My own studies of the middle classes in nineteenth- and twentieth-century England have, if anything, been more strongly influenced by Bourdieu's thought. First, his emphasis on the correspondence of cultural and social categories in the classification of social groups offers an important insight into how cultural events in Victorian society, such as the public concert or the Sunday sermon, could be transformed into a social rite by the well-to-do. 'High culture' and the ideas of cultivation and refinement that went with it mirrored and reinforced 'high society' with its intimations of power, wealth and status. Hierarchies of cultural and social classification were thus implicated in a complex rapprochement, meanings reverberating back and forth from one to the other (Gunn 2000). Secondly, Bourdieu's concept of cultural capital is important in explaining the transmission of position and privilege over generations in England, especially among an upper middle class. Patterns of inheritance show the significance not only of economic assets and social connections, but also of cultural dispositions transmitted through the key vectors of cultural capital, those of family and education (Gunn 2005). The combination of upbringing in the middle-class home and lengthy schooling in élite establishments enabled a social position based on wealth to take on all the appearance of a natural order. 'It confers the self-certainty which accompanies the certainty of possessing cultural legitimacy and the ease which is the touchstone of excellence; it produces the paradoxical relationship to culture made up of self-confidence amid (relative) ignorance and of casualness amid familiarity, which bourgeois families hand down to their offspring as if it were an heirloom' (Bourdieu 1992a, 66). Bourdieu's model in which forms of capital – cultural, economic, social – interact and can be transmuted into one another, in effect, provides a valuable framework in which the historical formation and reproduction of social groups can be analysed over time.

Also important is Bourdieu's concept of 'habitus'. Designed to overcome the age-old division between the individual as an active agent, on the one hand, and as the product of objective structures on the other, the habitus is defined as the system of 'durable, transposable dispositions . . . which generate and organise practices and representations that can be objectively adapted to their outcomes without presupposing a conscious aiming at ends or an express mastery of the operations necessary in order to attain them' (Bourdieu 1992c, 53). In simpler terms, Bourdieu sometimes referred to habitus as a 'practical sense' or 'feel for the game' that enables people to adapt to situations without prior calculation or conformity to pre-given rules. It represents dispositions, inculcated from earliest childhood, which are deep-seated and which work to organise people's practices and perceptions. Class and gender are both essential in shaping habitus, while habitus, in turn, contributes to the reproduction of social norms by adapting people's expectations to the possibilities of their situation. 'In reality, the dispositions durably inculcated by the possibilities and impossibilities . . . inscribed in the objective conditions . . . generate dispositions objectively compatible with those conditions and in a sense pre-adapted to their demands. The most improbable practices are therefore excluded, as unthinkable, by a kind of immediate submission to order that inclines agents to make a virtue of necessity, that is, to refuse what is anyway denied and to will the inevitable' (Bourdieu 1992c, 54). In the context of Bourdieu's larger theoretical framework, the concept of habitus is important in explaining cultural continuity and, in particular, the historical persistence of social inequality of all kinds. It has thus been invoked to explain the historical durability of sexual inequality and a specific gender ordering as well as to investigate the perceived invariability of social attitudes over time, such as alleged working-class indifference to art and museums (Lovell 2000; Prior 2002). Christophe Charle, Bourdieu's associate, has recently further proposed the idea of a 'national' habitus, defined by the forms of cultural dominance achieved by élites and bourgeois groups in specific national contexts (Charle 2001).

Bourdieu's theory and concepts have also been the object of extensive critique by theorists, sociologists and historians. Critics have attacked the apparent circularity of his arguments and their apparent resemblance – fiercely denied by Bourdieu himself – to functionalism, so that shared values and norms, internalised via the habitus, serve the purpose of maintaining social stability. How sudden or significant historical change comes about, whether radical political change or new cultural movements like modernism, can be difficult to explain within his theoretical framework, since continuity and conformity are routinely emphasised over rupture and dissent (Jenkins, R. 1992, 81–2; Minard in Corbin et al., 1999, 22).

Other historical theorists, including Michel de Certeau, have criticised Bourdieu's concept of habitus, seeing it as a superficial intellectual solution to the old paradox of agency and determination. For Certeau habitus removes the possibility for strategy and subversion that always remains open to individuals and groups in any social situation (Certeau 1984, 95–6).

In evaluating these criticisms one needs to take account of Bourdieu's own lengthy responses to them, including his dialogue over the years with cultural historians themselves. But his theoretical work contains a number of features that make it an especially fruitful resource for cultural historians. In the first place, his insistence on balancing the epistemological traditions of subjectivism and objectivism is pertinent for historical methodology. Among other ideas, this entails considering reflexively the categories implicit in the model of research itself alongside the evidence of the 'schemes of perception' and historical developments in the past. All historians, for instance, use concepts such as 'élite' and 'intellectual' that are anachronistic in relation to the periods they study; what requires to be considered is how this usage shapes the knowledge historians produce (Bourdieu 1992c, 25–9; Corbin *et al.* 1999, 20). Secondly, Bourdieu's array of concepts, including capital, habitus and field, offer historians the possibility of an analysis that gives full rein to the specific 'logic of practice' governing the subject under study, without having to refer mechanistically to external factors such as political, social or economic structures to explain it. Finally, Bourdieu's work is instructive in taking the cultural field as a whole as the object of study, not just part of it. In *Distinction* this enabled him to deal with both legitimate and popular culture, and to reject the conventional division of cultural knowledge into specialist areas – art history, music history, film studies – as an effect of the very historical processes being studied. In its rejection of dualism and reflexivity, as I shall argue in Chapter Eight, Bourdieu offers historians an important route out of some of the conceptual impasses of the cultural turn.

Evaluation

What, then, have these various thinkers in cultural anthropology, literary theory and sociology collectively contributed to the study of culture? Clearly, their thought has been shaped not only by distinctive intellectual disciplines and traditions but also by the very different objects of their analysis, ranging from tribal cultures in Africa to early modern cultures in Europe. Nevertheless, the theorists examined in this chapter share certain intellectual features. In the first place, their thinking about culture is marked by opposition both to structuralism and to psychologism. Anti-structuralism is evident in Bakhtin's critique of Saussure's linguistics, which serves as the starting-point for his own ideas of dialogism and heteroglossia. But it is also apparent in the rejection by Bourdieu, Geertz and Douglas of the more determinist elements of Lévi-Strauss's theory of culture as system (Bourdieu 1992c, 38–41; Geertz 2000; Douglas 1994, 305). At the same time, there is a refusal of the idea that language and culture can be understood as projections of individual or collective psychology, an emphasis reflected variously in the thought of Geertz, Bakhtin and Bourdieu. Similarities exist, too, at the level of concepts and methodology. Both Bourdieu and Douglas, for instance, evince a strong interest in classification systems, in the body as a social and cultural signifier, and in practice as a category for understanding human activity. Perhaps most fundamentally, at a methodological level, all the critics favour a form of micro-analysis through which larger concerns can be read. Ideas of 'taste' and of pollution, the study of the Balinese cockfight and carnival, represent categories or episodes through which other significant issues can be explored: the organisation of cultural meaning, for instance, or the relationship between symbolic practices, the social order and power.

These various perspectives, which together have contributed substantially to the cultural turn in the human sciences, have equally had an impact on the new cultural history. In some cases, the influence has been methodological, as in 'micro-history'; in others, it is manifested in conceptual insight, as in the Bakhtinian notion of carnival. Overall, however, the influence of the cultural turn has been partial and uneven. Historians have taken up some theorists, such as Geertz, more readily than others and this partiality extends into the various dimensions of their work itself. Thus historians are generally aware of Bourdieu's concepts of taste and capital, for example, but less familiar with his concept of habitus or his ideas about research methodology.

Since the late 1990s there have been signs of a move away from or beyond the cultural turn among certain (predominantly Anglo-American) historians formerly connected with it (e.g. Bonnell and Hunt 1999). Such a move combines a critique of aspects of the cultural turn with a search for alternative models of historical explanation. In part, this stems from anthropologists' own re-evaluation of the legacy of cultural anthropology, which has occurred in the last two decades, initiated notably by the American anthropologist James Clifford (Clifford and Marcus 1986; Clifford 1988). Echoing postcolonial perspectives, Geertz and his followers have been charged with exoticising the cultures they investigate, while simultaneously ignoring the positioned and positioning character of their own fundamental categories, including the act of anthropological observation itself (Dirks, Eley and Ortner 1994, 36–9). A similar criticism can be made of cultural historians, such as Natalie Zemon Davis and Robert Darnton, whose own choice of subjects – a mysterious case of impersonation in a sixteenth-century French village, a massacre of cats in eighteenth-century Paris – can appear as much an act of historical voyeurism as an attempt to understand peasant or artisan cultures (Davis 1983; Darnton 1985; Chartier 1993). Anthropologists, including Mary Douglas herself, have further posed the problem of the appropriate framework of culture and cultural analysis, which are likewise highly pertinent to historians (Douglas 1999, 77–8). To assume cultures are self-contained or framed by boundaries such as those of class or the nation-state, as much history as well as anthropology has tended to do, obscures the extent to which cultures of religion and ethnicity may be transnational and dispersed. As the historian William Sewell puts it, 'Anything we might designate as a "society" or a "nation" will contain, or fail to contain, a multitude of overlapping and interpenetrating cultural systems, most of them subsocietal, transsocietal or both' (Sewell 1999, 55).

As a consequence historians have begun to question the foundations of the new cultural history. The labour historian, Richard Biernacki, for instance, argues that, paradoxically, the cultural turn has had an essentialising effect on historical writing. 'Culture' has replaced 'society' as the ground on which all concepts and categories rest. 'Just as the old historians advanced their project by naturalising concepts such as "class" or "social community", so cultural historians construed their own counter notions, such as that of "sign", as part of the natural furniture of the human world, rather than as something invented by the observer' (Biernacki 1999, 63). In this view, cultural historians like Darnton and Carlo Ginzburg unwittingly exaggerated the coherence of the cultural worlds they studied, while extending the textual analogy to ever more abstruse objects of study. Biernacki cites an article taking a nineteenth-century parlour stove as a text as illustrative of the questionable lengths to which this model of 'sign-reading' can go. While some historians have called in response for the resurrection of social science analysis, Biernacki proposes a less foundational, more selective use of 'culture' and its categories; his intention is to 'shift historians away from their claims about the essence of cultural phenomena and move them towards questioning . . . . the isolable effect of particular cultural forms' (Joyce 2002; Biernacki

1999, 80). Culture, in short, is no longer the ground on which explanation occurs; rather, it represents only part of any explanation of historical change, whose effects – and limits – require to be precisely evaluated alongside other sets of factors, economic, political and so on.

Nevertheless, to indicate that the cultural turn has critical limitations is not to suggest that the theories of culture outlined in this chapter are exhausted. Far from it: in requesting that what is 'cultural' in any explanation be explicitly identified Biernacki echoes Geertz's own advice in *The Interpretation of Cultures*; in emphasising understandings of cultural activity, like reading, as bodily practices, he invokes Bourdieu (Geertz 2000, 27, 30; Bourdieu 1992c). Cultural theory, in effect, continues to be a major resource for new directions in historical study even among those who seek to move beyond now established forms of cultural history. Bourdieu's notions of 'practice' and bodily 'hexis', and Bakhtin's conception of language as dialogic, social and multi-layered can offer historians ways of thinking about human behaviour in the past that transcend the old dualities of representation and the real, subjective and objective, text and context. They hold out the possibility of a renewal of historiography, based on an understanding, first, of cultural activities – looking, listening, speaking – as embodied practices; and, secondly, of culture as made up of complex networks of interacting discourses, socially located and permeated by forces of conflict and power.

CHAPTER FOUR

Power

Both history and cultural theory share a profound interest in the concept of power. How power works and how it might be resisted or subverted are central themes of recent theory, from feminism to postcolonialism, as much of this book testifies. Power is also close to the heart of history as a field of study. It is not only that the state has provided many of the sources for the study of the past and that governments have had an important say in determining what counts as 'history' at any point. It is also that political history, understood as the historical study of power, is traditionally seen to be the dominant branch of history, the 'master topic' taught in every school and university (Tosh 2002, 108–19). Often, of course, such history is confined to 'high politics', the study of the monarchy, parliament and the relationship between nation-states. Yet those who urge a wider, more challenging view of historical enquiry also place power at its centre. Thus the title 'Subaltern Studies' was selected by a group of postcolonial Indian scholars for their radical brand of history, because it signified the 'centrality of dominant/dominated relationships in history' (Prakash 2000a, 122).

There are major differences in the way power and politics are understood by different historians, of course. Minimally, power is defined as the capacity to get people to do something they would not otherwise do. Max Weber, the classical sociologist, defined it as 'the chance of a man or a number of men to realise their own will in a communal action even against the resistance of others who are participating in the action' (Gerth and Wright Mills 1974, 180). Weber went on to distinguish it from a series of related concepts – domination, coercion, influence, authority, force, manipulation – that historians often use somewhat indiscriminately (Weber 1978). There are likewise both narrow and broad definitions of what constitutes politics, from the art of government and the activities of state, on the one hand, to the organisation of collective relationships and the management of conflict in society as a whole on the other. But whatever definitions are used, power and politics are integral to history as a subject. Indeed, one could argue that it is the study of power that organises the historical field as a whole, not only political and social history but also, less obviously, economic history and the history of ideas.

It is because historians are so interested in questions of power that changes affecting how it is understood have such significance. This chapter is concerned with ideas which have contributed to a radical rethinking of the ways that power is conceptualised. These ideas are associated very largely with a single figure, the theorist and historian, Michel Foucault. Most historians are familiar with Foucault's work through his studies of the emergence of the asylum and prison as institutions of disciplinary confinement, first published in the 1960s and 1970s. There is much less awareness of Foucault's later writing on what he termed 'governmentality', which has begun to exercise an influence on recent historical writing. In this chapter, I shall critically evaluate the theoretical transformation instigated by Foucault's later ideas about power, and examine how they have been deployed and developed in three studies of nineteenth-century Britain: of visual display (the 'exhibitionary complex'); the emergence of a discrete sphere of the 'social'; and the implementation of 'liberal governmentality' in the Victorian city. In order to register the scope and importance of this transformation, however, we need first to examine the pre-existing conceptions of power and politics implicit in historical analysis.

Conceptualising power

In a classic study published in 1974, the political philosopher Steven Lukes identified three different views of power used in political analysis. The first, which he called the one-dimensional view of power, focused on the act of decision-making in the political process. Power resided with those whose will prevailed where a conflict of interest or policy was apparent. What was significant in the one-dimensional view was that to count as such power must involve a visible conflict between actors with differing interests or preferences on a particular political issue. The two-dimensional view of power accepted this emphasis on conflict and decision-making, but added in the ability to control the political agenda – what counts as a political issue and what does not – and the fact that conflict and interests might be hidden as well as open. It thus criticised the previous view as overly concerned with the direct behaviour of participants and as ignoring the latent or contextual issues in any political conflict, including the potential significance of 'non' decision-making. Finally, Lukes proposed a three-dimensional or 'radical' view of power. While not excluding conflict and decision-making from view, this extended the concept of power from the immediate political process to include the 'socially structured and culturally patterned behaviour of groups and practices of institutions' (Lukes 1974, 22). Power was thus less an effect of individuals than of collectivities. It was not restricted to situations of overt conflict between observable interests, but might be exercised to prevent needs or grievances finding political expression in the first place, as in cases of manipulation or the imposition of authority. The radical view, favoured by Lukes himself, thus incorporated within the definition of power the possibility that any consensus might be artificial and that real interests could exist beyond those politically visible in any given situation.

Historians generally have shown limited interest in such abstract speculations on power (for an exception see Garrard 1983). Lukes' model is helpful, however, in mapping out the various theoretical positions which have implicitly underpinned historians' approaches to the study of politics and power. Thus according to G.R. Elton, the historian of Tudor England, political history:

. . . deals in people, even individuals, and not in statistical abstractions or notional groups (such as classes). . . Political history inescapably places people at the centre of the enquiry, and the framework provided by the structure of government and the relationship of political beings with one another minimises the danger of anecdotalism . . . The political historian's concerns drive him towards realities – towards what actually happened. They drive him away from dealing in abstract structures and forces which have reality only in the mind of the enquirer – if there (Elton 1988, 20–1).

Elton's insistence on power and politics as a matter of 'people' – politicians – their behaviour and inter-relationships as well as on the observable political agenda – 'realities . . . what actually happened' – indicates that he worked with the one-dimensional view. Not all studies of 'high politics', though, fit within this category. Lewis Namier's pioneering studies of eighteenth-century British parliamentary politics were predicated on the idea that the motive forces of politics lay below the surface of observable political behaviour in the networks of economic interest, patronage and ambition that determined the actions of MPs and their political patrons (Namier 1929). Equally, J.C.D. Clark's influential *English Society, 1688–1832: Ideology, Social Structure and Political Practice* (1985) depicted power as residing not with individuals but with institutions – monarchy, Anglican Church, aristocracy – in order to support his thesis that eighteenth and early nineteenth-century England was an ancien régime state rather than an industrial class society in the making. The recognition in these studies of control of the political agenda, of invisible as well as visible interests and of external institutional pressures on the political process, suggests that they accord with Lukes' two-dimensional view of power.

Like Lukes, however, other historians sought to go beyond both one- and two-dimensional views of power. In defining a three-dimensional, 'radical' view, Lukes was in part responding to the resurgence of interest in Marxist theory in Britain in the 1960s and 1970s stimulated by the work of historians like Eric Hobsbawm and E.P. Thompson (Kaye 1984a). Lukes drew on Marxist concepts of class and 'false consciousness', for instance, to argue for the inclusion of latent conflict and hidden, structural interests in any effective account of power (Lukes 1974, 24–5). At the same time, historians looked to Marxist inspiration for their own studies. In particular, they drew on the theory of two Western Marxists, Antonio Gramsci and Jürgen Habermas, in order to develop a three-dimensional view of power. Gramsci and Habermas loomed large in historical debates in the late twentieth century because they offered new and expanded ways of analysing power and politics in modern Western societies.

What Gramsci brought to the conceptualisation of power was the idea of 'hegemony'. In hegemony he sought to encapsulate the notion that the power of a ruling class was exercised less by coercion than by its intellectual and moral capacity to win the consent of the mass of the population (Gramsci 1982, 5–23; Eley and Neild 1980). Gramsci saw this as a complex process, not as a matter simply of propaganda and manipulation. Hegemony implied more than ideology in the narrow sense; it involved the construction of a whole lived reality such that the existing political, economic and social structures would be taken for granted by the mass of the people, seen as 'common sense' (Williams 1977, 109–11). Nor was the construction of hegemony a one-way, top-down process. It was the product of negotiation between the dominant and the dominated, so that hegemony was grounded in what Gramsci termed the 'national popular'. As this implies, hegemony was not a once-and-for-all condition, but a site of struggle. The consent of the masses was always provisional and therefore had constantly to be renegotiated and re-secured in historical circumstances which were themselves shifting. Especially important for Gramsci was the transition in early modern Europe from an aristocratic society, where the political class was kept aloof by an effective caste system, to a capitalist society, in which a bourgeois state actively sought to mobilise society as a whole in support of its aims and projects (Gramsci 1982, 260).

With its vision of power relations as extending beyond formal political institutions and its emphasis on the manufacture of consent as integral to the political process, Gramsci's concept of hegemony fits well with Lukes' three-dimensional view of power. It corresponded especially with Lukes' point that the exercise of power – and its analysis – does not require that power be expressed through an observable conflict. Thus for Lukes 'the most effective and insidious use of power is to prevent such conflict from arising in the first place' (Lukes 1974, 23). The impress of Gramsci's thought is widely evident in the social history of the 1960s and 1970s. It is variously apparent in E.P. Thompson's studies of eighteenth-century popular culture; in Eric Hobsbawm's account of the triumph of the European bourgeoisie, *The Age of Capital*; and in R.J. Morris' account of class and class consciousness in the industrial revolution (Thompson 1993; Hobsbawm 1975; Morris 1979; see also Kaye 1984b). One of the most thoroughgoing examples of Gramscian history is Robert Gray's essay, 'Bourgeois hegemony in Victorian Britain', originally published in 1977. Gray's intention was to 'deploy the resources he [Gramsci] provides in concrete historical research, with a conscious effort to purge conspiratorial and mechanistic formulations from the vocabulary of Marxist analysis' (Gray 1983, 235). The essay emphasised the complex power relations existing between different classes and fractions of classes (e.g. 'subaltern intellectuals', the labour aristocracy). Through his analysis Gray sought to distinguish between the 'governing fraction' of landowners, which dominated parliament and the state apparatus, and the 'hegemonic fraction' – the group 'whose interests preponderate in the exercise of state power' – identified with the industrial bourgeoisie. The complexion of government and politics concealed the real nature of power in Victorian Britain, according to Gray, which lay elsewhere in the exercise and interests of industrial capitalism. The operations of power were hidden, as it were, beneath the surface of politics.

Gramsci's concept of hegemony informed a series of debates in the 1970s and 1980s about the possibility of a reinvigorated Marxist history, the formation of power in modern states since the eighteenth century and the character of relations of dominance and subordination (Eley and Neild

1980; Eley and Blackbourn 1984; Kiernan 1995). Its influence continues to be registered in historical writing, notably in postcolonial history as will be apparent in Chapter Seven. From the early 1990s, though, it was the concept of the 'public sphere', developed by the Frankfurt School theorist Jürgen Habermas, which displaced hegemony as the most debated theoretical category among historians (Habermas 1992), for Habermas' theory attempted to explain how key categories of modern politics – public opinion, civil society – had come into being historically.

Habermas argued that in early modern Europe there existed no concept of a public – or private – realm. Power was vested directly in the person of the monarch and the court nobility – 'they represented their lordship not for but "before" the people' (Habermas 1992, 8). From the Reformation, according to Habermas, a public sphere gradually developed independent of monarch and court. It was first evident at state level, in the separation of the public finances from the monarch's personal holdings. The decisive historical development, however, was the creation in the eighteenth century of a bourgeois sphere of 'private people come together as a public' to engage in 'rational-critical debate' (Habermas 1992, 27). This public sphere was the product of the network of urban institutions, such as the coffee-house and the newspaper press, which promoted critical debate on the issues of the day, from novels and fashion to economy and politics. Out of this public sphere, which effectively mediated between the institutions of the state and those of society, came a new form of political power, the power of 'public opinion'. Between the late eighteenth and the mid-nineteenth century public opinion changed from the vehicle for criticism of government to the mainspring of government itself, starting with parliamentary and municipal reform in 1830s Britain, and subsequently took root in the political order of other West European nations. Consequently, the public sphere became the 'very organisational principle of the bourgeois constitutional states' (Habermas 1992, 74).

Much of Habermas' study of the public sphere was concerned with what he took to be its historical decline in the modern West, implicit in the shift from a 'culture-debating' society in the eighteenth century to a 'culture-consuming' society in the twentieth. Historians, however, have focused on that part of his thesis that dealt with the inception and formation of the public sphere between the seventeenth and nineteenth centuries. Habermas' thesis was influential in outlining how fundamental categories of politics and the political (private/public, state/civil society) took historical form and the different conceptions of power, monarchical, aristocratic and bourgeois, which underwrote them. In accordance with

Lukes' three-dimensional view, it showed how political categories were embedded in a wider constellation of power, in the structure and culture of the family, for example, and the dense layer of organisations that came to be termed 'civil society'. The thesis had particular influence on historians of eighteenth-century France, concerned with the relationship between the Enlightenment, popular political culture and the French Revolution (e.g. Baker 1989; Chartier 1991; Goodman 1992). Here Habermas' thesis was used to explore how the institutions of associational life – festivals, newspapers, clubs – served to link politics and the everyday 'lifeworld' in Enlightenment and revolutionary France; through the notion of the 'public' it was possible to show how politics at the period was grounded in the world of culture. The thesis has also been taken up and applied in the historiography of colonial and nineteenth-century America (e.g. Warner 1990; Newman 1997). In *Civic Wars*, for instance, Mary Ryan analysed the growth of democratic politics in nineteenth-century urban America through the meanings and practices of an emergent 'publicness', acted out on the city streets as much in meetings and committee rooms (Ryan 1997). More generally, Habermas' ideas have echoed through the historiography of urbanity, consumption and political culture in Britain and Germany since the eighteenth century (e.g. Bermingham and Brewer 1995; Eley and Blackbourn 1984; Vernon 1993).

As often as not Habermas' influence has been registered in critical qualification of his thesis as much as in endorsement of it. Historians have followed feminist critics in pointing out that Habermas failed to identify or analyse the ways in which the public sphere was founded on a specific gender order that excluded women and defined reason and rationality as a masculine preserve (e.g. Fraser 1989; Landes 1990). Others have questioned the chronology of Habermas' thesis and his tendency to associate the public sphere with the expanding influence of the middle class. As John Brooke has put it in relation to American history, 'Habermas essentially argued that the public sphere collapsed as an autonomously functioning arena [in the later nineteenth and early twentieth century] at the very point when many historians have found that public life began to become plural and democratic, and voices of class, gender and race began to challenge the authority of propertied masculine whites' (Brooke 1998, 53). Geoff Eley has further argued that there existed competing 'public spheres' in late eighteenth- and early nineteenth-century Europe, popular as well as bourgeois, comprising plebeian radicals and proto-socialists as well as liberals (Eley 1992). Even in its purest form, in effect, the public sphere was not fashioned within bourgeois culture alone.

Returning to our main argument, it is clear from this discussion that the three-dimensional view of power, identified here with the theories of Gramsci and Habermas, have been influential in social, cultural and political history. But they have also met with mounting criticism within these fields as the case of Habermas suggests. What such critiques indicated more generally, however, was the fact that by the 1990s many historians were finding existing models of power inadequate and were increasingly looking beyond them. With others in the human sciences, they turned to the work of the French cultural theorist Michel Foucault in order to rethink the categories of power and the political. The ideas elaborated by Foucault, particularly in his later work on governmentality, offered a radical challenge to both liberal and Marxist approaches to power. So important is his impact on thinking about power that it has been encapsulated in a single epithet: the 'Foucault effect' (Burchell *et al.* 1991; Bennett 1998).

Foucault: history and power

Foucault enjoyed an ambivalent relationship with the historical profession. His title at the Collége de France where he worked between 1970 and his death in 1984 was Professor of the History of Systems of Thought. He had lifelong interests in the history and philosophy of science and an abiding attachment to the arcane paraphernalia of historical labour: 'libraries, documents, reference works, dusty tomes, texts that are never read, books that are no sooner printed than they are consigned to the shelves of libraries where they thereafter lie dormant to be taken up only some centuries later' (Foucault 1980, 79). Foucault also regularly debated his methods and findings with historians (e.g. Foucault 1980, 146–65; Foucault 1991a). Nevertheless, it was true that Foucault operated at a critical distance from mainstream historians and developed his own concerns, methods and concepts (Jordanova 2000, 79). Understanding his specific and sometimes idiosyncratic approach to history is therefore important in order to appreciate his ideas about the historical operations of power.

In his historical investigations, whether on the treatment of madness or on governmentality, Foucault saw himself as pursuing a very particular form of enquiry. Rather than the study of the past, he was interested in what he termed the 'history of the present' – notably how certain ideas and practices in areas such as psychiatry and penal practice came to be installed as representing 'normality', 'rational conduct' and, especially, 'truth'. This philosophico-historical enterprise placed him at odds with established disciplines of knowledge. 'My books aren't treatises in

philosophy or studies in history: at most, they are philosophical fragments put to work in a historical field of problems' (Foucault 1991a, 74).
To generate the modes of historical analysis that this project required
Foucault adopted two different, though overlapping, methodologies or
'strategies'. The first he termed 'archaeology', the study of discourses
manifested in the archive, specifically the rules of formation governing
those discourses from which a particular knowledge was constituted
(Foucault 2004). Foucault did not interpret historical discourses in order
to discover their 'truth' or understand their author. Rather, he was interested in how such discourses themselves assembled a 'truth', how the
discourses of nineteenth-century psychiatry and criminal punishment, for
instance, instituted themselves as forms of expert knowledge, part of the
emergent 'human sciences'. At the same time, Foucault resisted viewing
his archaeological method as part of any semiotic or linguistic 'turn'. 'The
history which bears and determines us has the form of a war rather than
that of a language: relations of power, not relations of meaning' (Foucault
1980, 114). His second, related, approach to history was that of 'genealogy',
focusing on the historical existence of local or 'subjugated knowledges',
such as those of the patient or the nurse in medicine, and the 'disreputable
origins and unpalatable functions' which marked the creation of the
branches of modern scientific knowledge. While some have suggested that
'genealogy' increasingly superseded 'archaeology' in Foucault's thought,
the two approaches can be considered as separate but complementary:
archaeology represents an 'historical slice', genealogy designates the 'historical process' (Kendall and Wickham 1999, 29–31).

Foucault's history, then, is a history of knowledges rather than of ideas
and of power rather than of politics in its conventional sense. In his early
work especially, he was concerned to demonstrate the symbiosis of power
and knowledge, realised in the formation of major institutions of Western
modernity – the asylum, the clinic, the prison (Foucault 1967; 1973;
1977). 'My problem' he stated in a discussion with French historians 'is to
see how men govern (themselves and others) by the production of truth'
(Foucault 1991a, 79). Yet the highly specific nature of his enquiry should
not distract from the fact that Foucault also sought to break with what
he saw as basic tenets of Western historiography. He was hostile to
any notion of progress, for instance, as also to the idea of an historical
sequence of events linked by cause and effect, and his writings consequently emphasise rupture and disjunction in historical processes. Thus
in *Discipline and Punish* (1977) he saw the institution of the nineteenth-
century prison system as contrary to Enlightenment ideas of punishment.

The prison represented an unaccountable departure from, rather than a logical consequence of, previous penal developments (Foucault 1977, 293–308). As we noted in Chapter One, he was also antipathetic to social history, identified in France with the *Annales* school, considering its ambitions to encompass economy, society and culture to be totalising. Most radically of all perhaps, Foucault questioned the existence of a continuous human subject of history. The 'individual' in a modern sense, he argued, was a product of the nineteenth century. Historians' attempts to see social categories as subjects or agents of history (the bourgeoisie or women, for example) he rejected, along with the assumption that such entities necessarily possessed coherent interests.

One has to dispense with the constituent subject, to get rid of the subject itself, that is to say, to arrive at an analysis which can account for the constitution of the subject within a historical framework And this is what I would call genealogy, that is, a form of history which can account for the constitution of knowledges, discourses, domains of objects, etc., without having to make reference to a subject which is either transcendental in relation to the field of events or runs its empty sameness throughout the course of history (Foucault 1980, 117).

Foucault adopted an equally iconoclastic approach to power and the political and here too his thought changed over time. Whereas in *The Birth of the Clinic* (1973) and *Madness and Civilization* (1967) power was treated in conventional fashion as a repressive force, from *Discipline and Punish* onwards he viewed it more flexibly as a technology or strategy rather than as a possession. Power was more than merely repressive; it was also, in several senses of the term, productive. In his later work he began to study the political sphere more explicitly, through the developing concept of 'governmentality'. By governmentality Foucault designated a specific modern form of power targeted at 'population', which came to predominate over other types of power in Western Europe between the sixteenth and nineteenth centuries (Foucault 1991b, 102–3). The social theorist Mitchell Dean defines it more expansively as a 'novel thought-space across the domains of ethics and politics, of what might be called "practices of the self" and "practices of government", that weaves them together without a reduction of one to the other' (Dean 1994, 174; see also Dean 1999). Governmentality encompassed the 'conduct of conduct', the art and rationality of all forms of governance (Rose 1999).

Foucault clarified this concept by describing the historical conditions of its emergence. Between the sixteenth and eighteenth centuries, he argued, there was a rapid expansion in literature devoted to the problem of government at all levels, from the state to the school and family. In this literature it was possible to see a shift occurring from a form of government whose overriding purpose was to strengthen the ruler's relationship with his territory and subjects, as in Machiavelli's *The Prince* (1513), to other more complex forms of governmental rationality. By the eighteenth century government was seen as having not a single but multiple ends, such as the increase of wealth and population. Through new forms of knowledge, notably political economy, population itself was rendered visible both as an object and as an end of government. How to manage a population and how to maintain its wealth and security became an essential part of the art of government and its rationality. At the same time, 'politics' and 'economy' came to be understood as distinct, the former dealing with the techniques of government, the latter with a sphere of reality increasingly viewed as autonomous and self-regulating. These shifts themselves were linked to successive modes of rule: 'reason of state' associated with the rationalisation of the principles of state government; 'police' with its apparatus of surveillance which first constituted population as an object of knowledge; and subsequently with liberal governmentality, as we shall see (Foucault 2002, 201–22 and 298–325; 1991b, 239–64; Gordon 1991, 1–51; Simons 1995, 36–41).

Such ideas were a deliberate provocation to existing right- and left-wing views of power. On the right, Foucault attacked the notion of sovereignty, specifically the idea that ultimate power was located in a determinate body – the crown, the people or, as formulated in nineteenth-century Britain, the 'monarch in parliament'. 'Power must be analysed as something which circulates . . . It is never localised here or there, never in anybody's hands, never appropriated as a commodity or piece of wealth' (Foucault 1980, 98). This meant that power was to be analysed in its effects rather than its sources and at the margins rather than at the centre. To understand the power of the penal code, for instance, was not to view it as a set of abstract principles or a system of justice but to analyse its effects on the body of the punished. Historical analysis should therefore be concerned not with who possessed power but how power was exercised, its practices, strategies and technologies at micro-level. 'Mechanisms of power have never been much studied by history. History has studied those who held power . . .' (Foucault 1980, 51).

Foucault's critique of theoretical orthodoxy also extended to left-wing and Marxist views of power. He was sceptical of views which identified the modern state as the fulcrum of power, preferring to see the state itself as a set of practices rather than as an institution or (like Althusser) an 'apparatus', as dispersed rather than unitary, and as invested in domains usually associated with civil society, such as sexuality and the family. Whereas Gramsci tended to look *through* the modern state to its role as a vehicle for bourgeois interests, Tony Bennett has observed, Foucault sought to look *at* it, at how governmental power worked as a mode of rule (Bennett 1998, 69). By extension, Foucault did not consider that power and political agency lay, principally or perhaps at all, with social classes. 'I believe that anything can be deduced from the general phenomenon of the domination of the bourgeois class. What needs to be done is something quite different. One needs to investigate historically, and beginning from the lowest level, how mechanisms of power have been able to function' (Foucault 1980, 100). Furthermore, power itself was not to be regarded solely as an instrument of repression or domination, but as a circulating, omnipresent force, neither good nor evil. Consequently, resistance – the talisman of radical politics and history – was not the opposite of power, but its corollary. In Foucault's terms, resistance was the 'counterstroke' to power, the two always operating together. For if there can be no resistance without power, without resistance there can be no history (Kendall and Wickham 1999, 51).

Foucault argued that, ultimately, both liberal and Marxist conceptions of power shared a certain 'economism'. While in the liberal version power was seen as a right, to be possessed like a commodity, in the Marxist version power was understood to be rooted in the economy itself. It was with this pervasive economism that Foucault sought to break (Foucault 1980, 88–9). No less fundamental was his critique of sovereignty, the notion that power must ultimately reside in a specific location – in parliament, the state, the bourgeoisie, for instance. Here Foucault saw contemporary analysis of politics as immured in an old problematic, a discourse of 'despotism and legitimation, rights and repression'. By holding to this inherited idea of sovereignty, whose origins went back to the ancien régime, historians remained trapped in an anachronistic conception of power: 'we have still not cut off the king's head' (Gordon 1991, ix). Foucault's proposal for the study of the 'micro-physics of power' consequently went well beyond the model of analysis outlined by political theorists such as Lukes. Moreover, they are ideas that have exerted growing influence across various disciplinary domains in the decades since Foucault's death in 1984 (Bennett 1998; Burchell *et al.* 1991; Rose 1999; Simons 1995). In the following sections, I shall examine how his ideas have been deployed in three studies of nineteenth-century Britain.

The eye of power

One of the best-known aspects of Foucault's theory was his analysis of power as surveillance. Foucault identified the ability to control individuals' behaviour merely by watching them with the Panopticon, the principles of which were laid down by the utilitarian reformer Jeremy Bentham in the late eighteenth century. In Bentham's schema, the Panopticon represented a central tower, surrounded by a circular building comprising cells, each containing an individual inmate and open to view by a single overseer located in the tower. This was not only efficient in that one person could oversee a large number of inmates. It was also effective, in the sense that, according to Bentham, the simple fact that inmates knew that they might be watched at any moment was sufficient to modify and control their behaviour. Vision, here in the form of the overseer's gaze, operated at a distance as a mode of power (Foucault 1977, 195–230). Foucault invoked the model of the Panopticon as part of his account of the transformation of forms of punishment between the eighteenth and mid-nineteenth centuries. Whereas in the earlier period punishment was enacted on the body of the accused and treated as a spectacle designed to deter, by the later period it occurred in the closed site of the prison, was aimed at the mind and was designed to reform behaviour through repetition – for example, in the use of the treadmill (Foucault 1991b, 128). The nineteenth century witnessed, indeed, a 'swarming of disciplinary mechanisms' based on surveillance; the principle of the Panopticon was applied variously in schools, barracks, hospitals as well as prisons. The eye of power, in effect, became an essential component of the repertoire of 'security' in modern societies.

These ideas of vision and discipline informed the important historical study of the 'exhibitionary complex' by the cultural sociologist, Tony Bennett (Bennett 1995, 59–88). What Bennett designated by this latter term was a set of interrelated nineteenth-century, cultural institutions, such as the public museum and the industrial exhibition, which promoted new ways of displaying people and objects. By contrast with Foucault's disciplinary institutions, such as the asylum and the prison, which resulted in increasing withdrawal and confinement, the institutions of the exhibitionary complex represented an opening up to public use of older institutions like the museum and the library. Bennett therefore qualified Foucault's assertion of the installation of a 'carceral archipelago' during the nineteenth century. The spectacle of power and power as spectacle did not wither but flourished on new sites and in new formats. The exhibitionary complex was responsible for representing and disseminating in a visual fashion the ensemble of power and knowledge to a mass public.

How was this effected? Bennett noted that the opening of exhibitions and museums to great crowds of visitors was attended at first by a commensurate fear of public disorder. This was the case in Britain with the Great Exhibition of 1851, which attracted over six million visitors, and with museums such as that at South Kensington (later the Natural History Musum) which opened in 1857. Significantly, however, the fears proved groundless. The circulation of people in large open rooms and spaces around organised displays appeared to have an anaesthetising effect; the crowds were well behaved and the displays were left untouched. In explaining this phenomenon Bennett proposed an expansion of the panoptical principle. In the great halls and galleries of the exhibitionary complex everyone could see and be seen; events thus combined the 'functions of spectacle and surveillance' (Bennett 1995, 65). Through the spatial and visual technologies instituted especially by the major exhibitions of the second half of the nineteenth century, society came to be represented in the harmonious form of a spectacle. 'Expositions realised some of the ideals of panopticism in transforming the crowd into a constantly surveyed, self-watching, self-regulating and, as the historical record suggests, consistently orderly public – a society watching over itself' (Bennett 1995, 69; see also Sennett 1994, 292–304).

Exhibitions generated a further set of power effects by displaying knowledge in novel ways under the influence of emergent subject disciplines such as anthropology, archaeology and history. There were temporal and spatial dimensions to the principles that came to underpin displays of goods or pictures in the nineteenth century. In the first place such displays began to be organised chronologically, suggesting development and progress rather than universal values. Visitors would move through galleries which showed successive historical periods. The rapid growth of anthropology from the 1870s was especially important in this regard, enabling Western civilisations to be compared favourably with the 'primitive', 'pre-historical' cultures of peoples to be found in the outposts of European empire. By the period of high imperialism in the late nineteenth century, exhibitionary spaces had become organised on racial as well as national lines, reconstructions of 'native' villages complete with inhabitants proving especially popular attractions. Cultures were ranked on an evolutionary spectrum, in which the Western visitor, however humble, was placed firmly on the side of civilisation and progress. Disciplines from archaeology to art history were likewise mobilised within the exhibitionary complex to tell a single story of progress, based on crudely racist grounds and highlighting the achievements of the West in general and the metropolitan nation-states in particular.

The exhibitionary complex thus gave spectacular form to constellations of power and knowledge through specific technologies of representation or 'ways of seeing'. These technologies were novel and potent, reaching into the entertainment zones of popular culture (such as Blackpool) as well as the world expositions organised under the auspices of the state. Just as the Eiffel tower, built for the 1889 Paris Exhibition, enabled a panoramic dominance of the city, so the exhibitionary complex lent to the eye of power an almost Faustian dominion. It 'constituted an order of things and of peoples which, reaching back into the depths of pre-historic time as well as encompassing all corners of the globe, rendered the whole world metonymically present, subordinated to the gaze of the white, bourgeois and . . . male eye of the metropolitan powers' (Bennett 1995, 84). In Bennett's Foucaultian account of the birth of the museum, then, power was seen to reside not so much in a class (the bourgeoisie) or set of institutions (the state) as in the deployment of particular technologies of vision, assemblage and display, allied with new disciplines of knowledge. The powers generated in and through the exhibitionary complex circulated through the culture as a whole. While fairs and popular commercial entertainments might offer vicarious escape from the 'official' cultures of the industrial exhibition, they shared elements of its technology and ideological content (for example, the panorama and imperial themes). The museum, the public library and the art gallery were part of the disciplinary apparatus of nineteenth-century Western societies, distinct from but contiguous with carceral institutions such as the asylum and the prison. 'Where instruction and rhetoric failed', Bennett concluded, 'punishment began' (Bennett 1995, 88).

Historical epistemology

Bennett's study of the exhibitionary complex engaged critically with Foucault's ideas of surveillance and the disciplinary gaze. In *Making a Social Body: British Cultural Formation 1830–1864* (1995), Mary Poovey drew inspiration from a different set of writings by Foucault on the origins of the human sciences and the formation of modern rationalities. For Foucault, as we have seen, the emergence of objective, statistical knowledge of economy and society from the eighteenth century was an important political development. This knowledge, characteristically termed 'political economy', was to become the basis for forms of governance that for the first time took population as their object, its wealth, welfare and security. The development of political economy marked the transition from the view of government as an art to that of a science, 'political science' (Foucault 1991b, 95–101).

In *Making a Social Body* Poovey appropriated elements of this approach and applied them to the study of the preconditions for a unified 'mass' culture in later nineteenth-century Britain. Her conceptual framework owed an explicit debt to Foucault's mode of discourse analysis and, in particular, his account of the emergence of the human sciences. This framework Poovey termed 'historical epistemology', which she defined as the field that 'allows for the production of what counts as knowledge at any given time' (Poovey 1995, 1, 3). Here Poovey's analytic focus paralleled Foucault's concern with the 'politics of the scientific statement' and the construction of a 'régime of truth' (Foucault 1980, 112). The epistemological field consists of domains – what constitutes the boundaries and internal rules of a given area of knowledge-discourses, rationalities and disciplines. These were understood by Poovey to be the product of the epistemological field itself, not of external agents, such as the state, or of identities, such as gender and class. Epistemology – the formation of knowledge – shaped identity, not the other way round; it enables us to grasp how identities such as 'race' became visible at particular historical periods (Poovey 1995, 3). Adopting this perspective, Poovey's strategy was to uncover and analyse the process of disaggregation of the modern domains of knowledge – the 'economic', the 'political', the 'social' and so on. This disaggregation was seen as the precondition for the emergence of 'mass culture' from the later nineteenth century onwards. Poovey's enterprise was therefore an ambitious historical one: to show how fundamental categories of modern thought and governance took root in early and mid-Victorian Britain.

As her title suggests, part of Poovey's aim was to indicate how a concept of the 'social' developed as a relatively autonomous domain. The issue is critical given how routinely historical analysis (not to mention sociology) relies for explanation on reference to a social dimension, and the likelihood that the modern concept bears the marks of its origins. In the eighteenth century, Poovey argued following Foucault, the concept of the economic, previously related to the management of the household, was yoked to that of the political to refer to the governance of national resources, as in 'political economy'. Alongside this stood an older medieval notion of the 'body politic', referring to those recognised as political subjects (as against, for example, the excluded poor), which was steadily replaced by the term the 'body of the people'. By the early nineteenth century, both concepts were overtaken by the metaphor of the 'social body', which retained an important ambiguity of meaning: it could denote either the whole of the population of a nation-state or the poor alone. 'The phrase "social body" therefore promised full membership in a whole (and held out the image *of* that whole) to a part identified as needing both discipline and care' (Poovey 1995, 7–8). The term 'social' equally designated both an aggregated population (society, the poor) and a disaggregated domain of knowledge and action (social problem, social relations).

Poovey went on to describe how this emergent social domain was given increasing definition between 1820 and 1860 by technologies of 'population', such as empirical observation, 'fact-gathering' and, above all, statistics. Ian Hacking has argued that early nineteenth-century Britain was overtaken by an 'avalanche of numbers' in every area of enquiry from epidemic disease to social insurance. Statistical surveys showed time and again the 'taming of chance'; human actions appeared to follow laws as regular as those of physics (Hacking 1991, 185–9). The statistical societies established from the 1830s contributed to the creation of a separate social domain by identifying 'social' (as against 'economic') topics such as health, crime and education at the same time as focusing analytical attention on the poor. Poovey presented the New Poor Law of 1834 as a concrete example of these processes. The measure was framed on the basis of empirical 'facts' assembled by a Royal Commission and analysed by 'experts'. In 'solving' poverty its purpose was precisely to demarcate the social from the economic dimensions of the problem. Pauperism was distinguished from poverty, the former understood as a social phenomenon to be subjected to remedial action in the workhouse while the latter was deemed an economic category, to be left to the workings of a free market. The New Poor Law thus reflected the understanding of an emergent social domain while simultaneously giving material form to that domain through its institutional effects (Poovey 1995, 11).

Crucially, Poovey argued, the disaggregation of domains such as the social and the economic was predicated on a quintessentially modern model of scientific abstraction which allowed populations to be seen as internally homogeneous and therefore amenable to statistical calculation. The origins of this model of abstraction lay in the scientific method of the seventeenth century; its product was the powerful idea that space is abstract and empty. Abstract space was uniform, always the same and representable in the form of an empty grid. Because it encompassed both physical and social space (human relations) it enabled individuals to be viewed as functionally equivalent to one another and for persons to be identified with place. The concept of abstract space thus came to operate in the early nineteenth century as a paradigm of Foucaultian disciplinary power. It helped shape the view of the city itself as a 'social body', promulgated by influential medical men who, again following Foucault, were depicted as centrally involved in constructing and disseminating new forms of statistical knowledge and empirical method (Foucault 1980, 151; Poovey 1995, 37–42, 55–72). In the work of reformers such as James Kay, Edwin Chadwick and Thomas Southwood Smith between the 1820s and 1840s, the conditions of the poor were scrutinised, quantified and analysed prior to sanitary and pedagogic intervention. Through the process of abstraction, people were conflated with their environment; poor persons were transformed into 'slum-dwellers' (see also Mayne 1993). Intervention in the domain of the social, Poovey argued, left the market free as demanded by the principles of *laissez-faire*. Abstraction simultaneously served to relieve the emergent economic domain of moral obligations derived from earlier religious discourse. By the 1860s the effect of these processes was to produce a new conception of the individual, the 'disciplinary individual', self-reliant and self-governing, while simultaneously homologous with other individuals (Poovey 1995, 24).

Power and knowledge were thus synchronous in Poovey's account. While historical formations and processes operated at the level of domains in the epistemological field, their effects were registered materially on the bodies of the poor and the fabric of the city. Lest this model of power appeared too monolithic and determinist, Poovey argued that it accommodated complexity. The full logic of abstraction was never practically implemented; it was inhibited by religious obstacles in education and by popular resistance in the case of the New Poor Law. More fundamentally, power was never total because the process of the disaggregation of domains was uneven. In the field of historical epistemology emergent domains like the social had to co-exist and compete with residual domains of knowledge, notably the theological. The persistence of culturally and legally-sanctioned gender inequality, for instance, reflected the pressure of an older theological logic on the abstract rationality of the emergent economic domain of homologous individuals. In areas like philanthropy the complex interweaving of knowledges was especially evident, abstract rationality operating at the same time as old assumptions about God-given hierarchy and understandings derived from personal experience and face-to-face relationships (Poovey 1995, 43–52). Poovey's historical epistemology, the disaggregation of domains and the creation of the liberal individual, thus exemplified and extended Foucault's own genealogical account of the human sciences. While power worked in and through knowledge (Foucault's 'orders of discourse'), modern rationality simultaneously totalised and individualised its principal object, 'population'. In Poovey's words, by 1860 British society was 'free' 'in the sense that its members constituted individualised instances of a single subject, whose life was subdivided among the domains that claimed autonomy but appeared to be alike' (Poovey 1995, 24). Neither individuals nor classes made history; rather, these categories only came to the surface of historical visibility through the organisation and workings of knowledge.

Liberal governmentality

If part of the purpose of Poovey's neo-Foucaultian study was to explain the emergence of the modern individual, the political conditions of the 'free' liberal subject have been addressed directly in Patrick Joyce's *The Rule of Freedom: Liberalism and the Modern City* (2003). Like Poovey and Bennett, the context for Joyce's study was nineteenth-century Britain, but in this case the conceptual framework was provided by the notion of 'liberal governmentality'. After Foucault, Joyce defined liberal governmentality as a mode of rule whose lynchpin was the liberal subject itself, a self which was at once self-watching and watchful of power. 'In liberalism rule is ceded to a self that must constantly monitor the very civil society and political power that are once the guarantee of freedom and its threat' (Joyce 2003, 4). As this implies, the idea of freedom was integral to the liberal mode of rule; it represented not simply an end of government, an absence of restraint, but also, paradoxically, a technique of rule and thus a form of restraint. In liberal governmentality, Foucault observed, freedom is the condition of security (Gordon 1991, 19). In Joyce's study, moreover, liberalism referred to more than a political party, philosophy or ideology. It designated rather a form of governance that proclaimed its transparency, cultivated the reflexive and vigilant citizen, and sought to govern at a distance from its object. Consequently, liberalism was better understood as a series of practices than as a set of principles. Joyce's aim in *The Rule of Freedom*, therefore, was to re-evaluate politics in nineteenth-century Britain in the light of the substantial conceptual shifts wrought by the notion of governmentality.

Rather than taking the conventional frame for studies of governance, the nation-state, however, Joyce took the city. From the 1820s cities like

Manchester, Glasgow and, above all, London posed urgent problems of governance as their populations escalated and Britain shifted from a predominantly rural to the most highly urbanised society in the world. The city, Joyce argued, was the principal locus and object of liberal rule, the site where the techniques of rule were earliest and most systematically honed. Initially, at least, this necessitated the implementation of techniques from the repertoire of 'police', notably the amassing of information on populations. In order for power to be exercised in the name of liberal freedom, its object must be known, which was to say rendered visible. Joyce thus indicated the numerous media through which knowledge of the city and its inhabitants was acquired from the 1820s. They included not only statistical surveys and the census but also maps (the Ordnance Survey was active with ever-increasing detail at this time), newspapers, guidebooks and the spread of street signs and door numbers with the advent of the Penny Post in 1840. From this perspective, 'democracy' in its mid nineteenth-century incarnation appeared as a 'gigantic political technology based on number' (Joyce 1995, 24).

Liberal governance affected the way the city itself was viewed, as a vast self-regulating system akin to the human body. In the early Victorian period this meant that intervention by government was seen in pathological terms as restoring the urban body to its natural state of health. Circulation was a vital principle for the idea of the 'sanitary city', whether it involved circulation of water (drainage, water supply), air (ventilation of houses, parks as 'lungs') or people (crowds, traffic). Rather than viewing the history of the city as being defined by steadily increasing governmental jurisdiction over its running – a linear narrative that implicitly informs much of urban history – Joyce saw successive phases of liberal rule as based on changing governmental conceptions of the city. Thus the 'moral city' of the mid-Victorian decades was marked by a didactic historicism, expressed most strikingly in the architecture of the city centre, the monumental warehouses, public buildings and town halls. Architectural historicism was at this point an important way in which cities expressed their modernity, but buildings acted also as a form of moral address, providing a constant reminder of the ethical dimensions of citizenship. From the late nineteenth century the concept of the moral city was overtaken by the notion of the 'social city', predicated on what was now seen as the inherent sociability of populations which could be promoted by effective planning of the urban environment (Joyce 2003, 144–82). From Joyce's perspective, political will was not so much imposed on the physical infrastructure of the city as built into it, thus overriding conventional distinctions between government and people, state and civil society. Indeed, following currents of thought in science studies, Joyce argues that liberal rule inhered in and worked upon the very material fabric of the city. For not only were pavements, pipes and sewers designed so as to facilitate the freedom of the liberal subject by removing all impediments to movement, they were also developed in certain ways as self-regulating systems with their own forms of agency (Joyce 2003, 11–12).

In its incarnation in the nineteenth-century city liberal governmentality was characterised by a number of other features. Governance of self and society involved 'publicity': liberal freedom depended 'upon creating the conditions of a political legibility and visibility which would entail full knowledge of the subject's self, and just as much of the subject's society' (Joyce 2003, 100). The Municipal Corporations Act of 1835 required that local government should be opened up, made visible to itself and to the wider community. Likewise, the free library movement inaugurated in 1850 was intended to bring the light of knowledge to bear on urban society and its citizenry. The design of many public libraries, of which the British Museum Reading Room, built in 1847, was exemplary, itself contributed to the making of the liberal subject. As well as being free and public, the library offered private, silent reading overseen by a central supervisor; it promoted 'self-help and self-culture', knowledge of the world and, equally, of the local (Joyce 2003, 128–37). Moreover, it was not sufficient that liberal rule should invoke freedom; it had to be seen to enact it. This required what Joyce termed the 'performance' of liberalism in a variety of ways. The objectivity of government was performed partly by the separation of politics from administration, the former defined by party conflict, the latter identified with neutrality and expertise. Liberal freedom was also performed by walking the city, whether in the guise of the solitary wanderer or of the great public processions of the late nineteenth century which incarnated in bodily form ideas both of social hierarchy and of urban community. By means such as these, liberal rule was embedded in practices and technologies that provided it with great scope and flexibility. The continuing power and pervasiveness of liberalism, according to Joyce, lies not just in its connection to 'our sense of being free', but also 'to the way it is knitted into everyday life' (Joyce 2003, 8, 261).

Drawing extensively on Foucault, *The Rule of Freedom* provided a significant re-conceptualisation of nineteenth-century political history. Its focus was not parties, institutions or ideologies but techniques of rule, the strategies and practices by which governance was enacted. The study therefore accorded with Foucault's injunction to analyse the exercise of power instead of those who were deemed to hold it. By extension, power was seen as the product of abstract political rationalities rather than of individuals and groups with coherent wills and interests. Political change involved shifts in governmental rationality and the techniques of rule, not new policies or altered class alignments. Furthermore, Joyce's study departed from the conventional frame of political analysis, the nation-state or the specific locale used as a 'case-study' to investigate a wider historical issue or trend. While the focus in *The Rule of Freedom* was on nineteenth-century British cities, it encompassed also cities in Europe and beyond. In particular, liberal governance in Britain was seen as shaped by the encounter with colonial subjects, in Ireland and India, where modern techniques of rule were often first formulated and trialled. This emphasises, finally, how extensively politics and the political were expanded in Joyce's study. 'Power and also rule itself', he argued, 'are dispersed far beyond the areas and channels in which they are usually acknowledged' (Joyce 2003, 188). Power did not stop at parliament or town hall in the nineteenth century; it haunted the material world, the water pipes and paving stones of the modern city.

Evaluation

In their critical apparatus, then, each of the three studies outlined here moved beyond the one-, two- and three-dimensional views of power described by Steven Lukes. In none of the studies was power related specifically to the process of decision-making or to the ability of one individual or group to impose its will on another. Indeed, in the cases of Poovey and Joyce, there was an explicit rejection of the idea that power was identified with any specific group or institution. Furthermore, the studies had little to say about the conventional stuff of political analysis – parties, policy, politicians. Instead, their focus was directed towards the political in a broader sense, to the grounds of politics. How did a modern sphere called 'politics' come into being separate from, say, 'economy' and 'administration'? What kind of political subjectivities were envisioned by new techniques of governance? These questions are clearly derived from Foucault, but the authors engaged in critical development of his ideas rather than in slavish adoption of them. For this reason their work could properly be regarded as neo- or post-Foucaultian.

Foucault's ideas about power and history have themselves been the object of sustained criticism since the early 1980s (Weeks 1982; see also

Burke 1992). Some of this criticism came from historians and centred on differences of interpretation in the histories of punishment and madness, though it also extended to Foucault's cavalier and partial use of sources (e.g. Melling 1999; Zedner 1991). Other historians have expressed general reservations about his ideas and their application in historical study. French scholars such as Michelle Perrot and Arlette Farge suggested that Foucault had an 'anaesthetising effect': his historical work had an 'implacable logic' that left no space for alternative views (Foucault 1991a, 82–6). In a more partisan assault, the British historian Gareth Stedman Jones accused Foucault of a determinism that derived from the latter's exposure to Althusserian Marxism. 'His was a form of social theory imposed upon history; unremittingly grim and yet at the same time whimsical in its magnification of certain forms of evidence and its wilful disregard of others. Similarly, it remained parasitic upon Marxism, while at the same time stridently declaring its difference from it' (Stedman Jones 1996, 25). The stridency of Stedman Jones' own denunciation, however, overlaid a very partial reading of Foucault's work. While identifying a 'totalising' concept of power with *Discipline and Punish*, Stedman Jones ignored Foucault's response to his critics on this score and the nuanced treatment of the limits and resistances to power contained in the later work on governmentality. The elision of Foucault with a discredited species of Marxism in practice amounted to little more than a rhetorical defence of Stedman Jones' own more orthodox approach to the study of politics and society, based on the application of insights from intellectual history.

This is not to say that the Foucaultian approach in its historical applications is without problems. Two areas of difficulty in particular can be identified, apparent to a lesser or greater extent in all of the historical studies I have discussed. The first major issue is the 'top-down' tendency that characterises the analytic optic, despite the idea that power circulates rather than being imposed from above. In Bennett's study of the exhibitionary complex, for instance, the historian (and reader) partakes of the omniscient or panoptic view of the 'overseer'. The view from the gallery floor is hardly considered, nor the fact that exhibitions might be seen from – and engender – a variety of subject-positions rather than a single, uniform 'subject'. Nor, more generally, is there much concern to enable the subaltern voice – in whatever form – to speak. The 'rhetorical contest' between power/knowledge and its object, as one of Poovey's critics states, 'is entirely one-sided' (Gagnier 1999, 117). Equally, despite their critique of abstraction and emphasis on the practical nature of power/knowledge, Poovey and Joyce present the latter in highly abstract form, as 'epistemology' or 'rationality'. In part this derives from the sources and methods used: the tendency to select canonical texts or sources produced by the powerful and to undertake interpretation by a process of 'close reading', especially noticeable in the case of Poovey. But as another anonymous critic of *Making a Social Body* observed, 'Textualising non-literary events and interpreting them by the lights of even apparently non-formalist poststructuralist theories silently assimilates all kinds of events and texts to the ontology, language and professional work that were initially specific to the formalist, aesthetic and university-based treatment of literary texts' (Anon 1999, 137). Nor is this simply a function of a method or disciplinary viewpoint as the quotation itself hints. It is a product also of what might be termed the 'abstractionist eye' of the modern university itself, the preference of the academic institution for rationality over messiness, a 'reason' which historians and literary critics tend to reproduce in their own accounts.

Secondly, there is the question of agency or, rather, its absence. It is possible to agree with Foucault that power is not a commodity and history not a matter of sequential cause and effect, but this leaves unanswered the question of how historical change occurred and who or what contributed to it. What defines and generates change in a technology, a rationality or an epistemology? Foucault himself preferred to substitute the concepts of 'problem' and 'necessity' for those of 'will' and 'interest' but this deferred rather than resolved the issue (Foucault 1980, 206). It also creates difficulties for historians such as Joyce who seek to integrate this understanding into their analyses. Thus in *The Rule of Freedom* the reader is confronted by statements such as 'it was necessary to moralise' the city or the state 'felt its way into the future' (Joyce 2003, 15, 23). Why it was necessary, what impelled the state and, indeed, what specifically constituted 'reason' and 'rationality' in these contexts are all questions, however, that remain unexplained. The rejection of social agency becomes particularly acute in areas such as political rights or public health where the intervention of institutions, groups or even individuals clearly had a significant role in changing the relevant discourse (e.g. Baker 1989; Hamlin 1998). Furthermore, by placing the emphasis on historical phenomena as the effects of knowledge, neo-Foucaultian perspectives fail to explain certain persistent features of the organisation of power in modern societies. Why, for example, did all modern definitions of the social focus remorselessly on the bodies of workers and the poor while excluding the well-to-do? Why, if power is dispersed and multivalent, did it so often *appear* as unidirectional?

These are not the only conceptual problems, of course, though they are certainly significant ones. Nor are they necessarily damaging in the overall context of Foucault's thought and his attempt to go beyond the old duality between liberal pluralist and Marxist conceptions of power. Such is the transformative character of Foucault's enterprise that any serious student of power and the political will need to settle with it, as much as in historical studies as in other branches of the human sciences (see for example Barry, Osborne and Rose 1996; Hunt, A. 1999). Perhaps the central legacy of Foucault's thought is not his well-known ideas of disciplinary knowledge or even his critique of sovereignty, important as these are. It is, rather, that power is always an exercise, never simply an attribute. The task of the historian is consequently to make visible the techniques of power and to indicate how these might have cohered into something resembling a mode of rule, an 'ordering of order'. This, of course, is a reflexive task, amounting to what Foucault called a 'history of the present' as well as of the past. It is also part of that larger history of modernity to which we will now turn.

CHAPTER FIVE

Modernity

The modern and the postmodern have become some of the most widely used – and controversial – categories in cultural theory. In recent decades they have been the object of a series of fiercely contested debates conducted across a wide variety of disciplinary fields, from art and architecture to philosophy and the social sciences. These debates have involved complex questions of definition as well as of content. It is necessary to distinguish, for example, between postmodern*ism*, which refers to new modes of thought or stylistic categories, and postmodern*ity*, generally taken to designate a new stage or condition of society. Confusingly, perhaps, the term postmodern can relate to both of these two broad definitions, so that we can speak of a postmodern style of architecture and of a postmodern era. Much discussion, as we shall see, has revolved around the concept of the postmodern itself – whether it exists or not, what forms it takes, how its significance should be understood and so on. But increasingly theorists have begun to recognise that one of the most important consequences of the debate about the postmodern is that it brings into critical view the concept of modernity itself, so often overlooked or taken for granted (Wagner 2001, 5). All the questions of definition and substance that are asked of the postmodern apply equally – and perhaps still more urgently – to the category of the modern. This reorienting of critical attention from the postmodern to the modern in cultural theory has particular significance for historians since it impacts directly on their methods and – medievalists arguably excepted – their field of study.

For a long time historians were bystanders in the debates about modernity and the postmodern (Niethammer 1992, 1–5). Since the early 1990s, however, they have begun to engage, more or less tentatively, with the idea of modernity. In the Anglo-American world historians of science led the way, followed by social and cultural historians. Nevertheless, the concept of modernity has been received differently in particular national historiographies. In the case of British history, for example, recent historians have tended to emphasise the continuity between pre-modern and modern periods, so that the issue appears one of explaining a 'deferred modernity' (Conekin *et al.* 1999, 20). In the United States modernity is rendered invisible by its apparent ubiquity; not only has the United States epitomised modernity for much of the twentieth century, it has no existence as an independent nation state that is not in some sense 'modern' (Novick 1988). In parts of Continental Europe, by contrast, notably post-fascist and post-communist states, the question of modernity has an urgency that is directly related to the sense of rupture caused by political upheavals and the necessity of coming to terms with a problematic past (Hobsbawm 1995; Bessel 1996). Yet this differentiation on national lines is paradoxical, for while the nation-state is often understood as the creation of modernity, the concept of modernity itself assumes processes that are transnational and even global in scope. Much of the importance of modernity, and its heuristic value, reside in the fact that the concept overrides local and national contexts and encourages the historian to think about processes and frameworks that are simultaneously more wide-scale and fundamental (Bayly 2004).

The aim of this chapter is to explore the concept of modernity from an historian's perspective. In the process I shall look at some of the key debates in social and cultural theory about the modern and postmodern, though not as an end in themselves. I am interested, rather, in the interface between those debates and historical study – how ideas about modernity can be, and indeed have been, utilised by historians. We start by considering the definitions and meanings of modernity. While, as with the postmodern, there is no single, clear definition of modernity, this can be seen as a source of conceptual richness, enabling the historian to move between different analytical dimensions and perceive unexpected connections. The matter of definition is followed by a more familiar historical question, that of periodisation: when was modernity? Answering this question not only emphasises the reciprocal relationship between historical periodisation and interpretation, the one shaping the other, but also raises issues to do with temporality – the construction of time – and with nostalgia, whose presence may permeate historical accounts more thoroughly than historians generally allow. In the third section I discuss the recent historiography of the modern city as a case-study of the ways in which theories of modernity have come to inform historical research and have been enriched in the encounter. The chapter concludes with a critical evaluation of the category of modernity, its outstanding problems together with the possibilities it opens up for innovative historical practice.

What is modernity?

It is a truism to say that modernity is a concept with multiple meanings. The essential task is to unpick those meanings, to understand their context-specific character as well as the distinctions between the related terms 'modern', 'modernism' and 'modernity'. At its most basic the modern denotes the new, the contemporary, but it has also had particular historical significance. In the Europe-wide debate between the 'Ancients and Moderns' at the turn of the eighteenth century, for example, to be modern was to believe in the possibility of a present civilisation that might equal or even surpass in knowledge and beauty the achievements of classical Greece and Rome. The modern was here counterposed to classical antiquity, not simply to tradition (Gay 1973, 308–23). Yet the debate did not disrupt the belief that Europe's achievements were the direct product of the inheritance of ancient Greece and Rome. This was to be significant, as I shall argue, for it erased Europe's lengthy connections in this respect with Africa and Asia, and paved the way for a sharp contrast to be drawn between European modernity and the alleged 'backwardness' of other regions of the world at a period of accelerating imperial expansion (Bernal 1987). In the later decades of the nineteenth century 'modern' was used rather differently to describe a sense of restlessness, instability and disconnection from the past (Daunton and Rieger 2001, 5). These historical references to the modern, however, correspond only in part with the way the concept of modernity has been deployed by recent theorists. Indeed, we need to register at the outset the significant differences of meaning attached to the related terms involved: 'modernism', referring to movements in the arts and architecture between the later nineteenth and mid-twentieth centuries (Bradbury 1991); 'modernity', denoting both a framework of thought and an historical stage; and the 'modern', which in adjectival form might refer to any of these (e.g. 'modern art', 'the modern world'). There are obvious parallels here with the broad meanings attached to the term postmodern and its derivatives, but with a crucial difference: in simultaneously designating a structure of thought and an historical formation 'modernity' combines in one word meanings that are conventionally separated out in the terms postmodernism and postmodernity.

In understanding the notion of modernity it is therefore helpful to trace its conceptualisation in theoretical debates. Arguably the most important debate about modernity and the postmodern was the exchange in the 1980s between the French philosopher, Jean-François Lyotard and the German social theorist Jürgen Habermas, concerning what Lyotard termed the 'postmodern condition', which we have already touched on in previous chapters (Lyotard 1992). This debate, in turn, referred back to the early twentieth-century ideas of the sociologist Max Weber, one of the first intellectuals consciously to use the term modernity (Swingewood 1998, 137). Weber identified modernity with the break-up of the unified world-view provided by Christian religion, undermined first by the Protestant Reformation and subsequently by the philosophical rationalism of the eighteenth-century Enlightenment. Following the Enlightenment philosopher Immanuel Kant, Weber saw the principle of modernity as the division of knowledge into a series of autonomous spheres, notably science (identified with reason), morality (linked to justice) and art (associated with beauty). The creation of these spheres and the opportunities they held out for progress, emancipation and truth constituted the promise of the Enlightenment and of modernity. But Weber also saw this promise as being corrupted by countervailing pressures: the tendency for reason's emancipatory potential to be undermined by bureaucratic and capitalist rationalities; the propensity for the spheres themselves to be dominated by professional specialists and, thus, become exclusive; and the possibility of the values of the autonomous spheres spilling over into one another, as in the aestheticisation of politics, exemplified by fascist pageantry. The effect of these pressures was the decline of hopes for a society based on freedom and justice which modern reason had set in train and its replacement by an 'iron cage of rationality', characterised by the 'disenchantment of the world' and spreading bureaucratisation (Gerth and Wright Mills 1974).

In Weber's pessimistic reading, then, modernity is defined by the differentiation of spheres of knowledge which provide the basis for rational action. The debate between Lyotard and Habermas took place, as it were, in dialogue with Weber's formulation, subsequently embodied in the tradition of the Frankfurt School of critical theory (Adorno and Horkheimer 1973). Like Weber, Lyotard took the Enlightenment as his main historical reference point, together with the differentiation of knowledge which flowed from it. But in his interpretation the guiding principle was not the differentiation of knowledge into autonomous spheres but its legitimation in and through a series of 'grand' or 'meta'-narratives. These narratives included the 'dialectics of Spirit', which animated the search for objective and disembodied truth, and the 'emancipation of the rational or working subject', which put science at the service of the people (Lyotard 1992, xxiii, 31–7). The history of modernity since the Enlightenment, culminating in the disastrous wars, dictatorship and genocide of the first half of the twentieth century, has been the delegitimation of those grand narratives that assumed knowledge was pure, impartial and served the cause of progress – that truth, in short, must be aligned with justice (Lyotard 1992, 40). The necessary result was a loss of belief in grand narratives – what Lyotard termed 'incredulity towards metanarratives' – which was the hallmark of the 'postmodern condition'. Furthermore, Lyotard proposed that knowledge itself has become not so much differentiated as increasingly fragmented with the spread of information technologies – cybernetics, telematics and so on – in the second half of the twentieth century. Science consequently resembles a series of 'language games' where knowledge is no longer transferable from one domain or 'game' to another, or necessarily cumulative, building progressively on what has gone before. Instead, each 'language game' is discrete, accessible only through its particular rules of knowledge. But Lyotard did not view the postmodern condition as an evil, necessary or otherwise. On the contrary he saw it as representing an opportunity to abandon the maleficent effects of modernity, with its totalising, 'terroristic' forms of knowledge, and to explore the possibilities of 'difference' and respect for the alterity of the other. 'The nineteenth and twentieth centuries have given us as much terror as we can take', Lyotard declared; 'Let us wage a war on totality' (Lyotard 1992, 81–2).

On the other side of the debate, Habermas stood in defence of Weber, the Frankfurt School and what he termed the 'project of modernity' (Habermas 2001, 10). In his discussion of modernity he consequently reiterated Weber's account of the Enlightenment, the differentiation of the spheres of science, morality and art, and the baleful effects of professionalisation and intermixing of the spheres. But unlike Lyotard – and to a lesser extent, Weber – Habermas did not view modernity as exhausted or a postmodern condition as having been attained. Instead he described modernity as an 'incomplete project'. In so doing Habermas asserted the significance of the rupture between the modern and the pre-modern, the shift from a worldview based on faith to one based on reason. Equally, he upheld what he saw as the principal promise of the Enlightenment project, 'the prospect of a self-conscious practice, in which the solidary self-determination of all was to be joined with the self-realisation of each' (Habermas 1987, 337). Self-consciousness, self-determination, self-realisation – these were the products of the Enlightenment ambition to link critical reason to purposeful social change. Finally, Habermas charged Lyotard and other 'postmodernists' with conservatism, complicity with the status quo and wilful disregard for their own intellectual and institutional location. Against such critics he advocated a renewal of the Enlightenment project through an expansion of 'communicative reason', an expanding democratic dialogue (Habermas 1985).

What was significant in the Lyotard/Habermas debate, however, were not only the differences between the two theorists but also the fact that they agreed on much to do with the basic definition of modernity. For both theorists the Enlightenment was a crucial reference point. By extension, modernity was defined, first and foremost, in relation to knowledge or, more precisely, a conception of it identified with reason, objectivity and progress, in the sense that knowledge was understood as cumulative and as underpinning the advancement of society as a whole. At the same time, modernity was not confined to knowledge alone; it had implications for politics, culture (in the sense of modernism) and society, understood as what Lyotard termed the 'social bond' (Lyotard 1992, 11–14). So while the notion of modernity inherent in the debate might appear narrow, in so far as it did not invoke a clear set of historical changes such as industrialisation and democratisation, it did involve broader sets of issues than the purely philosophical. Nevertheless, the debate serves as an important reminder that modernity has at its definitional heart a particular conception of, and relation to, knowledge.

At the same time there are other ways of conceptualising modernity. In an important tradition linked also to the origins of modernism and traced back to the French romantic poet Charles Baudelaire, modernity is associated with the experiential impact of social life in the burgeoning cities of the nineteenth and early twentieth centuries: Manchester, London, Paris, Berlin, Vienna, New York (Frisby 1985). For Baudelaire, in a celebrated formula, the modern meant 'the transient, the fleeting, the contingent', qualities experienced most signally by the *flâneur*, the solitary figure who strolled the city's teeming streets absorbing the fluctuating impressions, in the crowds while not of them. The modern metropolis conjured up a 'phantasmagoria', a hallucinatory vision of people and commodities; it provided an endless succession of images of the new, the fashionable and contemporary (Baudelaire 1972; Benjamin 1992). Ambiguity and ambivalence were, indeed, fundamental components of the experience of modernity, suggested by the sense of exhilaration and anxiety, of freedom and loss that the individual encountered most powerfully in the modern metropolis. It is a perspective that was taken up and extended by the

American critic Marshall Berman in *All That is Solid Melts into Air: The Experience of Modernity* (1982). Like Baudelaire, Berman saw modernity as encapsulated by the visceral, dislocating experience of urban existence, which he traced from Second Empire Paris, through revolutionary St. Petersburg to later twentieth-century New York. But whereas Baudelaire related that experience only in passing to the processes of commercialism and commodification, Berman rooted it in capitalist urbanisation as articulated in Marx and Engels' memorable vision of the maelstrom created by the advent of capitalist society, outlined in *The Communist Manifesto* (1848).

All fixed, fast-frozen relations, with their train of ancient and venerable prejudices and opinions are swept away, all new-formed ones become antiquated before they can ossify. All that is solid melts into air, all that is holy is profaned, and man is at last compelled to face with sober senses, the real conditions of his life, and his relations with his kind (Marx and Engels 1969, 83).

Modernity, according to Berman, is therefore a condition or experience arising from the upheaval produced by capitalism, with all its ambivalent promises and perils. 'To be modern is to find ourselves in an environment that promises us adventure, power, joy, growth, transformation of ourselves and the world – and, at the same time, that threatens to destroy everything we have, everything we know, everything we are . . . To be modern is to be part of a universe in which, as Marx said, "all that is solid melts into air"' (Berman 1982, 15).

In Berman especially, modernity is tied closely to historical processes, not only to modernism as a cultural phenomenon but also to modernisation as an historical movement that is purposive and global. In much social and cultural theory, however, the emphasis remains on the epistemological: modernity as a form or way of knowing rather than of experiencing. As Alan Swingewood has noted, while wary of any epochal concept of modernity, Michel Foucault preferred to view it as a means of 'comprehending the present without recourse to transcendent principles enshrined in concepts such as totality' (Swingewood 1998, 142–3). The anti-essentialist element in poststructuralist and postmodern thought has tended to identify modernity, logically though often problematically, with certain epistemological foundations – the idea of a clear division between reality and its representation, of society as a totality, of history as a determinate process, and so on. Thus, in a theorist like Jean Baudrillard the postmodern signals precisely the collapse of these foundations – the implosion of the real and its supersession by the hyperreal, the dissolution of the 'social' and the end of history as a meaningful process (Baudrillard 1988). The social theorist Anthony Giddens, meanwhile, who distances himself from the notion of postmodernism, sees a defining feature of modernity as 'reflexivity', the capacity of individuals and institutions to respond and adapt to increasing, complex streams of information. In particular, this involves a 'reflexive project of the self' so that personal identity in modernity is understood to be fashioned from a continually adjusted series of 'self-narratives' (Giddens 1996, 20, 52–5). In all these theorists, therefore, modernity is tied to a series of philosophical and conceptual understandings, involving topics ranging from science and society to the self.

How, then, can we reach an understanding of the idea of modernity from these differing sets of interpretations? First, one does not have to accept Lyotard's prognosis of a postmodern condition to acknowledge that the debate about the postmodern has reactivated and altered the idea of modernity itself. As the sociologist Zygmunt Bauman puts it: 'If the concept of "post modernity" has no other value, it has at least this one: it supplies a new and external vantage point from which some aspects of that world which came into being in the aftermath of the Enlightenment and the Capitalist Revolution (aspects not visible, or allotted secondary importance when observed from inside the unfinished process) acquire saliency and can be turned into pivotal issues of the discourse' (Bauman 1992, 102–3). Yet one needs to accept the existence of a series of tensions or fissures in the general notion of modernity. To begin with, modernity combines within its overall meaning both subjective and objective dimensions. Modernity thus refers both to modern social and cultural formations *and* to the conceptual apparatus through which knowledge of these formations is acquired. This means that it is simultaneously an epistemological and an historical category. Even within the epistemological dimension, however, there is a split between two traditions of thought, one deriving from Weber that understands modernity in relation to a certain formation of knowledge, the other descending from Baudelaire that foregrounds the fragmentation of experience. Beyond all this there lies a further set of issues, only intimated here, about the politics of modernity – how far currents of thought associated with Western modernity can claim universal significance and what it means to do so. But before we can look in greater depth at these various aspects, we need to investigate a more obviously historical feature of the problem, the periodisation of modernity.

When was modernity?

To speak of modernity, or simply, the modern, implies a temporality, a (pre-modern) 'before' and a (post-modern) 'after'. Yet many theorists have rejected this idea of temporality, at least in its conventional historical form. The late nineteenth-century philosopher, Friedrich Nietzsche, for example, attacked the whole notion of history as a linear process, the unfolding of human potentiality across time. Nietzsche's role was to deny the historicist attempt to impose a single form and meaning on the past, and to free the present from the thrall of this species of historical 'determinism' (Nietzsche 1983, see also Ermath 1992). His philosophical successors went further, seeing linear temporality as an essential prop in the intellectual scaffolding of modernity from which they wished to escape. The German cultural theorist Walter Benjamin criticised the attachment of Rankean historiography to naturalism ('showing things as they really were') and to a narrative of chronological succession as the 'strongest narcotic of the [nineteenth] century'. Instead historians needed to rip objects and events out of their place in a temporal succession in order to grasp their meaning, and to understand that different temporalities existed in the same historical epoch, the archaic in the midst of the modern (Benjamin 1999, 25, 26, 463). Equally, at the end of his most celebrated work, discussing modernist painting, Lyotard paradoxically defined the postmodern as part of the modern: 'A work can become modern only if it is first postmodern. Postmodernism thus understood is not modernism at its end but in the nascent state, and this state is constant' (Lyotard 1992, 79). Even the most ardent advocates of the postmodern, however, have found difficulty in wholly escaping the temporal dimensions of their subject. Thus despite his denial of periodicity, Lyotard nevertheless dated the beginnings of the 'postmodern age' from the late 1950s with the completion of the reconstruction of the Western economies after the Second World War and the development of new information technologies (Lyotard 1992, 3–4). In his major study *Postmodernism or, the Cultural Logic of Late Capitalism*, Frederic Jameson likewise associated the postmodern with the advent of new cultural forms from the 1960s, though, borrowing from the Marxist theorist Ernest Mandel, he also equated it with a phase of 'late capitalism' since 1945 (Jameson 1993, 1, 35–6). The issue of periodisation, like that of history more generally, will not go away.

Historians themselves have had little if any input into the definition of any putative postmodern era, but they are habituated to the idea of periodisation itself. The historical record of the West is thus conventionally split into ancient, medieval and modern periods, the last category itself divided between early and late modern. Nevertheless, when the 'modern' started has long been a subject of debate. Historians have posited among other break-points the Renaissance of the fourteenth and fifteenth centuries as the moment at which a humanist culture broke free of the medieval inheritance; the discovery of America by Columbus in 1492, marking the beginnings of European expansionism and the foundations of the modern world system; the seventeenth-century scientific revolution and the dispute between the Ancients and the Moderns, as we have noted; and the dual revolutions of the late eighteenth century, the political revolution in France and America and the industrial revolution, which brought into being industrial capitalism and the idea of representative democracy. Breaking with this Eurocentric version of modernity, C.A. Bayly suggests it was an historical process starting in the late eighteenth century: 'It encompassed the rise of the nation-state . . . alongside a massive expansion of global commercial and intellectual links' (Bayly 2004, 11). Modernity was thus identified with the long process of globalisation in which China and Japan were as important as Europe and North America.

Modernism, meanwhile, is conventionally associated with the emergence of an artistic avant-garde and of non-representational modes of art in Europe from the last decades of the nineteenth century, though its origins too have been the subject of debate. While the onset of modernism can be dated differently between art forms – painting and the novel, for example – so too its inception can be debated within them. In architecture, for instance, modernism has been attributed not only to the florid style of art nouveau of the 1890s, but also to the ascetic formalism of inter-war architects such as Mies van der Rohe and Le Corbusier (Frascina and Harrison 1988).

Nevertheless, one feature is common to these different notions of the modern and of modernity. This is the idea that the modern marks a decisive break with what preceded it, a rupture between old and new worlds. Theorists such as Lyotard, Habermas, Bauman and Stuart Hall, each with different degrees of affiliation to postmodernism, all associate the moment of rupture with the Enlightenment (Bauman 1987; Hall, Held and McGrew 1992, 281–2). The Enlightenment is here seen as the cut-off point between a world-view dominated by faith, superstition and tradition, and one based on reason, science and progress. Jürgen Habermas puts it this way: 'The spell which the classics of the ancient world cast upon the spirit of later times was first dissolved with the ideals of the French Enlightenment. Specifically, the idea of being "modern" by looking back to the ancients changed with the belief, inspired by modern science, in the infinite progress of knowledge and in the infinite advance towards social and moral betterment' (Habermas 2001, 6). What was at stake in the Enlightenment was the division between the traditional and the modern; hence Anthony Giddens' definition of modernity as a 'post-traditional order' (Giddens 1996, 20).

Among historians, those who have contributed most actively to discussions about the periodisation of modernity have been historians of science. Stephen Toulmin has noted how, from the 1930s onwards, Western intellectual historians and philosophers tended to identify the onset of modernity with the seventeenth-century scientific revolution, and specifically the ideas of Descartes and Galileo in the 1630s. The hallmark of this revolution in the orthodox view was the 'adoption of rational methods in all fields of intellectual enquiry', the combination of empirical investigation in the sciences with abstract, 'pure' philosophy (Toulmin 1992, 13). Later intellectual movements such as the Enlightenment as well as the technological transformation associated with the industrial revolution all had their origins in the radically altered view of knowledge and the world that emerged in the scientific revolution over a century earlier. Descartes and Galileo between them laid the basis for a scientific method which was to create the possibility of continuous intellectual and material progress. This break with tradition at the level of ideas, so the conventional interpretation had it, was paralleled in the political sphere by the rise of the modern nation-state in Europe from the 1660s, independent of the power of the Papacy and older political constellations such as the Holy Roman Empire. While accepting much of this account, Toulmin argued for some modifications to it. He proposed, for example, that the intellectual origins of modernity owed as much to the tradition of sixteenth-century scepticism, associated with figures such as Erasmus and Montaigne, which was itself the creation of Renaissance humanism. The contribution of the tradition of humanist scepticism was a critical open-mindedness and a distrust of theoretical systems. Modernity, according to Toulmin, was therefore the product of 'twin trajectories', one sceptical, practical and experientially-minded, the other metaphysical, scientific and pursuing abstract universal laws. The history of modernity can be written in terms of the changing balance of power between these two poles of opinion. Toulmin thus interpreted the changes in thought evident in philosophy and the sciences since the 1960s not as a move from modern to postmodern, but as a shift in the axis of modernity; a reversal in emphasis from Cartesian rationalism to Montaignian scepticism, from 'the written, the universal, the general and the timeless' to the 'oral, the local, the particular and the timely' (Toulmin 1992, 167–201).

Other critics, however, have questioned more or less radically the whole notion of identifying modernity with science, reason and progress in this manner. Just as surrealism is to be understood as part of artistic modernism, so 'irrationalism' requires to be integrated into a history of Western 'reason'. As the social historian and theorist Craig Calhoun has argued in an important essay on 'Postmodernism as pseudohistory', romanticism was as significant an intellectual current in the production of nineteenth- and twentieth-century modernity as rationalism; the 'anti-modern' has, historically, always been embedded in the modern itself (Calhoun 1993, 75–96). Emphasising the scientific revolution or the Enlightenment as the foundation of modernity thus ignores the complexity of its actual historical formation. Indeed, Bruno Latour, the historian of science, has gone further, arguing the case that 'we have never been modern'. In the debate between the Ancients and the Moderns, Latour suggested, historians and theorists assumed that it was the Moderns that emerged victorious. In reality, though, modernity was only ever partially realised. For Latour, modernity implied a condition where the 'hybrid' ideas and imaginings of the pre-modern world would be excluded from a 'pure' science. Whereas in the pre-modern world the natural and the human were intertwined, in modernity nature and culture are understood as distinct spheres. But in reality this state has never been achieved according to Latour. 'We must speak as if nature and culture are clear and distinct realms but act as if they were not. We produce the modern world by mixing natural and cultural things into productive hybrids who [sic] can then promptly be ignored thanks to the purifying tendencies of modern thought' (Latour 1993, 46). The modern world is thus based on an obfuscation of the pre-modern with which it practically co-exists (see also Lee and Stenner 1999).

What appears as a technical question about the emergence of the modern therefore rapidly becomes a series of complex historical and philosophical questions about the definition and meaning of modernity itself. Even posing the question, 'when was modernity?' implies a nostalgic concern with origins evinced, not least, by the persistent attempts to identify it with a precise starting-point and definite historical periodicity. Nostalgia was built into the very inception of modernist ideas in the later nineteenth century, as even their champion, Habermas, recognised. 'The new value placed on the transitory, the elusive, and the ephemeral, the very celebration of dynamism [in thinkers like Baudelaire and Bergson], discloses the longing for an undefiled, an immaculate and stable present' (Habermas 2001, 7). For cultural theorists such as Walter Benjamin and Michel de Certeau, modernity is a condition haunted by the spectres of the past. In a discussion that prefigured in certain ways the arguments of Latour, Certeau observed that 'any autonomous order is founded upon what it eliminates; it produces a "residue" condemned to be forgotten. But what was excluded re-infiltrates the place of its origin . . . It resurfaces, it troubles, it turns the present's feeling of being "at home" into an illusion . . . [and] it inscribes there the law of the other' (Certeau 1986, 4).

It is partly against this pervasive historicism and attendant nostalgia that post-structuralism and postmodernism have been defined. Theorists such as Lyotard and Jacques Derrida predicated their arguments on a rejection of the search for origins and a concomitant refusal of nostalgia. We have to learn to think, in Derrida's phrase, 'without nostalgia', to give rein to the 'play' or 'agonistics' of language without reference to foundations or beginnings (Derrida 1982, 27; Lyotard 1992, 10, 41). While Derrida has subsequently expressed doubts about the possibility of such a stringent state of affairs, a number of cultural theorists like Jean Baudrillard and Frederic Jameson have continued to represent the absence of history as a cardinal feature of the alleged postmodern condition. This absence takes several overlapping forms. It implies, to begin with, the notion that knowledge of a real past is unattainable, not only for the epistemological reasons suggested in Chapter One, but because we live in a culture where effective relations with the past have been severed. To live in the postmodern is to experience a world that is depthless, history-less, a world in which we are condemned to an endless present. The postmodern therefore represents a rupture not simply with modernity, but with any sense of continuity with what has gone before. In his celebrated description of America, Jean Baudrillard took as one of its defining features an absence of history and historical memory, by contrast with European cultures, which he depicted as saturated by history, aesthetically and politically. 'For me, America is . . . the experience of the disappearance of Europe' (Baudrillard 1993, 252). Arguing somewhat differently that postmodernism represents the 'cultural logic' of late capitalism, Frederic Jameson depicted the postmodern as a condition of vitiated historicity, in which the past is relayed through stereotyped and nostalgic images, such as those evoked in Hollywood Westerns and the sanitised displays of the heritage industry. In architecture the past is cannibalised, but merely in the form of pastiche, the imitation of dead styles (classical, Georgian, etc.) that collectively go under the name of the 'neo'. This threadbare bond to the past is evident in the everyday world as much as in cultural expression, so that even for a committed Marxist like Jameson there no longer seems to be 'any organic relationship between the American history we learn from the schoolbooks and the lived experience of the current multinational, high-rise, stagflated city of the newspapers and of our own daily life'. History is stripped of its radical potential at the same time as it is evacuated of any realism, save the dawning realisation of a 'new and original historical situation in which we are condemned to seek History by way of our own pop images and simulacra of that history, which itself remains forever out of reach' (Jameson 1993, 22, 25).

From this ferment of critical opinions, then, one can discern a period-isation to modernity, loose and contested but apparent nonetheless. Modernity has a beginning and – in the view of postmodernists – an end. Much of the complexity of the term, as we have noted, derives from the fact that its meaning is simultaneously temporal and conceptual; it is both an historical formation and a philosophical one. Modernity designates not only a period of history but also a moment when 'history' itself comes to take on certain definite meanings as the progress of reason or, still more fundamentally, as a purposeful process of human development. The ideas of history and of the modern are therefore linked by a profound if covert synchrony. It is this conjunction that the postmodern disrupts, not by positing the 'end of history' as the conclusion to the continuous series of events so much as by articulating the waning of the belief that those events constitute a comprehensible process or that the past can be rendered meaningful. Even so, modernity can appear in this schema as itself akin to a 'grand narrative', with its own rise and fall. To understand the concept further we need to examine its application in a specific historical and the-oretical context. For this we shall turn to urban history, to the expanding literature on the city as exemplar and test bed of modernity.

Urban modernity

Since the later 1980s the cities of the nineteenth and twentieth centuries – especially the great metropolises of Europe and North America – have attracted growing attention from historians and others as the locus of new environments and experiences, experiments in modern living. This recent interest harks back to and builds upon a tradition of earlier sociological writing on the city associated with figures such as Max Weber, Georg Simmel and Louis Wirth. Such critics saw the city, as David Frisby and

Mike Featherstone have observed, as 'one of the crucial sites of modernity – the point of its intensification' (Frisby and Featherstone 1997, 12). Modernity here has, once again, a dual meaning, linked with but also different from the meanings attached to it in the larger conceptual context we have just discussed. Urban modernity refers to the built form of the city and to the ways city life was apprehended; it has, therefore, simultaneously spatial and experiential dimensions. These different aspects were well captured by Michel de Certeau in his widely cited essay, 'Walking in the city'. On the one hand, there is the knowledge of the city produced by the panoramic view from the top of a skyscraper. This is the 'god's-eye view', the view of the modernist architect, city planner or cartographer. On the other hand, there is the knowledge of the city of the walker or inhabitant, who moves through the streets as through a network of paths and buildings. The walker's knowledge of the city is a practical and sensuous one for Certeau, produced through repeated bodily experience. It is distinct from the planner's understanding, yet related to it, so that the particular spatiality of the myriad walkers 'insinuates itself into the clear text of the planned, readable city' (Ward 2000, 101–3). Here we shall examine successively the physical and the experiential dimensions of urban modernity, while attending also to the ways they persistently interact in historical and sociological analysis.

Throughout the twentieth century the built form of the city was seen as a powerful symbol and exemplar of the modern. This was partly a product of the much publicised association between urban form and modernism, the latter standing for continuous innovation in architecture and design combined with an emphasis on planning of the urban environment. Urban modernism can thus be variously exemplified by the functionalist design of Le Corbusier in France, the new towns of post-1945 Britain and the City Beautiful movement of the United States. But the process as a whole served to exemplify a still broader movement towards the implementation of a rational, expert-managed society of the kind which thinkers such as Weber and Habermas identified with modernity. In the words of the French architectural historian Paul Rabinow, 'Urbanism's synthesis of historical and natural elements into an object – the planned city as a regulator of modern society – can be seen as one of the most complete examples of modernity' (Rabinow 1995, 12). The planned city, with its grid-like symmetry and complex regulatory systems, appeared as the material embodiment of modern rationality. This modernity consisted, importantly, in the correspondence between ethico-political and practical considerations. As Rabinow made clear, in twentieth-century France urban forms, whether architectural, spatial or technical, had normative ends, in so far as they were intended to produce the model citizen alongside a 'modern' society.

Yet the spatial form of urban modernity was not simply the product of modern*ism*, of the city designed by the twentieth-century architect and planner. Its roots can be traced back to the almost wholly unplanned 'shock cities' of Britain's industrial revolution – Birmingham, Liverpool, Glasgow and, above all, Manchester – which seemed to presage the advent of a whole new society to contemporary observers such as Alexis de Tocqueville and Friedrich Engels in the 1830s and 1840s (Briggs 1968). The predominant tone of much of their description was apocalyptic. 'From this foul drain the greatest stream of human industry flows out to fertilise the whole world', Tocqueville wrote of Manchester in 1835. 'Here humanity attains its most complete development and its most brutish; here civilisation works its miracles and civilised man is turned back almost into a savage' (Tocqueville 1968, 96). It was not only the dramatic effects of industry on people and landscape that attracted attention, but also the changing socio-spatial configuration of the city itself. Engels' memorable account of Manchester in 1844 depicted the city as composed of a series of concentric rings, with warehouses and business premises concentrated at the centre, interspersed with slums, surrounded by a cordon of factories and workers' housing, and succeeded at a distance by an outer ring of semi-rural villas and suburbs occupied by families of the wealthier bourgeoisie.

For commentators like Engels what constituted the modernity of the industrial city was the supersession of the traditional model of the town, where different classes of inhabitants had lived and worked in close proximity to each other, by the growing separation of home and workplace, and a concomitant tendency to social segregation, amounting to a form of class apartheid. But the modernity of the industrial city also lay in the fact that the city as a whole appeared to have been geared to the priorities of the capitalist market, 'an economy of both time and wealth in production' as the French visitor Leon Faucher remarked of Manchester in the 1840s (Engels 1969; Faucher 1844; see also Marcus 1985). These patterns of urban form, first visible in early Victorian industrial cities and characterised by social segregation and functional specialisation, were to be taken as the blueprint of the modern city by the Chicago School of American sociologists, including E.W. Burgess and Robert Park, in the 1920s (Park *et al.* 1967; Savage and Warde 1993). What struck both contemporaries and later commentators as specifically 'modern' about Manchester, Birmingham – and later Chicago – was the degree to which the cities' spatial form and functional purpose appeared to mirror the demands of a new industrial, capitalist and class-divided society. They incarnated capitalist rationality in built form.

Between the mid-nineteenth century and the First World War it was the capital cities of the West that replaced the industrial centres as the spearhead of urban modernity: Paris, London, New York, Berlin, Vienna, Stockholm and so on. In regard to urban form what increasingly defined the modernity of these metropolises was not so much their spatial layout, which appeared increasingly amorphous, as their monumentality. Historians and geographers have followed Walter Benjamin in seeing the reconstruction of Paris under Baron Haussman in the 1850s and 1860s as a decisive moment in transforming the mass of narrow, winding streets of the old city into the broad, straight boulevards of the new metropolis. In the process, Haussman recreated the city as visual spectacle, opening up the monumental vista while simultaneously rendering the street a site of consumption, of window-shopping, promenading and surveillance (Benjamin 1992; Sutcliffe 1970; Clark, T. 1985; Harvey 1985). At the same period the construction of the Ringstrasse in Vienna after 1859 united a series of massive state and civic buildings via a broad, sweeping street (Schorske 1980). What was significant in all these reconstruction projects was the new priority given to circulation as the dominant principle of urban design, the flow of people and vehicles which contemporaries compared to the flow of blood around the human body (Sennett 1994). Nor were the capital cities unique in this regard. The major industrial cities similarly recast themselves after 1860 as metropolitan hubs, their centres given over to the display of people and goods, to shopping, entertainment and civic culture in a context of widened streets, open squares and florid architectural styles (Gunn 2000, 36–59).

Modernity was intrinsically urban in the nineteenth century and, indeed, in much of the twentieth; the city epitomised the new in its scale, layout and material fabric. But it was a newness that harked back to the past as much as to the future. Architecturally, the modern came dressed in neo-classical and Gothic styles. In what is perhaps the most famous evocation of the complex modernity of the nineteenth-century metropolis, Walter Benjamin's *Arcades Project*, temporalities were depicted as mixed and fluid. Second Empire Paris represented 'the new in the context of what has always been there', 'immemorial antiquity parading as up-to-date novelty' (Benjamin 1999, 25–6). The arcades themselves, built from the 1820s, were not only temples to the latest forms of commodity capitalism, they were also 'labyrinths', products of what Benjamin termed 'primal history'.

The built form, of course, was merely one part of the city's modernity. As we have already noted, the other important part lay in the experience it offered, perceived as both threatening and liberating to the individual. For the poet Baudelaire the rapid, transitory impressions of the city were the essence of modern experience, where truth, beauty – and horror – were located. In the 1860s Baudelaire was among the first to celebrate this experience and to propose that modern art should be devoted to capturing 'the passing moment and all the suggestions of eternity that it contains' (Baudelaire 1972, 5). His vision was to be influential in encouraging subsequent theorists to consider the phenomenology of urban life as an integral component of the meanings of modernity. In an important essay, 'The metropolis and mental life', first published in 1903, the sociologist Georg Simmel set out to study the socio-psychological impact of the city, identified here with turn-of-the century Berlin. How, Simmel enquired, did individuals preserve their autonomy in the face of detachment from tradition, an increasing division of labour and the 'intensification of nervous stimulation' caused by city living? Simmel's answer lay in the identification of a number of traits identified with the figure of 'metropolitan man'. The proliferation of sensory impressions meant that the city dweller was a creature of the intellect, of punctuality, calculation and precision. So complex an organism as the modern city, for instance, was dependent on an extreme attention to time among its inhabitants: 'If all the clocks and watches in Berlin would suddenly go wrong in different ways, if only by one hour, all economic life and communication of the city would be disrupted for a long time' (Simmel 1997, 177). This emphasis on the measurability of things, combined with the excess of sensory stimulation, inclined also to promote a certain blasé attitude in the metropolitan person together with a reserve towards others. The impact of the city in its scale and complexity of organisation on the individual was literally overwhelming, according to Simmel. It threatened the very sense of self. A further feature of 'metropolitan man' was consequently an exaggerated sense of individual personality, brought about at once by the freedoms offered by city life conjoined with the depersonalising effects of the 'overgrowth of objective culture' (Simmel 1997, 184). Through explorations such as this, Simmel sought to analyse in a systematic fashion the production of novel forms of metropolitan perception.

In his great study of nineteenth-century Paris, Benjamin also interested himself in the construction of a metropolitan mentality. The *Arcades Project* sought to catalogue modern urban states of mind: boredom, idleness, distraction, feverishness. Its most celebrated character, borrowed from Baudelaire, was the *flâneur* (see also Tester 1994). Drawing on the tradition of 'physiologies', portraits of urban types seen on the street, Benjamin depicted the *flâneur* as a new and significant metropolitan figure in Paris of the Second Empire. Detached from the workaday world of bourgeois and worker alike, the *flâneur* wanders the streets, studies the shops and passers-by, and allows himself to be carried along in the crowd without ever properly belonging to it. *Flânerie* itself demonstrates the primacy of the visual over the other senses, a characteristic feature of nineteenth-century perception. Through it, the city is represented as a spectacle: 'Landscape – that, in fact, is what Paris becomes for the *flâneur*' (Benjamin 1999, 417). He is also a consumer, at home in the new arcades and department stores, where goods are displayed, as much as on the street where the prostitutes ply their trade. For Benjamin, he symbolised the position of the educated bourgeoisie, who imagine themselves to be merely spectators of commodity capitalism but are, in reality, thoroughly enmeshed in the dreamworld which it has created. 'In the person of the *flâneur*, the intelligentsia becomes acquainted with the marketplace. It [the intelligentsia] surrenders itself to the market, thinking merely to look around; but in fact it is already seeking a buyer' (Benjamin 1999, 21). Urban modernity, which for Benjamin is both product and agent of the 'phantasmagoria' or dream state that capitalism induces, thus created not only a novel material environment but also new types of individual and new modes of human interiority.

This concentration on figures such as 'metropolitan man' and the *flâneur* has led feminist critics to question the gendered nature of the theorisation of the modern city. According to the sociologist Janet Wolff, 'the literature of modernity describes the experience of men'; within it women are rendered invisible (Wolff 1990, 34). While such an observation reflected the obvious masculine identity of the archetypal protagonists, it pointed at a deeper level to the predominance of the male gaze in constructions of urban experience. There was no type of the female *flâneuse*, not because women were absent from the streets of the city but because in the masculine vision of the authors of modernity women were invariably objectified, defined primarily as sexual commodities; the female equivalent of the *flâneur* was the prostitute (Pollock 1988, 50–90). A problem with this perspective is that it can collude in the alleged invisibility of women by assuming that their presence is irrecoverable, since that presence always appears vitiated by the male gaze. In response, a host of feminist historians have demonstrated the active engagement of women in the modern city, including middle-class women most commonly assumed to have been confined to the suburbs and the home. These spheres of urban engagement included department stores, specifically designed to attract women as customers, clubs and societies, sightseeing (sometimes accompanied by 'lady guides') and cultural events such as exhibitions and concerts (e.g. Nord 1995; Rappaport 2000 and 2001; Tiersten 2001). Attention to gender suggests that, alongside 'metropolitan man', it was through engagement in the modern city that figures such as the 'new woman' took shape. While they may have been discursively suppressed in representations of urban modernity, therefore, women were in fact active consumers and producers of a modern urban way of life (see also Wilson, E. 1991).

Other histories, too, have begun to be written of the modern city. Beyond the twin poles of urban form and social experience, planning and identity around which accounts of urban modernity have conventionally been written, new histories are emerging concerned with the material fabric of the urban environment and the bodily senses through which it was registered. Technologies such as gas and lighting and products such as pipes and asphalt can be understood as basic components of an urban 'system', the very fabric of modernity, but they too have their history of failed implementation and premature obsolescence as well as of triumphal progress (Nead 2000; Gandy 2002). Closely aligned with the material world was the experience of the senses, of sound, smell and vision, which not only shaped how the city was perceived but also the forms in which it was desired or, conversely, abhorred. Filth and stench dominated contemporary bourgeois responses to the 'slums', while an aesthetics of visual translucence, embodied in materials such as glass and buildings like the Crystal Palace, encouraged a ready identification of urban modernity with smooth, luminous surfaces (Corbin 1986; Otter 2002). What is evident through such historical studies is the increasing permeability of boundaries between domains previously considered separate: between the material world and human agency, or between what Simmel termed the 'objective structures' of the city and the individual's experience of them. One important result for historians is to render increasingly problematic a conventional historical narrative of 'urbanisation', understood as a cumulative and progressive process integral to modernisation (Gunn 2004).

Recent historical and sociological writing on urban modernity thus echoes many of the themes in the theoretical debate about the modern and the postmodern. Not only is the city represented as modern in cultural terms, serving as the catalyst for that intensification and fragmentation of experience seen as characteristic of both modernity and modernism. It is modern also in relation to its spatial form, its rationality (the city as grid or 'system') and to the knowledges, from planning to engineering, which attempt to manage its complexity. In this sense the historiography of the modern city reflects the different ways of understanding modernity we saw earlier, variously epistemological, historical and cultural. Yet in exploring themes such as perception and materiality this historiography has also proved fertile in opening up new meanings of the modern that are not simply reducible to these bigger themes. Such meanings are altering the terms of the theoretical debate, so that modernity may be understood in relation to developments at the micro-level of the street, to return to Certeau's analogy, as well as the 'god's-eye view' from the skyscraper.

Evaluation

How, then, can one estimate the value and significance of the concept of modernity for historical discourse? Looked at from a critical standpoint, what is apparent is the extraordinary elasticity and complexity of the term, so that at times it is difficult to know what is meant by it or which definition is in play. As a concept used in multiple discourses, from architecture to epistemology, modernity is context specific and it is not always clear that commentators are aware of its meanings in other disciplinary contexts. Limited agreement exists about when modernity started and if it has ended, or, indeed, if the notion has any historical referent at all. Consequently, when theorists or historians use the term it is often unclear whether they are talking about the same thing, even in a debate so apparently circumscribed as that between Lyotard and Habermas. As Stephen Toulmin has pointed out, where Lyotard identified modernity with the dominance of Cartesian rationality, Habermas associated it ultimately with emancipatory political practice. They were thus at cross-purposes. 'Many of the reasons that contemporary French writers give for *denying* the continued value of "modernity" refer to the same features of the twentieth-century scene that Habermas points to in *asserting* it. They take opposite sides on issues about modernity not for reasons of substance, but because – as seen from their respective points of view – the word "modern" means different things' (Toulmin 1992, 172–3, italics original).

From an historical viewpoint it can also be problematic to see modernity as based on rupture. Whatever criteria are used to distinguish between historical epochs, the continuities between the pre-modern, the modern and the post-modern are as striking to the historical eye as change. Historians of seventeenth-century science are used to the fact that the father of modern physics, Sir Isaac Newton, was simultaneously a devotee of 'pre-modern' ideas of alchemy and the 'music of the spheres' (e.g. Westfall 1993). Economic historians are likewise now well used to the idea of the British industrial revolution as a longer-term, more gradual process of economic transformation than earlier theories of a rapid 'take-off' between 1780 and 1830 suggested, and one in which many 'pre-industrial' structures and practices persisted (O'Brien and Quinault 1993, 1–30). Looking to the recent period, critics like Craig Calhoun question the shift from modernity to post-modernity on the grounds that key features of the former, such as political centralisation and capitalist accumulation, continue to operate in the latter. Understanding modernity consequently demands an account 'of historical change which does not mean epochal rupture' (Calhoun 1993, 90). Furthermore, no single element defines modernity, even 'reason' itself; thus the philosopher Alasdair MacIntyre has identified at least four separate conceptions of 'rationality' in European thought since the Enlightenment (MacIntyre 1988). Indeed, modernity may be defined by a tradition of irrationalism as much as of rationalism, a tradition identified with a Baudelairean celebration of transience and movements such as surrealism. All this suggests that the concept of modernity is unable to escape from questions of substantive historical definition. Yet the tendency for the term to take on board ever more historical and epistemological dimensions means that it risks capsizing into meaninglessness.

Finally, as I have indicated previously, the identification of modernity with the metropolitan West renders the concept suspect for many. Critics like Zygmunt Bauman and Paul Gilroy have pointed out that linking modernity with developments such as the rise of the European nation-state and the industrial revolution distracts attention from the fact that its emergence was historically coterminous with the creation of European empires from the sixteenth century. As a result, the concepts of history and knowledge that formed modernity also formed the West as the unspoken centre of history and knowledge, against which large parts of the world were defined as an ignorant and history-less other (Bauman 1987; Chatterjee 1993). Yet as Gilroy has suggested, a history of modernity from the point of view of the colonised and enslaved looks very different from the kinds of accounts of that process written from the vantage-point of the metropolitan West (Gilroy 1993). From this perspective, as we shall see in Chapter Seven, the end of modernity implies the end of the West as the inevitable and unreflecting reference-point of history and knowledge.

Consequently, accounts of modernity that continue to centre on Cartesian rationality or Haussman's Paris come to appear at best partial and localised. As Felix Driver and others have demonstrated, the empire was as much a part of the life and identity of European cities such as London, Marseilles and Seville in the nineteenth century as it was of the colonies themselves (Driver and Gilbert 1999). Conversely, the geographical dispersal of the intellectual legacy of the Enlightenment across the world over the modern period has meant that, since decolonisation in the mid-twentieth century, Europe has been 'provincialised' in more senses than one (Chakrabarty 2000).

So the modern remains a contested and problematic category. Yet this contestation can be seen as part of its conceptual richness. Modernity stands at a congested point of intersection between numerous discourses and disciplines; if it is a source of dispute it is also a site of exchange between different intellectual traditions and ways of knowing. That historians participate in this exchange is important, not least because it encourages critical questioning of those theoretical aspects which, as we have seen, are historically questionable or plainly ahistorical. After all, as the chapter has demonstrated, the debate about modernity is as much a debate about history as it is about sociology, philosophy or art. At the same time, however, participating in the debate also demands a critical questioning of some of the foundations of historical thought, history in its contemporary forms itself being understood as the product of modernity. These foundations include a teleology of progress (implicit as well as explicit), linear temporality and empirical methodology. Viewing history through the critical lens of modernity also involves questioning the assumption that the nation-state represents the basic framework for historical study, rather than, for instance, categories such as the self, humanity or transnational cultures.

One way of dealing with the complexity of modernity, adopted by some historians and theorists, is to pluralise it: just as there were many 'modernisms' in art, architecture and planning, so it is possible to speak of many 'modernities'. Such an approach recognises the different historical traditions bound up in the singular notion of modernity with which we started this chapter. While, for Baudrillard, America represented 'pure modernity' in the sense of a perpetual, history-less present, so Britain has been viewed by a series of historians and critics as exhibiting a 'conservative' modernity, based on lack of historical rupture and the gradual nature of change, and even a 'failed modernity', reflected in long-term industrial decline (Baudrillard 1993; Barnett 1984; Samuel 1998). The danger here, of course, is that rather than dissolving the nation-state as an analytical framework, pluralising the concept of modernity merely provides historians with a justification for reintroducing it. Ultimately, however, what subverts the idea of modernity predicated exclusively on metropolitan nationhood may not be theory or even the continuing process of globalisation so much as the new understandings of empire and migration which historians, among others, have been active in opening up. For these histories reveal the presence of the colonial other in the metropolitan heart of empire as well as the diverse conceptions of time and space that co-existed within the so-called project of modernity. The experience of empire and colonisation reminds us that modernity was shaped on the periphery as well as at the centre, in Delhi as well as in London, and that it contained within it not singular but multiple temporalities, geographies and histories. To speak of plural modernities, then, is to comprehend not only the divergent meanings of the term within the West but also the radically different ways in which the modern has impacted across territories and cultures over time, an awareness that still has the capacity to astonish even the most cosmopolitan traveller today. In the next two chapters we shall take these differences further by examining theories of identity and the postcolonial.

CHAPTER SIX

Identity

M atters of identity are part of the fabric of everyday life. Each time we show our passport, credit card or driving licence aspects of our identity are revealed: nationality, gender, age, occupation. When we talk with strangers they will place us – as we place them – according to appearance, accent and behaviour by ethnicity, class or status, education and so on. In the late twentieth century questions of identity became particularly urgent. Politically, they lay behind the development of an array of new social movements from the 1960s onwards, each concerned with a form of identity politics: the women's movement, black power, gay liberation. Academically, too, the concept of identity was everywhere in the social sciences and humanities during the 1980s and 1990s, from queer theory to postcolonial studies. 'All present struggles', Michel Foucault observed in 1983, 'revolve around the question: Who are we?' (Foucault 2002, 331)

These practical and political questions may seem remote from the activities of historians but they are in fact of determinate importance for them. In the first place, many current historians participated in the new social movements and were shaped by them. The historian of homosexuality, Jeffrey Weeks, describes the impact of joining the Gay Liberation Front while working at the London School of Economics in 1970. 'I assumed a new personal identity, found a new sense of belonging, and became committed to a new political project. And I began research on sexuality and sexual history' (Weeks 2000, 4). Even for those not directly involved, it was difficult to escape the intellectual impress of identity politics in the academy. Gender, race and class – the trinity of identity categories – impacted on history no less than other disciplinary areas, swiftly followed by categories such as sexuality and ethnicity, so that no historical study – or student essay – was complete without reference to one or more of them. At a still more fundamental level, however, history is concerned with identity since so much of historical study is about the changing identifications of people in the past, Catholics and Protestants, empire-builders and colonial peoples, workers and bourgeoisie. Where we find resistance in history, it is often resistance to overzealous forms of identification, the imposition of alien identities on subject groups.

On the whole historians are inured to essentialism in such matters. They are sceptical of the idea that historical identities are fixed or innate, and justifiably wary of arguments founded on the notion of a universal and unchanging human nature. At the same time, the concepts of identity used in historical studies are often simplistic and under-theorised. It is common to find identity invoked within a model of 'self' and 'other' vaguely assumed to derive from psychoanalytic or postcolonial theory and seen as imposed on societies or groups by means of 'discourses' and 'rep-resentations'. How identity is formed within this model is never specified. Nor is the question often raised as to whether different types of identity (individual/collective, race as against, say, gender) are formed in different ways by distinct practices and logics. How far can actors choose identities and how far are they determined for them? How do different identity cat-egories (class, sexuality, selfhood, for example) fit together and interact? Rather than just describing identities and various historical shifts in their meaning, it is necessary to account for the formation of identities and to explain how they work. Identities are a matter of doing as well as think-ing, of social practice as well as the social imaginary, and they require to be studied as such (Jenkins, R. 1996).

This chapter examines a number of forms of identity, related to nation, class, sex and gender, and the self. Race and ethnicity have been excluded since they are considered at greater length in Chapter Seven. The aim here is not to be comprehensive – an impossible task – but to encompass a number of the established identity categories in order to examine com-paratively their analytical workings. In so doing I shall examine the ideas of key theorists such as Benedict Anderson, Erving Goffman and Judith Butler, whose critical ideas have influenced, directly or indirectly, aspects of recent historical research. The historical examples themselves in this chapter are taken predominantly from the case of Britain between the later seventeenth and the early nineteenth century. This is by no means coincidental. Given that many historians have been interested in analysing the emergence of modern notions of human and social identity in the West, both the place and the period are understandable. Before proceeding to these topics, however, we need to consider in general terms what identity involves by way of a concept.

Defining identity

Etymologically, identity contains two distinct – and potentially opposed – sets of meanings. In the first place, it signifies what is unique about an individual or group. To speak of a person's identity is thus to indicate what distinguishes them and makes them different from others. At the same time, identity also denotes what is common to a group and the individuals who compose it. Here it signifies sameness, what such people share, so that to refer to a group as having a particular ethnic identity, for instance, is to highlight those features (culture, religion, place of origin, etc.) they have in common. There is also a temporal dimension to identity. It is necessary for it to be continuous over time in order for an identity to be recognised as such. If the behaviour of an individual or group is radically inconsistent, for example, their identity comes into question (as in the notion of 'identity crisis'). Equally, it is possible to gain and to lose identity; in some cases involving gradual memory loss or terminal disease this may be conceived as a dwindling of human identity itself (Bynum 2001).

In signalling both sameness and difference, the meanings of identity are not necessarily contradictory. The features that are shared by a social group are likely also to be precisely those that distinguish it from others; sameness and difference become two sides of the same coin. This points to a further duality: identity may be shaped both from within and without. The internal, self-determination of identity is evident in the case of both individuals and collectivities and is often the dimension most strongly emphasised in everyday discourse (and by historians). Indeed, as Anthony Giddens has described, the notion of self-identity as a 'life project', in which individuals are encouraged to construct their own narrative, is an integral aspect of Western society in late modernity (Giddens 1996). But identity may also be defined equally, if not more, by external attitudes and institutions. The identities of ethnic or sexual minorities are often shaped importantly by factors over which they have no control, such as popular prejudice. The modern state has also had a major role as a classifying agent. It is the modern state, for instance, that defines nationality and citizenship (sometimes stigmatising other 'alien' groups, as in Nazi Germany), reinforces class differences through occupational and other official social schema, and divides the population through education by underwriting the value of particular educational qualifications (Burleigh and Wipperman 1991; Higgs 2000; Bourdieu 1996). Historically, the balance of internal and external factors in the process of identity formation is variable. In the past, it was generally the latter rather than the former which were decisive. Membership of status groups such as the nobility, or of organisations such as the guild or trade, was more likely to define an individual's social identity than any act of self-determination. By contrast, since the nineteenth century the balance would appear to have tipped in favour of self-determination for both groups and individuals, at least in the West, although the scope for this varies substantially.

The internal/external dichotomy points to the further conventional sociological distinction between 'nominal' identity – literally, the name – and 'virtual' identity, the experience and meaning of possessing that identification (Jenkins 1996, 24–5). Thus, while the nominal identity of a group may remain constant (e.g. 'working class', 'women'), what it means to be part of that group may vary between members and over time. Moreover, as I have already indicated, the categories or types of social identity are not analytically coterminous or equivalent. Historians are used to the idea that the identities of the individual person and those of collective groups are formed by different means, although I shall also suggest that these may be more often linked than is sometimes assumed. Equally, some identities such as gender are 'primary', in the sense that they are instilled through the earliest socialisation and are thus deeply embodied. Others, however, such as membership of a religious group, may be acquired and changed, and are thus subject to a degree of choice. Consequently, a significant and, in some cases categorical, difference exists between the many types of social identity.

A substantial degree of complexity is therefore implicit in the concept of identity, which can be defined as the product of a mélange of self-description, contemporary social and political discourse, and historically sedimented categories. This complexity is reflected in the various theoretical approaches to the subject. A major division exists, for instance, between those who view identity as essentially determined from without and those who emphasise the self-determining agency of groups and individuals. In the case of Foucault, as we saw in Chapter Five, identities such as the autonomous 'individual' as well as categories such as class and criminality are historically produced by means of specific discourses and technologies. 'My objective', Foucault proclaimed, 'has been to create a history of the different modes by which, in our culture, human beings are made subjects' (Foucault 2002, 326). Influenced by Foucault, a number of sociologists have sought to extend this approach. Ian Hacking, for instance, has examined how an idea of the 'normal' was established in human behaviour during the nineteenth century, through systems of statistical classification (including the census) by which people could be categorised as 'fit subjects' as against others who were deemed deviant or dangerous (Hacking 1990). What emerges from many such studies is the central role of the state and its official knowledges in the institution of modern social identities, from class to welfare. As a result, identities and subjectivities tend to be viewed as constructed through external agencies and processes of 'subjection'. By contrast, in the hands of theorists such as Erving Goffman identity formation is largely though not exclusively the product of individuals and social groups themselves. Goffman, for example, stressed the importance of social interaction in the production of identity. Hence the significance for individuals and groups of techniques of 'impression management', adapted to specific social sites ('front stage' and 'back stage'), and the dramaturgical model of identity as the satisfactory performance of a particular 'role' or set of social expectations (Goffman 1969). Goffman did not ignore outside pressures, as his studies of stigma and of the asylum indicate, but his stress tended to be on the creative agency of individuals and groups in the formation of identities rather than on the operations of external forces (Goffman 1961; 1970).

Within the overall spectrum of interpretations, recent theorists tend towards the determinist end, as we shall see, paradoxically emphasising the opposite tendency to that implied by the historical movement towards increasing self-definition of identity. In part, this reflects the influence of psychoanalytic and linguistic models, so that identities are seen to be produced through language and the individual's insertion in the symbolic order (Lacan 1977). At the same time, such theories work to put identity itself at issue as a durable category; in the thought of Lacan and Foucault as well as in the 'deconstruction' of Jacques Derrida, identity, like meaning generally, is inherently unstable, incomplete and ultimately undecidable (Derrida 1981; Hall, S. 1994). The question for theorists such as Judith Butler is not 'what is identity?' but what is it that gives identity coherence or the appearance of an 'identity'. According to Butler – and, indeed, to every theorist mentioned here – there is no place or point of view outside of constructed identities, no authentic self or essence to which we can retreat (Butler 1990, 147). Yet the implication of determinism or closure in this position tends to be rejected by feminists and queer theorists, such as Joan Scott and Butler. Instead, what such analyses constantly emphasise is the contrived nature of identities, their plasticitv which derives in part from their very historicity. Identities are se having been constructed historically; they are therefore, if not transient, at least open to the possibility of change and subversion. In some cases, as with sex and gender, temporality is hidden underneath a veneer of permanence, belying the historical transformations that have continually reshaped their meanings. In other instances, however, identities are the explicit outcome of struggle about the past and its appropriation. This is the case with the first historical example we shall look at, that of national identity.

National identities

Nationalism is a highly developed and contested subject in historical and political studies. Most historians and theorists of nationalism are agreed that its origins are relatively recent, located in the eighteenth and nineteenth centuries (Smith, A. 2001; though see also Hastings 1997). In the influential interpretation of John Breuilly, for instance, nationalism developed in Western Europe after the French and American revolutions, in response to the crisis of legitimacy following the dissolution of the ancien régime and its replacement by a state reliant on popular sovereignty. Nationalism replaced theology and dynasticism as the principal means deployed by the modern state to justify its powers and activities. The idea of the nation as co-existent with a territorial state and an ethnically or culturally homogeneous population was thus not the result of any essential 'need' for identity. Rather, such a need was fabricated by state institutions themselves; the 'nation' was the product of the state, not, as nationalist mythology or functionalism would have it, the other way round (Breuilly 1982). Nationalism is generally considered a modern phenomenon but not all theorists follow Breuilly in viewing it as the consequence of politics and the state. Others have emphasised the significance of cultural factors in creating an idea of national identity rooted in an alleged commonality of culture, territory and memory (e.g. Gellner 1983; Nora 1996). Among the most important such accounts is that of the historian of south-east Asia, Benedict Anderson, which a recent critic has termed one of the 'last "great theories" of nationalism' (Anderson 1991; Low 2000, 364).

According to Anderson, nationalism was not a result of self-conscious political ideologies, but of the dissolution of the 'large cultural systems that preceded it' (Anderson 1991, 12). In Europe, these included the religious community of Christendom and the dynastic realm of monarchical states and empires, such as the Habsburg Monarchy, whose borders were porous and populations diversified by language, ethnicity and religion.

The waning of these systems between the sixteenth and eighteenth centuries was partly political, involving dynasticism in an increasing search for principles of legitimacy – here Anderson is in agreement with Breuilly. But its causes were also cultural. They included the discovery of lands and peoples overseas, which worked to relativise Christianity and weaken the hold of existing religious authority; a new awareness of linear time, which made possible the idea of a society existing at a particular temporal point, with a past, present and future; and the spread of print capitalism, and with it vernacular languages. As an ideology predicated on the nation as a primary source of identity, which emerged in Europe in the half-century following the American War of Independence, nationalism was intimately bound up with these cultural processes. The new sense of time and the spread of a vernacular language, for instance, made possible the emergence of the nation as the focus of history and, indeed, its natural frame and reference point (Anderson 1991, 72–82). Similarly, Anderson demonstrates how literary forms such as the novel and newspaper, both of which took shape in eighteenth-century Europe, were dependent for their comprehension on certain basic understandings. These included the notion that strangers were connected through membership of a 'society', whose existence in secular, historical time was assumed by all those within it. To read a daily newspaper was to engage in a solitary activity whose meaning was shared with millions of other, unknown individuals whose mutual interrelationship was nevertheless implicitly recognised. In effect, the emergence of national identity was predicated on people's capacity to imagine the nation as a particular form of community. Novels and newspapers 'provided the technical means for "re-presenting" the *kind* of imagined community that is the nation' (Anderson 1991, 25).

Anderson's thesis is a sophisticated one in which the nation exists as an imagined identity and relation, produced historically from a dense matrix of political, material and cultural processes. No doubt partly as a consequence of the work's complexity and brilliance, it is not a model that has been utilised in subsequent studies of national identity, even though it is frequently cited. Linda Colley's *Britons: Forging the Nation 1707–1837* (1992), which covers a similar period and themes, albeit in a specific context, adopts an altogether more conventional approach. Colley's subject is the creation of Great Britain as an 'invented nation' (the debt to Anderson as well as to Hobsbawm and Ranger (1984) is immediately evident) during the 'long eighteenth century' following the Union joining Scotland with England and Wales in 1707. In particular, a specifically British identity, capable of overriding other national and regional allegiances, is seen as forged out of the successive wars against Spain and France between 1715 and 1815. In the patriotic ferment of these wars, British identity was powerfully linked with Protestantism as well as with trade and empire. By the early nineteenth century this identity was being celebrated in regular performance of the national anthem and the first royal Jubilee in 1809 (Colley 1992, 209, 217–28). But the formation of British national identity, Colley insists, was at root relational. The British 'came to define themselves as a single people not because of any political or cultural consensus at home, but rather in reaction to the Other beyond their shores' (Colley 1992, 6). Britishness was formed in opposition to what was perceived as a threat from Continental and Catholic rivals in a time-honoured dialectic between Self and Other, Them and Us.

What, then, do these accounts say about the formation of identity in general and national identity in particular? The answer is perhaps less than might appear. Anderson's thesis is more convincing in outlining the conditions for identification with the nation than in explaining the particular historical forms which that identification took. Moreover, he depicts national identification as a deeply embedded form of modern consciousness, a primary identity (Anderson 1991, 203). But more recent historians have argued for the shallowness of late eighteenth-century notions of national identification, suggested by the welcome given to the supranational 'friends of humanity' at the French National Convention in 1792. From such a perspective nationalism did not come to be seen as natural in this period but, on the contrary, something that needed to be constantly asserted, constructed and imposed (Bell 2001). By comparison with Anderson, Colley's account appears theoretically underpowered, reliant on a model of Self and Other borrowed loosely from psychoanalytic theory but lacking proper explication. Within this model any manifestation of national consciousness may be taken for a sign of identity, while one nation merely replaces the next as the source of 'otherness' (Mandler 2004, 109–13). So the status of the nation as a category of identity remains problematic; we shall return to this in the conclusion to this chapter. In the meantime we need to turn to a further difficult category, that of class.

Class and social identity

Class is part of the litany of categories routinely invoked under the heading of identity, but its qualification as such is debatable. Its equivocal position in this respect is related in the first instance to the multiple different understandings of class that circulate in the humanities and social sciences, including history (Joyce 1995b). These can be divided for schematic purposes into 'strong' and 'weak' class idioms, with a spectrum of positions between the poles (Holton 1996). In the strong idiom, class is the fulcrum of a structural account of power and exploitation in society, based on an analysis of economic relations of production which are seen to permeate all dimensions of social life, including politics and culture. Marx and Engels remain the obvious reference points here, but 'identity' was not part of their conceptual vocabulary. In their classic distinction between 'class in itself' and 'class for itself', the latter category was equated with 'class consciousness', seen as going beyond identity to a deeper and, in some cases, revolutionary, realisation of collective interests and historical mission (Marx 1955, 195). In the weak class idiom, on the other hand, class becomes one source of power and inequality among others in society and has limited or variable impact on politics and culture, or even necessarily on group formation. Here a notion of identity might appear to have greater purchase, but it is noticeable that the concept did not have a place in the work of Max Weber, who has been the major theoretical resource for this type of class analysis (Weber 1978).

There are those in both idioms who consequently resist viewing class as an identity on the grounds that it represents a category of a qualitatively different order. A recent advocate of this view is the political philosopher Diana Coole, who eloquently opposes the tendency to absorb class into discourses of identity and difference associated with cultural, linguistic and psychoanalytic theory (Coole 1996). Eschewing the strong class idiom of Marxism, Coole proposes a definition of class as structured economic inequality, a 'stubborn and systematic economic division' which has consequences for a whole range of 'life chances', from income level to mortality rates (Coole 1996, 17). Class is therefore to be understood pre-eminently in economic not – as in discourses of difference – in cultural terms. It is characterised by relative invariance over time by contrast with identity, which is fluid and mutable. Class is not structured like a language and its members, in Coole's words, 'do not ask "who are we?" first, or even at all' (Coole 1996, 21). Finally, class implies a reality independent of discourse which can be represented objectively. Class and identity, in short, are incommensurate categories for Coole since they have different epistemological foundations. One result of this disparity is that while nominally encompassing class, discourses of identity in practice work to silence it as a source of significant difference and oppression (Coole 1996, 24).

Coole's arguments are incisive and may be instructive for those who assume a too easy correlation between the conventional markers of social difference. Within history, they can be seen to provide an angle of critique on those historians associated with the 'linguistic turn' and the deconstruction of the working class (e.g. Joyce 1990; Stedman Jones 1983). However, Coole's approach is not without limits for understanding either the theoretical and historical dimensions of class or its conceptual relationship with identity. By defining class simply as structured economic inequality she overlooks the variety of other social forms which economic inequality has taken historically, from the feudal estates of medieval Europe to Asian caste societies. Even historians of nineteenth-century Britain, which many including Marx considered to be the exemplar of a modern class society, have become wary of assuming class to be the necessary complement of the changes wrought by industrialism and rapid urbanisation. 'Class formation was a possible not an inevitable result of the interaction of urban growth, social and environmental tension', R.J. Morris puts it; the resulting social formation might have emerged differently (Morris 1990, 15). Furthermore, in a familiar elision, Coole identifies class exclusively with the working class, the putative 'underclass' and the poor. These are the groups in effect whose definition may be most strongly material since it is they who bear the consequences of economic inequality. But this excludes from view other historical groups, such as the aristocracy and the middle class(es), whose formation may take place on rather different terms. In the case of the aristocracy the defining feature of membership was not so much wealth as kinship – in many places it was essentially a landed and military order, though one that might accept new members through ennoblement or marriage (Bush 1992). Equally, the 'middle class' or bourgeoisie represented less a class based on common economic position than an amorphous space between the notables on the one side and the mass of manual workers on the other (Kocka and Mitchell 1993). While nominally part of the same socio-economic class, the families of wealthy merchant bankers and those of white-collar clerks inhabited different social and material universes.

Indeed, recent historical research on the middle class has suggested that, far from an invariant category, it exhibited many of the protean qualities normally associated with identity. In the case of late eighteenth and early nineteenth century Britain, the meanings of 'middle class' were predominantly political not social, according to Dror Wahrman, representing moderate reforming opinion between the excesses of both Jacobin radicalism and intransigent Toryism (Wahrman 1995). In the crisis-ridden 1830s and 1840s the title took on strong moral bearings, referring 'less to a social group than to the right-thinking, morally upright core of British society' (Crossick 1991, 158). For the Victorian period as a whole, recent studies have drawn attention to the cultural basis of middle-class membership, regulated by codes of gentility and consumption, and shared across the Anglo world of Britain, Australia and the United States (Bushman 1992; Young, L. 2003). Indeed, in the case of the United States, Daniel Walkowitz sub-titled *Working With Class*, his important study of social workers in twentieth-century America, 'the politics of middle-class identity'. Social workers were seen as a key group precisely because their role was to patrol the boundaries of classes and mediate social relationships across them. As a liminal group they were especially significant in illuminating shifts in class identity over time. Walkowitz describes how in the early twentieth century social workers were defined – and defined themselves – as 'middle class' in vertical terms, that is by distinction from the group of élite philanthropists and organisers above them and the ranks of relief recipients below. By the later twentieth century, however, this hierarchical conception had become fractured along lines of race and gender. While the objects of welfare were now predominantly blacks and Hispanics, members of these groups were increasingly drawn into the welfare services themselves as cheaply paid aides. Under attack from federal governments and political parties, the professional status of social work weakened. At the same time gender lines were drawn more sharply, men occupying management roles, women those of counselling and therapy, often in a freelance capacity. Social work thus mirrored the crumbling of a solid sense of middle-class identity in late twentieth-century America, associated with lines of economic division. What remained was race, the sense of whiteness as the core of middle-class identity, with African Americans as the racialised Other or 'underclass' (Walkowitz, D. 1999).

For these historians, then, the concept of class is historically highly specific; its meanings are produced through public discourse in relationship to – and conflict with – other categories, not exclusively or even primarily through shifts in socio-economic formation. As Pierre Bourdieu noted, struggle over categories and titles is an integral part of the 'class struggle', not simply an outcome of conflicts occurring elsewhere in the economic domain (Bourdieu 1992a, 479–81). Coole's admonition notwithstanding, class here bears a marked resemblance to other types of identity and is seen to be produced by similar kinds of process. However, it is important that class be understood as one form that social identity can take, not as a master category into which all such forms are collapsed. Rather than assuming class, it may be more illuminating to examine the micro-politics of relationships of power and status, to take the ideas of the social psychologist Erving Goffman, for instance, rather than those of Marx. Goffman's notion of the 'interaction order' provides a framework for such an analysis, based on the detailed analysis of what occurs in the face-to-face encounters between historical agents. His concepts of 'region' – where an encounter takes place, whether it is frontstage or backstage – and 'frame' – the social setting with its specific codes and rules – can be helpful in situating interaction. Focusing on self-presentation, ritual exchange and the choreography of bodies involved, Goffman provides the historian with a set of tools for analysing a social event (Goffman 1969). Like Clifford Geertz's concept of local knowledge discussed in Chapter Three, Goffman's approach enables the elucidation of wider social relationships from the small-scale encounter. Thus the ritual exchange of gifts or testimonials between employers and workers is suggestive of the complex, delicately balanced set of relations between capital and labour in Victorian society (Gray 1996, 219–29). Similarly, the rites of gentility performed in front of acquaintances and strangers represented a critical means for regulating the boundaries of class, status and gender among the Victorian well-to-do (Young, L. 2003). As the metaphors here suggest, social identity for Goffman is constructed on dramaturgic lines; it works as a performance. The task of the historian is to understand how the performance is staged and what its meanings are for participants, spectators and the larger social entity of which it is part. Goffman's work has been criticised, among other things, for its focus on the individual rather than collectivities and for prioritising consensus over conflict in social relationships (MacIntyre 1985). But it can help the historian situate and analyse the dynamics of social relationships without assuming they can be immediately understood as examples or expressions of abstract categories like class.

Sex and gender

Class is not a visible marker of social difference, although processes of identification may seek to make it so. By contrast, sex and gender are highly visible forms of identity, inscribed in or on the body. They are primary identities, formed in early socialisation and resistant to change. And they appear to operate within all societies as fundamental categories in the social organisation of similarity and difference (Bourdieu 2001). Gender here refers to the cultural organisation of sexual roles – masculine, feminine, androgynous, etc. – whereas sex is conventionally defined as biological, rooted in bodily difference (Eder, Hall and Hekman 1999). Thus, whereas sex is conventionally seen as stable over time, gender is historically variable; how femininity and masculinity have been understood in different periods and cultures has changed. Or at least this is what might be described as the orthodoxy of gender history which has recently come under challenge from both historical and theoretical standpoints, as we shall see.

Under the influence of post-structuralist thought, the concept of gender has come to have great significance for historical studies since the late 1980s. In this theoretical context gender is freed from its former identification with women and specific sexual roles to become a principal determinant of political and social organisation as a whole. In the seminal account of Joan Scott, it is a 'useful category of historical analysis' at two levels: 'gender is a constitutive element of social relationships based on perceived differences between the sexes, and gender is a primary way of signifying relationships of power'. In the latter case, gender has been a constitutive feature of class relationships, workers, for instance, frequently being coded by employers and officials as feminine, weak, dependent and exploited, but by labour leaders as masculine, representing physical strength, productivity and protectiveness (Scott, J. 1988, 42, 48). At the same time, the historical record is important to feminism because it indicates not merely the formal subordination of women to men but also the perpetual struggle over what the category of 'woman' (and 'man') means. The identity of women as a category is far from a settled matter, according to the historian Denise Riley. ' "Women" is historically, discursively constructed, and always relatively to other categories which themselves change; "women" is a volatile collectivity in which female persons can be very differently positioned, so that the apparent continuity of the subject of "women" isn't to be relied on' (Riley 1988, 1–2). Riley provides examples of this historical mutability, first in the gradual sexualisation of the soul, and hence of religious experience, in the seventeenth and eighteenth centuries; and secondly, in the implication of women in the emergent idea of the 'social' during the nineteenth century, in philanthropy, domestic economy and, by the twentieth century, the complex institution of social welfare. 'Woman' is thus a malleable and fluctuating identity, shaped by and in response to a myriad of historical pressures.

In the wake of Scott and Riley's pioneering studies, historians have applied analyses of gender to widening areas of the past, including the constitution of history itself as an institution (Smith, B. 2000). In particular, they have investigated the origins and formation of modern gender identities, seeking in the seventeenth and eighteenth centuries the emergence of what were to become normative ideas of relations between (and within) the sexes in the nineteenth and twentieth century. Focusing for the moment on Britain, debate has centred on the putative development of 'separate spheres' between 1780 and 1850, whereby men became increasingly identified with a public sphere of politics and business while women were confined to the home and childcare. Articulated most cogently by Leonore Davidoff and Catherine Hall in their study of middle-class families, the thesis has since come under increasing attack (Davidoff and Hall 1987). Critics have suggested that there was nothing new about the concept of separate spheres in the late eighteenth century; it can be found in other periods and societies. Nor was it confined to the middle class, but was apparent in other social groups such as the landed gentry. The extent to which it informed actual behaviour has been exaggerated; middle-class women continued to operate in public domains such as organised religion, philanthropy and the arts while men's responsibilities in the private sphere simultaneously expanded. Indeed, the ideology of separate spheres may have been a response to the increased public activity of women, not to its diminution (Shoemaker 1998; Tosh 1999a; Vickery 1993). The concept of public and private spheres, so historians have recently argued, does not provide a reliable guide to understanding masculine and feminine identities or behaviour in this period.

Nevertheless, changes there were in gender identities between the late seventeenth and early nineteenth centuries. In tracking these changes the key seems to lie at the level of sex rather than gender, or in the relationship between these two. In the mid-seventeenth century sexual difference was explained by a humoral model, in which the male was seen to consist principally of hot and dry fluids, the female, of cold and wet. The bodies of men and women were viewed as basically similar; it was humoral differences which caused genitalia to develop in what were regarded as inverse ways. Equally, the distinction between hot and cold fluids was a matter of degree and did not denote a sharp division between the sexes. 'Sex before the seventeenth century was still a sociological and not an ontological category', according to Thomas Laqueur. Sex was the 'epiphenomenon, while *gender*, what we would take to be a cultural category, was primary or "real"' (Laqueur 1990, 8). Between the late seventeenth and early nineteenth centuries, however, this 'one-sex' model of sex and the body was gradually overturned by both medical and public opinion. An idea of anatomical difference replaced that of the humors, rooting sex more firmly in the body and the reproductive organs. Whereas women's orgasm had formerly been considered essential for conception, the new model of sexual reproduction made women merely receptacles for the all-important male sperm. Similarly, whereas women had formerly been viewed as the more lustful sex, now they became passive while men took on the active role (Schiebinger 1994). What was emerging by the late eighteenth century was thus a 'two-sex' model of the body whose overriding consequence was sexual polarisation.

Alongside other cultural shifts, the change from a one to a two-sex model of the body had major implications for gender identities. For the one-sex model of the early modern period envisaged gender as organised on a spectrum. Accordingly, it was possible for men and women (who shared the same prototype body) to possess a variety of masculine and feminine characteristics, determined by their particular humoral mix. The tradition of masquerade in which sexual, gender and other kinds of identity were put in play was one cultural expression of these ideas, especially notable in England from the 1720s (Castle 1986). And the legacy lingered. Joan Scott gives the example of the French feminist and revolutionary Olympe de Gouges who 'refused the differentiation of bodies into fixed binary categories, insisting instead on multiplicity, variety, ranges of difference, spectra of colours and functions, confusion of roles', before meeting her end at the guillotine (Scott, J. 1996, 22–3). As the fate of Gouges implies, by the late eighteenth century these ideas had come to be seen as threatening to social order, challenging the polarised view of gender relations, the division into two naturally opposite sexes prevalent by this period. Such a view rested, in turn, on acceptance of the two-sex model of sexual difference in which gender was no longer seen as an independent variable but as deriving directly from the sexed body. Sex, in Laqueur's terms, had moved from a sociological to an ontological category, a reality or 'nature' which determined all gender characteristics. Thus the medicalised image of the Victorian woman as permeated by her sex and ruled by the biological imperatives of menstruation, pregnancy and menopause.

The shift to the two-sex model in the course of the long eighteenth century had consequences for men, women and sexual relations. Sexual behaviour is difficult to research historically but there is evidence for Britain to suggest a stronger emphasis on penetrative sex after 1750 as compared with an earlier period when petting appears to have been a popular sexual practice (Hitchcock 1997). This has been linked to the growth of 'compulsory heterosexuality' and with it a stricter, more assertive masculinity from the mid-eighteenth century, contrasted with prior forms of libertinism. One aspect of this was the predatory masculinity Anna Clark found among English artisans, a 'drunken misogyny' based on the alehouse and workshop, which nevertheless gave way by the 1840s before 'respectable patriarchy' (Clark, A. 1995). Moreover, the two-sex model also required that the masculine be defined in opposition not only to women but also to effeminacy and homosexuality. Before the mid-seventeenth century homosexuality was condemned but it was nevertheless understood as part of a continuum of sexual behaviours, not as something inherently alien or noteworthy. With the spread of the two-sex model in the eighteenth century, however, homosexuality came to represent a distinct sexual category, and one which was increasingly the object of intolerance: from 1699 homosexuals began to be prosecuted in the courts, while terms such as 'molly' and 'sapphist' became forms of abuse (Trumbach 1991). At the same period, a homosexual subculture came into being in London for the first time, with its own language and codes of conduct; as John Tosh has observed, this subculture was effectively the only space at the period where a choice of sexual identity was on offer (Tosh 1999b, 233). While consolidating a specific hegemonic masculinity, therefore, the two-sex model also witnessed a fracturing of masculine and sexual identities.

There are undoubtedly problems with this reinterpretation of the formation of modern sexual and gender identities. It is better at describing the changes concerned than at explaining them; and the evidence for the changes themselves is patchy, stronger on attitudes than actual behaviour, on the metropolis than the provinces, and on élites rather than the population at large. But significant changes there clearly were between the seventeenth and nineteenth centuries, the result less of separate spheres and the division of gender roles, as was previously claimed, than of sexual polarisation and discursively constituted identities. Identity changes were themselves predicated on shifts in understandings of the body and, in particular, of the articulation of sex and gender. In this respect historical research over the last fifteen years has mirrored trends in cultural theory, notably the important ideas of Judith Butler on sex, gender and performativity. It is to these that we now turn.

Performativity

We have noted the idea of performance in certain interpretations of identity, borrowed from social psychology and anthropology. Identities are thus seen as akin to roles that individuals play on a variety of sites or stages. The concept of 'performativity', elaborated by the feminist and queer theorist Judith Butler, has some analogies to this larger notion of performance, but it departs from it in critical ways. Butler's ideas, expounded most systematically in her early work, *Gender Trouble*, represents the most significant and radical theory of gender identity of recent years (Butler 1990). Its impress has been registered widely across the humanities and social sciences. Although Butler's ideas have been promulgated by the feminist historian Joan Scott, with whom she has worked closely (e.g. Butler and Scott 1992), their influence within history has more often been indirect. It is common, indeed, to see them grossly simplified or travestied, as Butler herself has complained (Butler 1993). Yet Butler's theory of sex and gender has implications for all historians concerned with identity and its formation, not least because she arrives at startlingly similar conclusions to those of recent historical research.

Butler's argument in *Gender Trouble* starts from the statement by Simone de Beauvoir, the novelist and philosopher, that 'one is not born a woman, but rather becomes one'. What this is taken to imply is that neither sex nor gender are natural, innate categories; they are attributes which a subject learns in the course of socialisation. This may appear uncontentious, but Butler uses it to set up a number of fundamental questions about the status of 'sex' and how gender is practically constructed. Implicit here is a critique of forms of feminism that assume (in the manner of much women's history) that sex can serve as the unquestioned, pre-discursive basis of identity between women as well as of Foucault's depiction of the body as a blank medium on which cultural and historical processes are inscribed (Butler 1990, 1–6, 129–30). In this critique Butler begins to unpick the connections assumed to link together sex, gender and sexuality. Sex is no longer the invariant biological grounding of gender, just as sexuality does not follow from gender. Following Riley among others, she argues that sex no less than gender has a history and that the relationship of the two categories needs to be untangled in order to understand how identities formed in their name are set to work. Of particular importance in Butler's analysis is the idea, originating from the psychoanalyst Joan Rivière, that femininity (termed 'womanliness' by Rivière) represents a type of masquerade, what Butler describes as 'the performative production of a sexual ontology' (Rivière 1986; Butler 1990, 47). This idea enables Butler to develop the argument that gender itself is something that is enacted, not given, and that what the masquerade 'masks', among other things, is precisely this disjunction with biological sex: 'gender is a kind of persistent impersonation that passes as the real' (Butler 1990, x).

Gender in Butler's account is therefore not the expression of a deep-seated inner nature, but a 'regulatory fiction' enacted on the body, whose purpose is to maintain in place a heterosexual order and which creates the illusion of stable, unified and, above all, natural gender identities.

In other words, acts, gestures, and desire produce the effect of an internal core or substance, but produce this on the surface of the body, through the play of signifying absences that suggest, but never reveal, the organising principle of identity as a cause. Such acts, gestures, enactments, generally construed, are performative *in the sense that the essence or identity that they otherwise purport to express are* fabrications *manufactured and sustained by corporeal signs and other discursive means (Butler 1990, 136, emphasis original).*

What is argued here is that neither the body nor sex serves as a basis for gender. Gender is not therefore expressive, since there is no underlying essence to which it refers; rather, gender is 'performative', in Butler's sense of the term. In the linguistic theory of J.L. Austin, 'performativity' refers to speech acts, like promises or declarations, that serve to constitute the very reality they represent (Austin 1975). In Butler's study gender is understood as performative because its attributes 'constitute the identity they are said to express or reveal' (Butler 1990, 141). Rather than being the cause of certain masculine or feminine ways of behaving, in other words, gender is the effect of those ways of behaving.

How and by what means, then, is gender identity produced? Butler again provides an answer: 'Gender is the repeated stylization of the body, a set of repeated acts within a highly rigid regulatory frame that congeal over time to produce the appearance of substance, of a natural sort of being' (Butler 1990, 33). Gender identity is something that is embodied, not just a mental or discursive category, and it is produced through bodily acts, gestures, 'styles of the flesh' that give all the appearance of being produced by the body, by sex itself. Moreover, these acts are repeated so that they become mundane; like ritual or habit, what is enacted by gender is a social performance that is neither conscious nor arbitrary, but acquires meaning for both performer and spectator through its capacity to produce a coherent, 'natural' subject over time. Gender performativity is also social not individual, intended to sustain those norms of sexual difference on which a heterosexual order depends. The creation and maintenance of identity, Butler insists, is hard work, since it relies on the consistent repetition of rule-governed practices which render identity culturally intelligible. This process also has its 'failures', of course, in individuals or groups who do not properly – that is to say, credibly – 'fit' the requirements of particular identity categories (e.g. the good parent, the heterosexually desiring or desirable object): 'indeed, we regularly punish those who fail to do their gender right' (Butler 1990, 140). At the same time, the failure inherent in the lack of fit with norms is one way in which the allegedly natural relationship between sex and gender is revealed to be nothing more than a 'regulatory fiction'. It is this gap between sex, gender and gender performance that is also disclosed, according to Butler, in cultural acts such as drag and cross-dressing, which a knowing audience comprehends as parody. And while parody is not of itself radical, it points to the way in which normative gender identities might be subverted, that is to say 'rendered thoroughly and radically *incredible*' (Butler 1990, 141, italics original).

In subsequent work on gender performativity Butler has shifted her interpretive emphasis. Gender, she affirms, is not to be thought of as a matter of choice or as akin to a performance in the theatrical sense. Instead, Butler emphasises the discursive aspect of performativity, the 'reiterative power of discourse to produce the phenomena that it regulates and constrains' and seeks at the same time to develop the psychoanalytic dimension of the concept (Butler 1993, 1–23). This turn to language and the symbolic are less likely to be of interest to historians than the earlier identification of performativity with bodily practices related to socially regulated norms. But in *Gender Trouble* especially, Butler provides historians with a theory of how gender identity is produced and works, for masculinity as well as femininity. It is not directly transferable in her view to other identity categories, such as race or class, which have distinct conceptual histories and operate on different lines (Butler 1993, 18). Even so, Butler's notion of performativity may prove helpful in interpreting those rituals and symbolic events where what is at stake is precisely the authoritative institution of social difference. Here performativity's 'social magic' can explain the symbolic transformation of bodies into categories of power and authority – kingship, governance, aristocracy (Butler 1999). But it is in the field of gender identity and sexuality that Butler's work has had most purchase, finding resonance in the very historiography we examined in the previous section, which has similarly prised apart the histories of sex, gender and the body in order to reassemble them in new, historically-informed ways. Such ideas are equally important to the analysis of the final identity category examined here, that of the modern self.

The emergence of the modern self

The thrust of both cultural theory and cultural history has thus been to denaturalise those categories that appear most fundamental and transhistorical: gender, sex, the person. To these one can add a further identity category, that of the self, a move which appears to confound intellectual as well as popular assumptions. Is not the concept of the self, the individual's innermost being, basically unchanging over space and time? Is it not part of that essential humanness that allows people to speak to one another, through art and culture, across historical time? And if there have indeed been shifts in how the self has been understood even within Western culture, how can historians investigate what is largely a private and hidden subject? The idea that the self has a history is, in fact, not a new one. It forms part of the established narrative of the rise of individualism and received extensive treatment during the course of the twentieth century in fields such as anthropology, social psychology and sociology (Mauss 1985; Mead 1934; Sennett 1976). It also derived theoretical impetus from Michel Foucault's studies of the transformation of human individuals into subjects, through the discourses of the human sciences, the construction of binary oppositions (e.g. self and society), and the processes of identification or self-fashioning (Foucault 1990). But the self – and particularly, the making of the modern self – has recently come under intensive scrutiny from historians and it is their arguments that I shall briefly examine here.

What is meant by the 'self'? The term refers in principal to the inner, private world of the individual, which represents their essence or core, and finds its complement in the idea of the 'person', designating the public, social face of the individual (Jenkins, R. 1996, 30). It denotes introspection and independence – the self as different from and autonomous of others. However, as anthropologists have frequently pointed out, this concept of the self is culturally and historically specific to the modern West. How a modern Western idea of the self came into being and from what previous conceptions of personhood are questions which historians such as Charles Taylor and Dror Wahrman have investigated, seeking their answers in Europe of the eighteenth and early nineteenth centuries. The selection of period is significant here, since not only is it considered a key period in the creation of Western modernity, as we saw in Chapter Five, but it is also the historical point at which other identity categories – sex, gender, class – were themselves coming to take recognisably modern forms. Thus Charles Taylor traces the emergence of a tradition of thought that emphasised both the interiority and uniqueness of self-identity and which he sees as culminating in Romantic 'expressivism', the urgent voicing of an inner truth (Taylor, C. 1989). With Romanticism the self has become an organic essence which must be nurtured, developed and find expression through the individual's life. We are close here to Anthony Gidden's notion of the modern self as a reflexive project, which requires the person to construct a 'trajectory of development from the past to the anticipated future' (Giddens 1996, 75).

Whereas Taylor focuses on a tradition of intellectual and artistic thought, Dror Wahrman's account is cast in broader social and cultural terms. Wahrman views the making of the modern self as emerging out of an *ancien régime* of identity' in the late eighteenth century (Wahrman 2004). What distinguished the latter was the idea that identity was something that the individual assumed and that, like a role, it could be modified and even discarded. By contrast, in the modern regime post-1780, identity was understood to be innate and ultimately unchanging; thus the self might develop from a budlike state in infancy through the whole life-course, but its essence remained the same. Wahrman similarly characterises this shift as a move from 'intersubjective identicality' to 'individual identity', which in turn involved a change in the balance of emphasis within the definition of identity itself. What was emphasised in the *ancien régime* understanding of identity was sameness, what people shared with others; in the modern version, by contrast, the stress was on difference, what distinguished the individual from others and made them unique. It was this shift in the conception of identity, Wahrman argues, that lay behind the precipitate decline of the masquerade in England from the 1770s. Identity play came to be seen by the time of the American and French Revolutions as socially subversive and inimical to the unique integrity of the individual self (Wahrman 2004, 158–65, 265); similar transformations can be observed in spheres as diverse as politics and portraiture. The Romantic notion of childhood as a distinctive stage of human development also played its part, as Carolyn Steedman has argued, in popularising the idea of an interiorised essence, present in every child, which formed the basis of the individual's personal history (Steedman 1995). For Wahrman, too, the emergence of the modern self was inextricably entwined with the transformation of other identity categories, of 'race', class and, above all, gender. Thus the 'gender panic' which he sees as overtaking English (and French) society in the late eighteenth century was coincident and interlocking with the shift in understandings of the self indicated here (Wahrman 2004, 40–4). Both were concerned to stabilise and essentialise identity, to root gender in sex and the self in the person.

Consequently, the emergence of the idea of the self as a unique, private domain of the individual was the product of the gamut of changes affecting identity (or identities) as a whole (see also Reddy 2001). What these changes shared, among other things, was a hardening of the categories concerned so that it became difficult to comprehend any particular identity as malleable or fluid. 'Just as it became harder to imagine a person's gender roaming away from his or her sex (without severe consequences), or civilisation from race, or political behaviour from class', writes Wahrman, 'so it became harder to imagine . . . that personhood, or the self, could roam away from the man' (Wahrman 2004, 278). There are problems with Wahrman's thesis, not least its tendency to rely on a narrow evidential frame (educated, eighteenth-century London) to construct an argument for a cultural revolution in Western society as a whole. But if Wahrman is at least partly correct – and his arguments mesh with those of sex and gender, as we have seen – then historians may have indeed begun to expose the historical foundations of those ideas of identity which cultural theorists have seen as integral to the concept of the modern subject.

Evaluation

This chapter has depicted a series of historiographical and theoretical transitions in the study of social identity. The first and most obvious is the shift in intellectual focus over the last twenty years from what might be termed historically self-evident identities, such as those of the nation, to ever more 'natural' and, hence, less visible identities, like sex and self. One can discern, secondly, a change at the level of theoretical approach and sophistication. Among historians, this is apparent in the increased questioning of identity as a categorical given (as in the treatment of 'women' as a unified group) as well as in the growing critique of models of identity posited in terms of a simplified dialectic between 'self' and 'other'. In their place has grown up the recognition that identity is theoretically complex and the outcome of multi-layered historical processes. The forensic analysis of the body, sex and gender, demonstrated most brilliantly in the theory of Judith Butler but reflected also in the work of cultural and gender historians, bears witness to a new level of conceptual sophistication in this regard. Identity formation is likewise revealed as a process of doing, not just thinking; identities are formed in action through repeated patterns of behaviour, bodily practices such as gesture and cultural forms such as masquerade and drama. Further, research suggests how identity categories were operationally linked to one another with long-term material effects. The polarised perception of male and female sexualities in the later eighteenth century, for instance, was clearly pivotal to the reshaping of gender relations in the modern West which, in the twentieth century, would underpin, among other things, the policies of the welfare state.

Nevertheless, questions remain about the literature of identity. With reference to the historiography, the questions concern both sources and methods. Evidence of sexual practices is, unsurprisingly, limited before the twentieth century and, as with the study of the self, historians are reliant on accounts of and by the educated. Consequently, whether patterns discerned at this social level extended more widely in society is largely conjectural. In effect, it is doubtful whether the evidence base for certain aspects of identity is sufficiently robust to sustain claims of widescale historical change. One result of the limitations of the sources is that historians may, wittingly or not, exaggerate the evidence of change. Reviewing recent research on masculinity, John Tosh has drawn attention to those aspects of gender that did *not* change between the mid-eighteenth and mid-nineteenth century, including the structure of household authority and forms of masculine behaviour (Tosh 1999b, 223–38). Equally, while the historical literature on class is vast, we know remarkably little about how ordinary men and women saw the social world and their own position within it. Historians who have set out to explore social class in its various forms have been accused of using sources such as autobiography merely to confirm their own preconceived interpretations, rather than acknowledging the fluid and ambiguous subject positions articulated in these sources. 'Identity' here may become an anachronistic label affixed to groups and individuals, instead of an active process ('identification') which is at issue in any particular historical conjuncture (Host 1998, 60–90).

As a number of these examples imply, problems of sources frequently spill over into method and methodology. While historians have explored identities extensively in the currents of public discourse, for instance, it is much less clear how far these were actually internalised and became part of individual subjectivities. This is a methodological issue partly because so much of the historical study of identity proceeds by description, a form of documentary bric-à-brac held together by loose association, or what Dror Wahrman terms 'weak collage' (Wahrman 2004, 45). The temptation in such an approach is to collect instances of the patterning of identity over a given historical period without enquiring in detail as to its breadth and depth. However, the interpretive significance of a pattern can only be gauged if its limits are established within a larger field of social and cultural representation. Only at this point does it become possible to assess, with anything approaching rigour, the place of a pattern of identity and its

effective influence. What is suggested here is also the problem of prioritising discourse as a source over the study of specific practices. The issue here
is not simply epistemological – the difficulty of separating 'discourse' from
'practice' – but methodological, since attention to the last of these frequently undermines arguments based on the first, as demonstrated by the
historical critique of 'separate spheres'.

Questions also extend to the theory and politics of identity. As we have
seen in this chapter, identity is closely linked to the problematic concept of
representation. 'Representation' holds out the promise of making visible
groups as political subjects while at the same time conveying in a normative sense the assumed essence or truth of that group (Butler 1990, 1).
Moreover, in so far as representation is conceived as akin to an object or
image it designates a product rather than a process, jostling for the attention of historians among a host of other representations at any given time.
In these respects the concept of representation mirrors the difficulties associated with identity itself: an ambiguity inherent in its definition which
easily leads to conceptual confusion, together with a vagueness about how
representations practically work. The study of representations, like that
of identities to which it is so often linked, tends be descriptive, merely
indicating the passage from one set of representations (or identities)
to another without illuminating the means by which this transition is
effected. Although this criticism is not confined to historiography, it
remains the case with many of the accounts discussed in this chapter.
Despite the wealth of recent historical research on social identities this
body of work has not produced a theory of identity of equivalent explana-
tory power to that of Judith Butler. Yet Butler's theory is itself confined to
the operations of sex and gender, and is not intended to apply to other
identity categories. Following Butler, 'identity' itself becomes problematic
to the extent that it serves to conflate different categories under a single
heading, such as race and class, which have their own histories and regulatory principles. Historians like Mary Poovey have sought to explore
these histories in epistemological terms, as we saw in Chapter Five, and
in his account of the origins of the modern self Wahrman follows suit
(Poovey 1995). But while this approach avoids some of the problems
associated with the concept of representation, it too relies heavily on
description in demonstrating the shift from one epistemological regime to
another.

Finally, the study of identities raises political issues. One major paradox is that while the political thrust of much historical and theoretical
work on identities is to denaturalise and even dissolve them, the effect is

the reverse, to reinforce them. It is by no means clear, for example, that to deconstruct the category of women is advantageous to the cause of feminism; indeed, many feminist historians would argue that is in fact politically disabling (Hoff 1994). Equally, to argue that the category of homosexual is an historical invention can be seen as diminishing its status as a legitimate sexual identity, rendering gay men vulnerable to attacks from social conservatives. In general, while the frequently stated aim of identity politics has been to make distinctions based on race, gender or sexuality socially meaningless, arguably such politics has not only strengthened the visibility, activism and sense of community associated with these identities but also entrenched the very categories themselves (Weeks 2000, 7).

There are, then, considerable problems and complexities in the field of identity studies that warn against the unreflective use of terms such as 'representation'. Yet identity is a concept that history, perhaps above all among the human sciences, can ill afford to do without, for it is difficult to conceive of a species of historiography that is not concerned in some form with the character and composition of human identities in the past. It is a field, moreover, that has given rise to some of the most engaged and engaging historical work of the last twenty years. Indeed, its influence has been such that it has contributed substantially to the growth of what is perhaps the single most significant area of recent theoretical and historical research, that of postcolonial studies. It is to this area that we now turn.

CHAPTER SEVEN

Postcolonialism

O f all the successive waves of cultural theory that have swept across the human sciences since the late twentieth century it is postcolonialism that arguably provides the greatest challenge to conventional historical practice. This is partly because it is a body of thought that specifically targets 'history' as an object within its broader enquiry into the geopolitics of knowledge, the relations between 'the West and the rest', the imperial powers and their former colonies. Postcolonialism provokes questioning *inter alia* of the conceptual framework of historical study (classically, the nation-state); of accepted models of periodisation (the traditional, the modern) and conceptions of historical time; and of categories deemed capable of universal application, such as capitalism and religion. It also interrogates the processes of historical research, the kinds of knowledge that can be derived from the archive and the status of historical 'evidence'. Not surprisingly, while some historians have received such ideas enthusiastically, and, indeed, have shared in elaborating them, others have treated postcolonialism with hostility or indifference. The historian of imperialism, John Mackenzie, for example, has vigorously rebutted Edward Said's theory of Orientalism, accusing Said among other things of grossly over-simplifying the complex history of cultural interchanges between East and West (Mackenzie 1995). Major historical studies of empire and globalisation continue to be published, meanwhile, with only passing reference to the detailed postcolonial literature (e.g. Cannadine 2001; Bayly 2004; see also Hall, C. 2004 for comments).

There is a long-established and voluminous historiography of empire. In Britain the tradition stretches from J.R. Seeley's *The Expansion of England*, first published in 1883, to the official Oxford and Cambridge University histories written over a century later (Seeley 1883; Louis

1998–9; Marshall 1996). Postcolonialism likewise has a history, if more recent and slight. Critics such as Robert Young have pointed to the historian Arnold Toynbee's denunciation of the illusions of Western cultural imperialism at the time of the Second World War, notably Toynbee's criticism of the 'Late Modern Western convention of identifying parvenue and provincial Western Society's history with "History", writ large' (Young, R. 1990, 19). Others have identified as an intellectual precursor the classic historical study *The Black Jacobins* by the West Indian Marxist C.L.R. James, first published in 1938, which explored the interaction between the French revolution of 1789 and the San Domingo (later Haitian) revolution two years later, culminating in independence from French rule in 1804 (James 1980). What is particularly significant about James' account is that not only are the two events seen as historically interrelated, but that it also clearly showed the way in which political influences had flowed both ways between metropole and colony. Among French intellectuals of the 1950s, as we saw in Chapter One, the war over the colony of Algeria which ended in Algerian independence in 1962 provoked anguished public debate about European imperialism and its effects, involving figures such as Roland Barthes, Jean-Paul Sartre and Frantz Fanon. This experience, in turn, had a significant impact on French post-structuralist theory.

But such debates were by no means universal in the former imperialist powers. In Britain, where decolonisation occurred steadily over the three decades from the ceding of independence to India in 1947, the legacy of empire was for a long time met in intellectual circles by what Stuart Hall has termed a 'resounding but unconscious silence' in which historiography itself was complicit (Hall, S. 1996, 270). An influential strand of labour history in the 1960s and 1970s, for example, denied that imperialism had a significant cultural or political impact on the British working class in the nineteenth and early twentieth centuries (e.g. Pelling 1968; Price 1972). It was not only that empire occupied a shadowy place in debates, historical or otherwise, about British society, but that even the most cosmopolitan 'world histories', such as those of Perry Anderson and Fernand Braudel, proceeded on the implicit assumption that Europe was the centre and progenitor of History as a unified, unfolding process (Said 1985b, 22). One consequence was that Europe was deemed to be the place where historical processes of change, like industrialisation and modern democracy, first occurred, later to be replicated under local conditions in other parts of the globe. Thus from the vantage point of Australia, as the cultural critic Meaghan Morris laconically put it, the modern can appear only as 'a *known history*, something which has *already happened elsewhere*, and which is to be reproduced, mechanically or otherwise, with a local content' (Morris, M. 1993, 10).

This chapter considers the interrelationship of postcolonial theory and historical studies. To begin with I shall examine the influential ideas of a group of theorists – Edward Said, Homi Bhaba and Gayatri Spivak – who have shaped the whole field of postcolonial thought. This includes the school of Indian historiography known as Subaltern Studies that has proved most receptive to this and other kinds of cultural theory, and whose own collective output has implications both for the practice and understanding of history in the West. I shall also look at how postcolonial theory has been used to rethink the impact of the 'Empire at home', in Britain and elsewhere, as well as some of the major criticisms that have been levelled at it. In particular, I shall argue that while postcolonialism puts in question the whole geopolitical framework of history, its application in certain contexts, notably British history, has had the paradoxical consequence of reinforcing staple elements of that framework, including the concepts of Europe and the nation. But before proceeding to these larger issues we need to define more precisely what postcolonialism means.

Defining postcolonialism

Like 'modernity', the term postcolonial implies both an historical periodisation and a mode of analysis or critique. It relates to the notions of colonialism and imperialism, concepts that are often used interchangeably. If both concepts imply the domination of one state or people by another, colonialism is normally used to refer to the informal, economically driven process whereby a metropolitan power exerted influence over parts of the world primarily for trading purposes. Imperialism, on the other hand, designates a project of domination carried out politically as an instrument of state policy (Young, R. 2001, 16–17; Porter 1975, 2–3). The historian of empire Catherine Hall thus uses the term colonialism to cover the processes of European 'discovery' and expansionism between the fifteenth century and the 1800s, and imperialism to refer to the late nineteenth and early twentieth century when the pursuit of empire reached its zenith and became an active part of the politics of many European nation-states (Hall, C. 2000, 5).

The concept of postcolonialism is related to both these terms, but it has also accrued further distinctive meanings. It designates, first, a period after the dissolution of the world empires which had reached their apogee between 1880 and 1920 when a quarter of the world was partitioned up between the major European imperial states, the United States and Japan (Hobsbawm 1987, 57–9; Bayly 2004, 228–33). The dismantling of empire was hastened by increasingly militant nationalist movements after the Second World War so that by 1970 the imperial era was effectively over, though its aftershocks were still felt in brutal wars in Vietnam and parts of Africa. By this period too the economic and cultural effects of globalisation were increasingly recognised by politicians, policy-makers and intellectuals. In an essay entitled 'The muse of history', first published in 1974, the Caribbean writer Derek Walcott reflected on the bitter legacy of slavery and spoke of the 'monumental groaning and soldering of two great worlds', the Old World and the New, in the historical present (Walcott 1995, 374). The waves of migration from the former colonies which accompanied these processes provide another vantage-point from which to view the postcolonial moment. In Britain in particular the 1980s witnessed a growing recognition of the emergence of new ethnic identities as the children of migrants from the Caribbean and the Indian subcontinent came of age. Among members of this new generation identities (black, British, Asian, Caribbean) were no longer fixed by reference to a clear sense of 'home' and there was a tendency to reject all racialised and essentialised categories (Gilroy 1987; Hall, S. 1988). But if the concept of postcolonialism reflects a strong sense of historical transition, this is not taken to assume that colonialism and imperialism are 'over'. One of the central purposes of postcolonial critique is to combat the cultural and other legacies of colonialism as these persist and are renewed through a capitalist international division of labour and Western politico-military hegemony. Thus, a critic like Gayatri Spivak, professor of humanities at Columbia University in New York, refers to herself as situated within the 'current academic theatre of cultural imperialism' (Spivak 1996, 232). A striking and little remarked aspect of this neo-imperialism is the globalisation of English itself as the dominant language of academic exchange.

At the same time as it evokes an historical conjuncture, postcolonialism also represents a specific mode of critique, concerned in the first instance with the analysis of identity, 'race' and place. It is inherently an interdisciplinary project, deliberately calling into question conventional academic divisions between literature, history, and anthropology – the study of peoples assumed to be without 'history'. Postcolonialism also links bodies of thought not usually brought together or seen as compatible, such as Gramscian Marxism, literary deconstruction and psychoanalysis. Its working concepts – ambivalence, hybridity, difference – are developed out of these theoretical traditions, while undergoing redefinition within postcolonial thought itself. The dimensions of postcolonialism are therefore geopolitical and epistemological. Within its bounds, geography matters – where a text (or history) is written from becomes equally (or more) important than who it is written by. An essential part of the postcolonial critique is thus concerned to effect the decolonisation of Europe's intellectual legacy. If, following Robert Young, postmodernism 'can best be defined as European culture's awareness that it is no longer the unquestioned and dominant centre of the world', then postcolonialism is the principal instrument for the unravelling of European thought on a global stage (Young, R. 1990, 19). As such, it brings into question the plethora of disciplines and categories, from history and anthropology to reason and objectivity, through which what was in fact a local – European or Western – knowledge came to stand as something universal, as knowledge *tout court*. Postcolonialism, in short, represents the intellectual moment at which, to quote the title of a pioneering study, the empire strikes back (Centre for Contemporary Cultural Studies, 1982).

Orientalism, hybridity and difference

We have already seen that the origins of postcolonial thought can be traced back to the first half of the twentieth century and, indeed, earlier. But the emergence of postcolonialism as a distinctive intellectual constellation is conventionally associated with the work of three critics: Frantz Fanon, Edward Said and Homi Bhaba. Originally from Martinique, Fanon trained as a psychiatrist in France. Moving to North Africa in the 1950s, he participated in the Algerian struggle for national liberation from French colonial rule before dying in 1961, a year before Algerian independence. His first book, *Black Skin, White Masks*, published in 1952, was an attempt to understand the psychology of colonialism and the colonised subject; his last, *The Wretched of the Earth*, which appeared in 1961, represented a revolutionary manifesto on behalf of anticolonial movements.

In his writings Fanon contributed a number of influential themes to subsequent postcolonial thought. In the first place, the lengthy historical process of European expansionism was seen not simply as remaking the rest of the world, but Europe itself. 'The settler makes history' in the act of colonial expropriation, Fanon argued. 'The history he writes is not the history of the country which he plunders but the history of his own nation in regard to all that she skims off, all that she violates and starves.'

Consequently, in an ironic reversal Fanon depicted Europe as the product of its other: 'Europe is literally the creation of the Third World' (Fanon 1991 [1961], 51, 102). At the same time Fanon paid detailed attention to the complex, divided character of black subjectivity created in and by colonial relations. 'Not only must the black man be black; he must be black in relation to the white man . . . Overnight the Negro has been given two frames of reference within which he has to place himself' and to which he simultaneously submits and resists (Fanon 1982, 110, 140). In adopting this issue as a central problem, Fanon constituted the colonised subject as the object of critical enquiry within the discursive framework of colonial power. Finally, in the revolutionary coda to *The Wretched of the Earth* Fanon called for a rejection of European humanism as an intellectual resource, since humanism had revealed itself through the imperial project to be no more than a rhetorical sham. 'Let us waste no time in sterile litanies and nauseating mimicry. Leave this Europe where they are never done talking of Man, yet murder men wherever they find them, at the corner of every one of their own streets, in all the corners of the globe . . . Today we know with what sufferings humanity has paid for every one of their triumphs of the mind.' European fascism from this perspective was merely the violence of colonialism brought home (Fanon 1991, 101, 311–12). Fanon thus set in train a number of arresting critical themes which have resonated through much of the later literature of postcolonialism.

However, the figure who more than anyone is credited with inaugurating postcolonialism (though he himself disliked the term) was the Palestinian intellectual, Edward Said. Said's book *Orientalism*, first appearing in 1978, represents one of the foundational texts of postcolonial studies, initiating not so much a new object of study – the history of Western attitudes towards the East – as a new mode of critical, interdisciplinary analysis spanning literature, historical studies and anthropology. In its critique of cultural imperialism and its political engagement *Orientalism* looked back to Fanon, but in its methodology the study drew on the early work of Foucault, notably the latter's conception of discourse and power. According to Said, Orientalism is the product of European or Western discourses and forms of knowledge which define 'the East' as fundamentally other and – in the context of imperialism – as culturally subordinate to the West. He thus defined Orientalism as a '*distribution* of geopolitical awareness into aesthetic, scholarly, economic, sociological, historical and philological texts; it is an *elaboration*, not only of a basic geographical distinction (the world is made up of two unequal halves,

Orient and Occident) but also of a whole series of "interests" which, by such means as scholarly discovery, philological reconstruction, psychological analysis, landscape and sociological description not only creates it but also maintains it' (Said 1985a, 12, italics original). As this implies, Western academic, administrative and cultural knowledges were not viewed as in any sense neutral or disinterested. While Said dismissed the notion of a simple relationship between Orientalism and imperial power, he nonetheless described the former as depending on a 'flexible *positional* superiority, which puts the Westerner in a whole series of possible relationships with the Orient without ever losing him the upper hand' (Said 1985a, 7).

Orientalism, then, is the ensemble of discourses through which the East was (and is) produced as alien, exotic – and inferior. But when and how was it formed historically? Said was ambiguous about the periodisation of Orientalism. On one side he claimed it to be an endemic feature of European culture, apparent in the writings of classical Greece and regenerated through events such as the late medieval Crusades against Islam (Said 1985a, 55–60). On the other, however, Said also argued that Orientalism took distinctive shape in Europe from the eighteenth century and was thus coterminous with the expansion of the European empires from this period. In this latter case Orientalism was seen as deeply implicated in the cultural forms and disciplinary knowledges of the nineteenth century. Included here were the travel writing of figures like Charles Doughty, the poetry of Lamartine and Chateaubriand, and the novels of Flaubert and Conrad. Orientalism was identified too with the emergence of new academic disciplines: philology (the science of language), anthropology, history, and, not least, the scientific study of the Orient itself, whether by enthusiastic amateurs, like Edward Williams Lane who wrote on Egyptian customs, or by specialists at the many European universities which offered Orientalist subjects by the 1850s (Said 1985a, 190–1). Yet these literary and scholarly texts were not seen by Said as 'merely cultural', in Judith Butler's ironic phrase. Drawing on Gramsci's concept of hegemony, Said argued that they were central to imperialism as a military, administrative and governmental project. They were part of the 'enormously systematic discipline by which European culture was able to manage – and even produce – the Orient politically, sociologically, militarily, ideologically, scientifically and imaginatively during the post-Enlightenment period' (Said 1985a, 3). In the final part of the book, entitled 'Orientalism now', Said showed how Orientalist ideas have continued to inform cultural and political practices in the West, from academic 'area studies' to state policy formation. An example, which Said drew attention to in a subsequent interview, was Samuel Huntington's polemical analysis of contemporary global politics as defined by the 'clash of civilisations', Western and Islamic, which took on increased potency following the attack on the World Trade Center in 2001 (Said 2002, 4; Huntington 1997).

In *Orientalism* and the subsequent *Culture and Imperialism* (1993) Said's principal contribution to intellectual debate was to establish 'colonial discourse' as an object of analysis and to delineate its cultural and political scope. Discourses described as Orientalist are thus revealed to underpin much of the history of Western relations with the East (and the South), not just attitudes that can be seen as obviously idealised or exoticising. But while this is generally recognised, his approach has been questioned by subsequent critics. Said has been accused of adopting the stance of Western humanism, which assumes a universalism of experience, and even of Eurocentrism in his attention to literary texts derived from the Western canon to the exclusion of other non-Western texts and voices (Clifford 1988). Moreover, his thesis can be seen as ahistorical in certain respects, as I have intimated, rendering Orientalism a more or less permanent feature of European culture, marked only by differences of degree or form. It also leaves minimal scope for resistance on the part of the colonised who were its principal objects, despite plentiful evidence of opposition wherever such ideological confrontation occurred. Consequently, Said's work can be deemed – ultimately and perversely – to reinforce the very binary opposition between East and West which he set out to undo, since it offers no historical or realisable space outside this fundamental division.

Certain of these weaknesses in Said's thought have been picked up and worked upon by the postcolonial theorist, Homi Bhaba. Bhaba's debt to Fanon is likewise evident, not only in the application of psychoanalysis to the situation of colonialism, but also in the insistence on the temporal as well as spatial situatedness of politics and culture. Thus Bhaba opens his major collection of essays, *The Location of Culture* (1994) with Fanon's statement from *Black Skin, White Masks*: 'Every human problem must be considered from the standpoint of time'. What Bhaba principally questions in Said's work is the idea that within the parameters of Orientalist discourse power resides exclusively with the colonisers; Said's abrupt division between power on the one side and powerlessness on the other contributes to and exemplifies the way in which his arguments tend to reproduce binary oppositions. Instead, Bhaba portrays colonial power as fractured and ambivalent, especially in colonial settings such as nineteenth-century India and the Caribbean. The existence of the colonised is registered in the discourses of their rulers by signs of a persistent unsettling presence, a subtle subversion that does not require outright resistance to achieve its destabilising effects.

How more exactly, then, does Bhaba depict the relationship between coloniser and colonised? He points first to a certain ambivalence or split in the colonial discursive system, evidenced in a range of texts from novels to administrative reports. At a primary level the discourse of the coloniser is split on the one hand between the necessity to represent the colonised, in the political and administrative senses of the term as well as in the cultural and imaginary; and on the other the need to disavow them, to recreate the native population as alien and inferior. This produces a tension if not an actual contradiction: for while the former strategy seeks to identify coloniser and colonised as mutually comprehensible and therefore similar, the latter insists on their fundamental difference. As a consequence, colonial mastery is flawed and incomplete; the identity of the colonised always eludes the grasp of authority.

At the same time, the power of colonial discourse produces in native subjects a certain 'hybridity'. What this involves is the formation of a subject who identifies with (or 'mimics') the colonising authority and is simultaneously alienated from it. Particularly notable among that segment of the native population most closely linked to the colonial power, such as minor officials, hybridity designates a subject-position defined by Bhaba as ambivalent: 'not quite/not white' (Bhaba 1994, 89–92). Yet the fact that assimilation is never fully achieved is also disturbing to colonial authority, since it points to an unknowable element in what is construed as the native 'character'. The problem for authority of the mimicry of the native subject is conveyed by Bhaba in the notion of 'sly civility', which he identifies, among others, in the writings of English missionaries to early-nineteenth century India (Bhaba 1994, 93–101). It is a notion that conveys, together with a certain indecipherability, the suspicion of insubordination and subversion. 'To the extent to which discourse is a form of defensive warfare, then mimicry marks those moments of civil disobedience within the discipline of civility: signs of spectacular resistance. When the words of the master become the site of hybridity – the warlike sign of the native – then we may not only read between the lines, but even seek to change the often coercive reality that they so lucidly contain' (Bhaba 1994, 121). Bhaba's notions of mimicry and hybridity here are close to the idea of the 'hidden transcripts' of everyday defiance that James Scott has reported in his comparative study of forms of popular resistance, symbolised in the Ethiopian proverb that forms the epigraph to his book: 'When the great lord passes, the wise peasant bows deeply, and silently farts' (Scott, J.C. 1990).

In Bhaba's work, then, colonial hegemony is never total; it is always partial, prone to the destabilising effects of ambivalence and difference. Resistance figures, however, not as an opposition outside hegemonic relations so much as a permanent pressure within them. Drawing on Derrida's notion of *différance*, the discursive element that persistently works to unsettle stabilities of meaning, Bhaba argues that the 'space of the adversarial . . . is a pressure, and a presence, that acts constantly, if unevenly, along the entire boundary of authorization' (Bhaba 1994, 109). Elsewhere he refers to this as a 'Third Space' between the subject and object of discourse which disrupts the smooth transfer of discursive meaning, including that designed to affirm the 'historical identity of culture as a homogenizing, unifying force, authenticated by the originary Past, kept alive in the national tradition of the People' – whether it be the historical identity and culture of the native or of the coloniser (Bhaba 1994, 37). Ultimately, then, Bhaba's arguments regarding ambivalence, hybridity and difference aim to undermine not only the idea of coloniser and colonised as operating within clearcut relations of power, but also the Western conception of history as a unified process that underpins such a view. 'The struggle against colonial oppression not only changes the direction of Western history, but challenges its historicist idea of time as a progressive, ordered whole' (Bhaba 1994, 41).

Unsurprisingly given their complexity and controversial nature, Bhaba's arguments have not gone without challenge. Bhaba has been accused of expropriating historical examples for his own theoretical purposes – he himself acknowledges the use of 'reckless historical connection' – and of analysing the relations between coloniser and colonised within a static, universal model, ignoring the evidence of variations in those relations over time and space (Young, R. 2001, 347; Bhaba 1994, 199; Sinha 1995, 18). Moreover, and in contrast to Fanon, there is little sense in Bhaba's writings of the native as an independent agent in the theatre of colonial relations, since to envisage this agency is seen as reverting back to the terms of a discredited humanism (Parry 1987; 2002, 77). But just as Bhaba's conceptual lexicon – ambivalence, hybridity, mimicry – has proved highly influential, so many of his theoretical insights have shaped the character of subsequent enquiry in postcolonial studies. They include the attempt to work within and against the binary oppositions set up by colonial discourse: East/West, power/agency, coloniser/colonised. In particular, Bhaba raises the key question for postcolonial historians: how is it possible to locate and interpret the historical significance of those – the overwhelming majority of people, especially in the so-called developing countries – who leave no documentary record and whose traces have been obliterated in the colonial experience? If the work of Bhaba, together with that of Said and Fanon, can be said to provide much of the theoretical foundation for postcolonial studies, then it is a collective legacy that continues to resonate. Just how far this is so will be apparent by examining what is the most important movement in postcolonial historiography, Subaltern Studies.

Subaltern Studies

Literary studies, psychoanalysis, and philosophy: these represent the dominant intellectual ingredients, in various admixtures, in the work of Fanon, Said and Bhaba. 'History' is consequently seen through the particular lens which these disciplines provide. However, as we previously saw in considering definitions, they are not the only provenance of postcolonial studies. The earliest debates on this subject took place in political theory, as Aijaz Ahmad has observed, involving discussion of the 'postcolonial state' within the context of Marxist theory (Ahmad 1995, 5). The school of historiography known as Subaltern Studies may be seen as located within this tradition of social science research as well as that of literary theory. Thus the original issue around which the group emerged in India in the 1980s was that of the history of Indian nationalism. As the leading figure in its foundation, Ranajit Guha, put it in what came to serve as the manifesto of Subaltern Studies, 'it is this study of the failure [of the nation to come to its own] which constitutes the central problematic of colonial India' (Guha 2000, 6). In characteristic postcolonial fashion, however, the intellectual resources from which Subaltern Studies historians have drawn inspiration is very eclectic. They include Gramscian Marxism and 'history from below', associated with British historians such as Eric Hobsbawm and E.P. Thompson, together with Foucaultian post-structuralism and the literary deconstruction of Derrida. As befitting its central task – how to write history after colonialism – Subaltern Studies is a productive mélange of widely different intellectual currents, many of which are seen as frankly incompatible in more orthodox approaches to history and theory.

The project originated with a group of predominantly Bengali Marxist intellectuals who established Subaltern Studies as a series of collected essays on South-Asian historiography, under the editorship of Ranajit

Guha, in 1982; by 2000 ten such volumes had been published under this title (Guha 1982; Chaturvedi 2000, vii). What united the original group was a dual opposition: on the one hand towards the existing nationalist historiography of India, which concentrated heavily on the role of the nationalist leadership and the bourgeois parties; and on the other, towards the Cambridge school of historiography, which provided a less flattering counter-image that depicted Indian colonial history as a perpetual internecine struggle between rival elites (e.g. Seal 1968). Guha's manifesto for Subaltern Studies, modestly titled 'On some aspects of the historiography of colonial India', addressed the problem in stark terms. The existing historiography of Indian nationalism, whatever its provenance, was 'dominated by elitism' for it deliberately omitted the political contribution of the mass of the population to the ending of colonial rule, independent of the actions of the élite. 'The involvement of the Indian people in vast numbers, sometimes in hundreds of thousands or even millions, in nationalist activities and ideas is thus represented as a diversion from a supposedly "real" political process . . . or is simply credited, by an act of political appropriation, to the influence and initiative of the elite themselves' (Guha 2000, 2, 3). The task of the historian was therefore to reject this élitism, to recognise the existence of an autonomous sphere of popular politics and to analyse the interrelationship between élite and subaltern domains in the colonial history of India and its aftermath. Significantly given the later thinking of the group, Guha also stressed at the outset the role of the subaltern as an active political agent; it was necessary 'to focus on consciousness as our central theme, since it is not possible to make sense of the experience of insurgency merely as a history of events without a subject' (Guha 1985, 11).

The initial project of Subaltern Studies thus bore certain clear traces of the influence of Marxism and 'history from below' in its ambition to recuperate the voices of those marginalised in the dominant historiography. E.P. Thompson had been elected President of the Indian History Congress in the late 1970s and famously rode into the proceedings on the back of an elephant (Chandavarkar 1997). The group also borrowed from the work of Antonio Gramsci the conceptual framework of hegemony and, crucially, the notion of the subaltern. In his 1982 introduction Guha described the term 'subaltern classes' as synonymous with the 'people', defining them as representing 'the demographic difference between the total Indian population and all those whom we have described as "elite"' (Guha 2000, 7). The subaltern thus encompassed a wide variety of social groupings, from the rural poor and urban working class to wealthy peasants and even, in some cases, impoverished landowners and landlords. Both history from below and Marxism brought with them difficulties, however. In the first place there was the view of Eric Hobsbawm that the peasants who made up the vast majority of the population of India (and of other parts of the world) were 'pre-political', lacking a coherent political conception of the forces that oppressed them and of the increasing penetration of capitalist market forces into the countryside during the twentieth century (Hobsbawm 1959). Behind Hobsbawm's opinion lay the orthodox Marxist view that saw the urban, industrial working class as evidence of a more 'developed' state of capitalist relations and therefore more capable of authentic revolutionary (or anticolonial) action. In opposition to such views, Guha refused to interpret peasant political consciousness as 'backward' or, in Hobsbawm's term, 'archaic'; the peasant masses, he asserted, were an integral part of the modernity which colonial rule had imposed on India (Guha 1983a).

Problems of a more practical kind also confronted the group as they attempted to uncover the subaltern presence in histories of popular politics, protest and labour. For traces of that presence were few and far between in the historical record, especially the voices of subalterns themselves. Such sources as did exist on India prior to independence tended to be products of the colonial administration or filtered through them. Consequently, what Rosalind O'Hanlon called the 'recovery of the subject' was a project fraught with difficulty. For to the problem of sources was added the sensitivity of Guha and his colleagues to the dangers of historians merely adding a further layer of appropriation by interpreting evidence of insurgency in such a way as to confirm their own preconceived models and categories (O'Hanlon 2000; Guha and Spivak 1988, 26–33).

In their studies, therefore, the historians attempted to develop inventive methodological strategies. Once again Ranajit Guha was to the fore in this endeavour. In a highly original essay, 'The prose of counter-insurgency' (1983b), he suggested that for the study of peasant insurgency in nineteenth-century India, three types of discourse were available, each defined by its proximity in time to the events the discourses described. Primary discourse represented reports written by officials, who were also often eye-witnesses, in the immediate aftermath of the events, usually to alert the authorities elsewhere to disturbances. Secondary discourse referred to memoirs or histories of the events, written some years later by administrators or army officers who had directly or indirectly participated in them. Tertiary discourse designated histories written at a considerable distance in time by historians who had no direct affiliation to the events and who could thus claim some independence and objectivity. What Guha sought to show was that each of these levels of discourse was written in the 'code of counter-insurgency'; in different ways each opposed the rationality of the colonial administration or of authority more generally (including the authority of 'history') to the irrationality of the peasant. While the nineteenth-century administrator might speak in the name of the 'civilising mission', nationalist and Marxist historians assimilated the peasant masses to the larger struggle for freedom. All sought the causes of peasant revolt in external factors, whether hunger, oppression or troublemakers, and consequently denied reason to the peasant themself. At the same time, the creative agency of the insurgents was at least partly visible in the challenge to the official codes manifested in both primary and secondary discourses. Guha thus demonstrated how the prose of counter-insurgency bore the stamp of the insurgents, 'the signifiers of the subaltern practice of "turning things upside down"', as well as the predominantly religious framework of insurgent consciousness (Guha 1983b, 1–42). Even in the circumscribed and ideologically invested remains of the colonial record, Guha suggested, it was possible for the attentive historian to 'read history against the grain' and identify the evidence of an alternative moral economy.

Nevertheless, the questions of whether or not the historian can recuperate the subaltern presence in the sources and whether agency can be imputed to subaltern groups have remained troubled ones, as much for Subaltern Studies as a collective as among its critics. Indeed, it was the collaborator and critical friend of the group, the postcolonial theorist Gayatri Chrakravorty Spivak, who further problematised the issue in a classic article entitled 'Can the subaltern speak?' (Spivak 1993). Spivak was well qualified to comment; not only had she co-edited a volume of *Subaltern Studies* with Ranajit Guha but she had worked in the 1980s on the archive of the East India Company, researching the Company's construction of 'India' as an object of representation and of Indian women in particular (Spivak 1985, 128–51; 1999, 199–311). In 'Can the subaltern speak?' she undertook a critique of many of the assumptions that underpinned the work of Guha and the Subaltern Studies group. The whole project of recovering the consciousness of peasants and other subaltern groups, according to Spivak, was rendered problematic, if not impossible, by the 'epistemic violence' of Western colonialism. For it was through this act of colonial violence that certain forms of knowledge, including 'history', had been installed as the normative version of reality, relegating native understandings to the status of 'subjugated' or illegitimate knowledge.

Spivak acknowledged the appropriateness of the semiotic approach which Guha and other historians had taken in seeking to decipher the subaltern presence in the interstices of the colonial text and their awareness of the dangers of a misguided appropriation of the subaltern voice inherent in the act of historical interpretation. 'With no possibility of nostalgia for that lost origin, the historian must suspend (as far as possible) the clamour of his or her own consciousness (or consciousness-effect, as operated by disciplinary training), so that the elaboration of insurgency . . . does not freeze into an "object of investigation"' (Spivak 1993, 82). But severe difficulties remained, ideological and philosophical as much as historical. The traces of the subaltern could be found but only in the sources of the native élite or colonial administration. Consequently, while the subaltern had undoubtedly spoken in the past, that voice could never be authentically recuperated (Spivak 1996, 292). Moreover, if the consciousness of Guha's male insurgent was beyond retrieval that of the native woman was doubly effaced by the effects of colonialism and patriarchy. Thus Spivak reached a sceptical conclusion: 'If, in the context of colonial production, the subaltern has no history and cannot speak, the subaltern as female is even more deeply in shadow' (Spivak 1993, 83).

In other writings Spivak has elaborated these positions and indicated certain ways of analytically circumventing the problems she identified. While the subaltern as historical agent with a distinctive 'consciousness' remains beyond recovery, in her view, what is recoverable in certain cases is a subject position or 'effect', located in the spaces and silences of discourse. The subaltern is thus defined as a 'difference rather than an identity', 'the absolute limit of the place where history is narrativized into logic' (Spivak 1996, 213, 217). In a manner similar to Bhaba, therefore, Spivak urged the historian or critic to decipher the subject effects of the subaltern within the discourses of colonialism. Some of the difficulties involved in this approach are evident in her analysis of the nineteenth-century debate about *sati*, the Hindu practice of widow sacrifice outlawed by the British in 1833. Drawing on the studies of the Indian historian Lata Mani, Spivak sought to show how, despite the apparently irreconcilable opposition between the Hindu tradition which authorised the practices of *sati* and the British authorities who deemed them barbaric, both sides in the debate looked to the same sources in scriptural tradition to justify their positions. The object of *sati*, the widow, was trapped and rendered mute by the arguments of native patriarchy on one hand and colonialist liberalism on the other. For Spivak, this meant that the widow was not merely absent in the sources (that is, there was no direct documentary evidence of her viewpoint), but that she had no subject position from which she could speak. Her position could only be spoken for by others. The case of *sati* thus symbolised for Spivak in an extreme form the general process by which the effacement of the subaltern woman was effected: 'The case of *sati* as exemplum of the woman-in-imperialism . . . mark[s] the place of "disappearance" with something other than silence and non-existence, a violent aporia between subject and object status' (Spivak 1993, 102). All that remained of the voice of the subaltern woman was an absent presence, a vacant space left by the double violence of colonialism and patriarchy.

Spivak's argument poses in graphic form the problems of writing the subaltern back into history, especially in societies such as India where the 'epistemic violence' of imperialist rule has transformed the conditions under which knowledge of the past (or indeed any scientific knowledge) can be obtained. Even 'India' itself represents an artificial concept, whose unity is comprehensible only as an effect of the history of British rule. What is therefore required of the critical historian is not simply to write counter-histories – Spivak has in any case shown such a project to be flawed – as to question the basis of Western notions of 'history' and the categories of thought which go with them. It is a task which Subaltern Studies' historians such as Dipesh Chakrabarty and Gyan Prakash have begun to undertake with great acuity. For following Spivak the Indian historian is also subaltern in relation to the traditions of Western academic historiography. Thus for Chakrabarty the institutions of Western and non-Western history exist in a relationship of 'asymmetrical ignorance'.

Third-world historians feel a need to refer to works in European history; historians of Europe do not feel any need to reciprocate. Whether it is an Edward Thompson, a Le Roy Ladurie, a George Duby, a Carlo Ginzburg, a Lawrence Stone, a Robert Darnton, or a Natalie Davis . . . the 'greats' and the models of the historian's enterprise are always at least culturally 'European'. 'They' produce their work in relative ignorance of non-Western histories, and this does not seem to affect the quality of their work. This is a gesture, however, that 'we' cannot return (Chakrabarty 1992a, 1–2).

Still more profound in the view of such historians, is the manner in which Europe continues to figure as the subject and referent of all histories, even those of the non-Western world. One of the fundamental premises of historical writing, for example, is that the sources used are verifiable. This assumes the existence of a public archive and of

information which is accessible to anyone who desires it. But in societies like India, knowledge is often restricted to the educated élite and access to historical information is limited since there is no clearly demarcated domain defined as 'public'. The historians' notion of the archive as the repository and testing ground of historical knowledge is thus revealed to be a local, Western supposition rather than a universal reference point (Chakrabarty 1992b; Prakash 2000a).

Dipesh Chakrabarty especially has pursued the project of 'provincialising Europe' by calling into question the very categories – reason, temporality, the archive – on which Western or European history is predicated. He refuses, for instance, the use of concepts such as 'religion' because it assumes a universal context which can assimilate and explain all 'gods and spirits', rather than understanding such local manifestations, like the subaltern itself, as an element of radical, untranslatable difference (Chakrabarty 2000, 76–7). Chakrabarty attacks equally what he terms Western historicism, which he defines as the perception of history as a singular, unified process of development over time, common to both liberal and Marxist traditions of historical writing. Taking the example of E.P. Thompson's classic article, 'Time, work-discipline and industrial capitalism', he seeks to illustrate the effects of historicist thought (Thompson 1967). Thompson depicted British workers in the industrial revolution as undergoing a profound transformation in living and working habits, through subjection to the dictates of clock-time and factory discipline. This transformation is seen by Thompson as a fate awaiting the workers of the third world; with the spread of capitalism workers in developing countries will be required to submit to the same forces. Thus capitalism provides the mechanism through which history is represented as a continuous process that reduces all geographical and cultural specificities to a single logic: first here, then elsewhere (Chakrabarty 2000, 48). Because such processes are always seen as originating in Europe and as being transported elsewhere at a later date, they are also only rendered comprehensible beyond Europe by the categories of thought through which they have already been apprehended: that is to say, as 'industrialisation', 'class formation', 'democratisation' and so on. From the perspective of historicism, according to Chakrabarty, all history turns out to be Western or European history, since Europe is understood to provide both the originating point for global historical developments and the intellectual categories for defining them.

Western historicism as outlined by Subaltern Studies scholars thus condemns the third world to a history of successive 'failures' (to industrialise, effect a bourgeois revolution, etc.) and, consequently, to a never-ending game of catch-up with the West. Unsurprisingly, therefore, such historians have sought to escape this determinist logic by questioning the premises on which Western historiography is based. Gyan Prakash calls for 'post-foundational histories' that critique all essentialised categories, such as 'race' and nation (Prakash 2000b); Ashis Nandy demands histories that are politically principled yet also psychological and post-rationalist, 'mythographies' through which the submerged and strange voices of post-colonial consciousness may be heard (Nandy 1983). Meanwhile, Dipesh Chakrabarty envisages a history which combines Marx's commitment to social justice with a critique of totalising thought that allows the supernatural to disrupt the secular world and a non-linear conception of historical time that puts the present 'out of joint' with itself (Chakrabarty 2000, 16). For none of the Subaltern Studies group, however, is it possible to construct histories outside or beyond the intellectual legacy of colonialism and the West. All that can be done is to turn the intellectual tools bequeathed by the West, including Marxism and psychoanalysis, against the West's own categories of modernity – reason, progress, linear time – and to adapt these tools to create anti- and post-colonial histories of difference. As a result, history-writing in a postcolonial vein becomes a paradoxical enterprise. Thus in Chakrabarty's words, while Subaltern Studies necessitates the project of provincializing Europe, it is a project that can be undertaken 'only in an anticolonial spirit of gratitude' (Chakrabarty 2000, 255).

The empire at home

As part of its critique of traditional historiography, postcolonial criticism dissolves the conventional division between metropole and colony, 'home' and 'away'. 'Europe is literally the creation of the third world' wrote Fanon and subsequent critics like Paul Gilroy have echoed the theme, seeing in the encounter with its colonial others the foundations of Europe's sense of its own modernity (Gilroy 1993, 17). Postcolonial historians have equally argued that it is impossible to understand the histories of Britain, France or Spain as separate from those of their colonies. Cultural and political influences, like trade, flowed both ways, from metropole to colony and back. If native societies were altered ineradicably by the impress of colonial rule, so too were the imperial powers. 'Empire was . . . not just a phenomenon "out there"', Antoinette Burton has observed, 'but a fundamental part of English national identity and culture at home';

by 1914 it was to be found 'in spaces as diverse as the Boy Scouts, Bovril advertisements and biscuit tins; in productions as varied as novels, feminist pamphlets, and music halls; and in cartographies as particular as Oxbridge, London and the Franco-British Exhibition' (Burton 2000, 138–9; see also Burton 1998).

By the later nineteenth century the British empire was the largest of the European empires, extending over five continents and a quarter of the surface of the globe. Within this network colonies had a varied status, from the self-governing dominions of Canada, Australia and New Zealand, to direct dependencies such as India, ruled by a British colonial administration. 'Britain' itself was a complex colonial formation, made up of four nations, two of which (Ireland and Scotland) had been brought into union with England and Wales in the previous two hundred years; Ireland's peculiar status as a 'metropolitan colony' meant that the issue of imperialism was always close to home. The 'British' empire was therefore predicated on the hegemony of England in Britain and of an Englishness, which, as a hegemonic identity, could deny its ethnicity altogether (Hall, S. 1988).

Under the postcolonial impulse historians have begun to rewrite not only the history of the British empire but also of Britain itself as an imperial society – the empire at home. This empire was, of course, not unchanging. Rather than the moment of 'high imperialism' in the late nineteenth and early twentieth century, recent historians have looked to the growth of Britain's sea-based, trading empire of the seventeenth and eighteenth centuries as the progenitor both of later imperialism and of English national identity (e.g. Daunton and Halpern 1999; Wilson, K. 2004). The effects of empire were indeed visible in Britain at this period, not only in the products of the colonies but in the population at large. Rosina Visram has traced the origins of the Asian community in Britain to the nabobs, servants and lascars who arrived, in London especially, from the 1600s onwards (Visram 2002). A 'black' population, predominantly made up of Africans and West Indians, is estimated at between ten and fifteen thousand by the 1770s, concentrated mainly in London and ports such as Bristol and Liverpool. They included figures such as Olaudah Equiano, a Nigerian former slave, and Ottabah Cuguano, a Ghanaian, whose writings and speeches were to play an important part in the campaign in Britain to abolish the slave trade (Meyers 1996).

At still more profound levels the experience of empire permeated the political culture of eighteenth-century Britain. While Linda Colley stressed the importance of the wars with France in developing a distinctive sense of

British identity in the later 1700s, as we saw in Chapter Six, more recent historians like Kathleen Wilson have emphasised the contribution of empire to the same process. Building on Benedict Anderson's notion of the nation as an imagined community, Wilson sets out to show how large a part empire played in that imagining in mid-eighteenth century provincial England. The rapidly expanding newspaper press represented the mercantilist worldview of the period and regular news of politics and trade related to the Americas, the West Indies and elsewhere filled its columns (Wilson, K. 2003, 32–3). Alongside newspapers both politics and club life promoted a vision of citizenship and social order that prioritised trade, rationality, independence and masculinity. The result was a version of the nation, both English and British, that was at once participatory and exclusionary. 'Decades of war had tended to bolster a militaristic, masculinist version of national identity that privileged the claims of the white, trading and commercial classes while excluding a range of "effeminate" others who threatened their supposedly distinctive goals: not only the French or francophilic, but also the aristocratic, the foppish, the irrational, the dependent and the timid' (Wilson, K. 2003, 37). These last three categories, in particular, were aimed at marginalising those who were already placed at the edges or outside the community of citizens and nation, both women and the black populations who, as we have already seen, were present 'at home' as well as in the colonies. Yet this was also a highly flexible discourse of 'participatory patriotism', capable of upholding liberty and the rights of the 'freeborn Englishman' at home while withholding them from slaves and others in the colonies. The effects of the 'first British empire', in Wilson's terms, were thus less to place metropole and colony in binary opposition than to create complex hierarchies of citizenship and belonging in which the national polity was mapped onto the empire while imperial imaginings worked to reconfigure political identities in Britain itself (Wilson, K. 2003, 52–3).

Both the forms and the representations of the British empire changed over time. This was not only apparent in the uneasy shift in the mid- and later nineteenth century from an 'informal empire' based primarily on trade, to a formal one defined by territorial domination in which imperialism increasingly became a direct instrument of state policy (Porter 1975, 3). It also revolved around specific issues such as the politics of slavery and the ideology of 'race', as Catherine Hall has demonstrated in *Civilising Subjects* (2002), a study of Birmingham, England and Jamaica in the mid-nineteenth century. Hall's work is a good example of the attempt to write a new history of empire informed by postcolonial criticism. This ambition necessitates, first, viewing metropole and colony not as independent entities – the standard historical approach – but following the arguments of Ann Stoler and Frederick Cooper, dialogically, in a single 'analytic frame' (Hall, C. 2002, 9; Cooper and Stoler 1997). In particular, Hall is interested in tracing how Jamaica – a British colony seized in 1655 which became highly profitable in the following century for its sugar plantation economy – came to figure as an 'other' in the English imaginary: 'Jamaica was one form of the constitutive outside of England' (Hall, C. 2002, 10). By exploring attitudes to 'race' and empire in Birmingham and the activities of Baptist missionaries from Birmingham in Jamaica, the study analyses the 'making of colonising subjects, of racialised and gendered selves, both in the empire and at home' (Hall, C. 2002, 13).

At the centre of Hall's argument is the identification of a significant shift of outlook towards questions of 'race' and empire in Birmingham, and in England more generally, between the abolition of slavery in the British colonies in 1833 and the passing of the Second Reform Act in 1867. Birmingham was renowned as a centre of radical politics and religious Nonconformity, and figures such as Joseph and Sophia Sturge, John Angell James and Thomas Morgan were to the fore nationally in the anti-slavery movement of the 1820s and 1830s. Such peoples' view of slaves in colonies like Jamaica was fundamentally liberal; black people were part of the 'family of man' and as such should be treated like all other British subjects. Given the right conditions, which included, first and foremost, the abolition of slavery as an institution, former slaves could become industrious, independent, respectable men and women. At the same time, abolitionists tended to produce images of black people as essentially childlike. They promulgated a 'stereotype of the new black Christian subject – meek victim of white oppression, grateful to his or her saviours, ready to be transformed . . .' (Hall, C. 2002, 321). As Hall makes clear, what this represented was a form of cultural racism, predicated on a 'splitting' of the black subject by attaching to that subject a number of stereotyped characteristics in an act of what Pierre Bourdieu termed 'symbolic violence' (Hall, C. 2002, 322; Bourdieu 2000, 168–72).

A generation later, in the 1860s, however, attitudes had changed, in Birmingham and England generally. While the issue of 'race' was once again politically prominent, this time in the issue of slavery in the American Confederacy, the old liberal consensus was breaking up. Support existed in Birmingham for both sides in the American Civil War, but in the debates for an extension of the franchise in Britain Birmingham Liberals like John Bright and Nonconformist ministers like R.W. Dale argued that experience had proved that Englishmen were especially suited to self-government, whether at home or in the white settler dominions such as Australia. Their arguments increasingly rested, according to Hall, on a view of the superiority of the Anglo-Saxon 'race', bolstered by ideas derived from the evolutionary thought of Darwin as well as by a broad-based notion of economic and social 'improvement'. 'In the late 1860s the emphasis of the men of the midland metropolis was on the hierarchy of races, peoples and nations and their own assumed position in that hierarchy' (Hall, C. 2002, 432).

Ideas of progress and superiority reflected also a view of developments in colonies such as Jamaica, to which men and women in Birmingham were connected through the missionary endeavours associated with church and chapel. Among liberals there was disappointment that the emancipation of the slaves after 1833 did not appear to have led to the social improvement of the native population for which they had hoped. While Jamaica had a British Governor, directly responsible to the Colonial Office in England, it also had a form of representative government, including a small group of black voters, which was expected to expand in numbers following emancipation and the acquisition of land by former slaves. Yet political unrest remained endemic, culminating in a major rebellion at Morant Bay in 1865 which was savagely repressed by local troops under the order of Governor Eyre. While public opinion in Birmingham was not generally sympathetic to Eyre, the episode resulted in the British government withdrawing rights to any form of representative government; Jamaica became a crown colony ruled from London. Consequently, the dominant logic of the later 1860s was that while the vote might be extended to the 'respectable' working man in Britain, self-government was unsuitable to 'coloured' colonial populations abroad, whose inherent savage or childlike characteristics disqualified them from political rights. The late 1860s therefore witnessed a new 'racial mapping of rights' across the British empire (Hall, C. 2002, 424). This change, in turn, was predicated on a discursive shift from cultural to biological racism, prefigured in the views of Thomas Carlyle, the Victorian polemicist, in his 'Occasional Discourse on the Nigger Question' published in 1853. In the words of Catherine Hall, by the 1860s a 'structure of feeling dominated by the familial trope and a paternalist rhetoric had been displaced by a harsher racial vocabulary of fixed differences' (Hall, C. 2002, 440).

Hall's detailed account shows how events in two different locales, Birmingham and Jamaica, can be seen to have interacted and been part of the same historical dynamic at a particular historical moment, the early to mid-Victorian period. Other historians, too, have examined the variety of ways in which 'home' and 'away' became linked, materially and discursively. In *Imperial Leather*, for instance, Anne McClintock has shown how deeply imperial imagery pervaded late Victorian advertising in Europe; through products such as soap, the colonies were implicated in the most intimate spheres of bourgeois domesticity and sexuality (McClintock 1995). Conversely, in her study of colonial masculinity Mrinalini Sinha has demonstrated the ways in which gender perceptions originating in debates in Britain shaped the categories on which controversies in India, concerned with the relations between native and European subjects, rested in the 1880s and 1890s (Sinha 1995). Stereotypes of the effeminate Bengali 'babu' or intellectual were contrasted with the figure of the 'manly Englishman', that of the European 'new woman' with the perceived traditionalism of Indian womanhood. In so doing Sinha sought to reorganise the framework of historical analysis, arguing 'that metropolitan and colonial histories were both constituted by the history of imperialism' (Sinha 1995, 182; see also Sinha 1998). From this perspective colonial masculinity was not the product of one national context or another, of Britain or of India, but of a single historical dynamic constituted by imperialism. In studies such as these the categories of metropole and colony, 'home' and 'away', begin to disintegrate in front of imperial currents and flows that had no exclusively national belonging or linear determination.

Evaluation

In the preface to *The Writing of History* Michel de Certeau begins with an image of the encounter between the fifteenth-century European explorer, Amerigo Vespucci, and a naked native woman representing Latin America. Certeau describes this as a foundational moment for the writing of history. 'An inaugural scene: after a moment of stupor, on this threshold dotted with colonnades of trees, the conqueror will write the body of the other and trace there his own history' (Certeau 1988, xxv). The whole institution of modern Western history, Certeau suggests, emerges from the colonial encounter between Europe and the other. The corpus of postcolonial theory and history proceeds from this same insight. For postcolonialism is concerned not only with the historical content and political legacy of colonialism, but equally – and at the same time – with the categories of Western thought, including the institution of history, through which that experience and inheritance are represented in the present. It holds up for scrutiny the position of the investigator as well as of the investigation. Postcolonial criticism is distinguished, in the words of Gayatri Spivak, by 'its insistence that in disclosing complicities the critic-as-subject is herself complicit with the object of her critique; [by] its emphasis upon "history" and upon the ethico-political as the trace of that complicity – the proof that we do not inhabit a clearly defined critical space free of such traces' (Spivak cited in Young 1990, 170). In effect, postcolonialism invokes history as a mode of critique at the same time as it unmasks the supposed neutrality of 'history' as an institutional practice.

Nevertheless, postcolonialism has not been without its own critics. Within historical studies, a number of issues have emerged from a critical assessment of Catherine Hall's *Civilising Subjects*. Hall's ambition to overcome the 'home' and 'away' dichotomy of much imperial history by attempting to comprehend England and Jamaica within a single 'frame' is only partly successful. The limits to this effort are exposed in the very division of the book into two main parts, the first dealing predominantly with events in Jamaica, the second with those in Birmingham. The resulting narrative therefore tends to be conventionally sequential rather than structurally synchronous, as Hall originally proposed. Moreover, as David Feldman has pointed out, although Hall ranges widely in her study to Australia and West Africa, the focus on the interrelationship between England and Jamaica means that the wider colonial matrix that bore on that relationship, including events such as the Indian Mutiny and the American Civil War, is obscured (Feldman 2004, 239–40). The lines of influence were not so much bilateral as multidirectional; colonies like the metropolitan countries were implicated in complex networks of power. By extension, and in a more general perspective, historians' attempts to demonstrate the impact of imperialism in Britain as in other colonial powers can have the paradoxical effect of reinforcing the idea of the nation as a fixed historical referent and of shoring up a hierarchical relationship between metropole and colony: first 'here', then 'there' (Burton 2000, 140–1). Recognition of this problem suggests the need to disrupt the deep-rooted connection between history and the nation-state and to begin to engage with the idea of 'post-national' histories. This is indeed a theme that has begun to emerge with the establishing of new frames for historical study, such as the 'the Atlantic world', which question established geographical boundaries and reveal unsuspected networks of social and cultural interconnection (Gilroy 1993; Linebaugh and Rediker 2000).

It is a standard accusation of historians, of course, including historians of empire, that postcolonial theory is unhistorical, abstract and lacking specificity. This criticism is flawed in so far as it treats history and theory as separate compartments and falls back on the false assumption that conventional historical writing is itself in some sense theory-less. However, it remains the case that much of postcolonial thought, including that of many Subaltern Studies historians, works with unified and ahistorical ideas of Europe and 'the West' as well as of empire. Historians are only too well aware of the many different kinds of 'empire' – the Holy Roman Empire, the Ottoman Empire and so on – which differ significantly from each other as well as from later imperial formations in their organisation and modes of rule. And what of one of the major empires of the twentieth century, that of the Soviet Union, which has yet to be constituted as an object of postcolonial study? In short, the focus on the British empire in postcolonial studies, as to a lesser extent on the French and Dutch empires, could be said to have obscured wider questions about the effects of imperialism and decolonisation in other parts of the world, though some studies of areas such as the Middle East and Africa have emerged (e.g. Mitchell 1991; Werbner and Ranger 1996).

In constructing Europe and the 'West' as monolithic entities, postcolonialism tends to reproduce the very ahistorical, essentialised categories that, ironically, Said saw as defining features of Orientalism. But as we have glimpsed here, 'Europe' itself was remade in its relationship with its colonies during the nineteenth century, positioned at the apex of a hierarchy of 'civilisation'; it too was not an historically static category (Ahmad 1992). Moreover, even if one accepts the idea of Europe as an intellectual abstraction, a form of shorthand for a cluster of hegemonic traditions of historical, sociological and philosophical thought, then it is necessary to see this as linked to very particular locations in modern Europe, notably to England, France and Germany. Europe, one could argue, has its own subalterns in its midst. While French and Anglo-American historians and theorists are assumed to have universal significance, how many British intellectuals could name a Norwegian or Portuguese historian, or a contemporary Spanish or Hungarian theorist? Asymmetrical ignorance, in other words, does not operate simply in relation to metropolitan centres and their former colonies, but within the ideological configurations of Europe and 'the West' themselves (Griffin and Braidotti 2003).

A still more fundamental criticism of postcolonial theory is that it tends to reproduce the very structures of thought which it aims to dissolve. We have already seen how Edward Said's Orientalism thesis repeats the essentialised ideas of East and West that it seeks to critique and this kind of internal contradiction is a sufficiently frequent feature to think of it as almost a trope of the genre. Concepts such as Bhaba's 'hybridity', for example, appear to posit two previously undifferentiated knowledges, Western and native, which the hybrid both articulates and subverts. In the process, however, Bhaba conjures up precisely the type of essentialised categories – including the category of 'race' – that his arguments have sought to disavow. Essentialism and binary opposition, in other words, enter by the theoretical back door just as they appear to have been banished from the front. Such analyses can seem determinist in so far as it becomes difficult if not impossible to imagine any effective, permanent transformation in the conditions that they describe. As with certain forms of feminist and queer studies, noted in Chapter Six, postcolonialism can sometimes appear fixated on the very categories of 'race' and its associated relations of power that it claims to set out to abolish (Goldberg and Quayson 2002, xiii).

Rather than betokening retreat, however, these criticisms suggest the need to push the arguments described here further. Certainly, as I indicated at the outset of this chapter, postcolonialism poses a radical challenge to all types of history as it is currently practised and not only in the West. It shifts attention from purely epistemological or philosophical questions about the status of historical knowledge to the contemporary political ramifications of history as an institution. It suggests the need to expose the deep-seated complicity between the state, the nation and historical production, and the effects of this constellation on the ways histories continue to be apprehended and written. Following Foucault, postcolonial theory throws into the relief the spatial dimension of power relationships; power is not be considered merely in vertical terms as a matter of 'higher' and 'lower', but horizontally, across surfaces, networks and territories (Foucault 1986, 22). Not least it challenges historians to find fresh ways of thinking about historical time rather than as 'empty and homogeneous', to countenance the possibility of multiple simultaneous temporalities, and to think creatively about what might qualify as historical evidence outside the false universalism of the archives and the documentary record. Finally, and above all, postcolonialism invites the historian to revisit anew one of the oldest aspirations of historiography: to imagine the past as comprehensible while at the same time ineradicably other.

CHAPTER EIGHT

Theorising History

In the aftermath of the debate about Marxist structuralism in 1981 Raphael Samuel commented on the 'climate of anxiety around the very notion of theory' apparent among British historians (Samuel 1981, xliii). Almost twenty years later, the political historian Michael Bentley noted an equivalent anxiety in historical circles towards the term 'postmodernist': 'It is meant to carry the same force that "Are you a Protestant?" might have exerted during the Counter-Reformation' (Bentley 1999, xi). The persistence of such attitudes in a period which saw the spreading influence of cultural theory across the human sciences in Britain and elsewhere raises a number of questions. What have been the effects of cultural theory on historiography? How far is it continuing to shape historical practice? And what kinds of theoretical history are being developed in the wake of the cultural turn?

The chapters of this book have variously sought to address these questions. Cultural theory has been seen to impact on contemporary historical writing both widely and, in some cases, deeply. In the course of the book we have ranged from questions of narrative to matters of personal and social identity, from the dialogic to the postcolonial. The critics and theorists examined under the name of cultural theory have likewise been very diverse, encompassing names well known to historians, such as Michel Foucault, and those less familiar, like Paul Ricoeur. Despite this diversity, however, it is possible to discern in the range of theories explored here a number of common, interlinking themes. The first is a concern with history, whether in the form of a critique of historicism or in a direct engagement with the limits and possibilities of historical representation. Far from being indifferent to history as is sometimes assumed, cultural theory might more accurately be regarded as obsessed with it. Secondly, many of the theories have engaged in and been marked by a continuous dialogue with Marxism, sometimes finding common ground in radicalism, more often adopting a critique of Marxism's totalising ambitions. Thirdly, cultural theorists exhibit, in keeping with social and political historians, a profound concern with power relations. How power can be understood to work, its dynamics, ramifications and limits, represents a central problematic of theoretical investigations. As these shared features imply, cultural theory can be understood as a coherent if recalcitrant body of thought rather than as a random assemblage of individual thinkers. And as a body of thought it has undergone its own shifts in formation so that postcolonialism, for example, can be understood as recombining earlier ideas drawn from Marxism and post-structuralism as well as contributing its own ingredients to what is a distinctive intellectual mix.

Since the turn of the twenty-first century, however, a growing number of voices have asserted that the heyday of cultural theory and the attendant crisis which it provoked in the discipline of history are in some sense over. What this might mean for the role of theory or the practice of history is by no means clear. The purpose of this final chapter, therefore, is to pull together the threads of the book, to examine how cultural theory has impacted on history and to evaluate its ambiguous legacy. In order to do this I start not from theory, but from two histories which exemplify a variety of the ideas and themes explored in the previous chapters. They have been selected not because they are typical of new forms of theorised history – no histories could be – but because they illustrate the very different ways in which strands of cultural theory have been taken up and woven together in recent historical writing.

Two histories

In 1992 Cambridge University Press published a book by Greg Dening entitled *Mr Bligh's Bad Language: Passion, Power and Theatre on the Bounty*. Dening was Professor of History at Melbourne University, one of Australia's most established institutions. Unusually for a historian entering the profession in the 1950s he had also undergone training in anthropology and part of *Mr Bligh's Bad Language* was written during a year spent at Princeton, working in the company of Clifford Geertz. Dening's book is complex and multilayered. At one level it can be read as a conventionally researched history of the voyage of the Bounty from Portsmouth to the Pacific island of Tahiti between 1787 and 1790, of the mutiny that occurred at sea and the fate of the various mutineers and seamen, including the captain William Bligh. In recounting this history Dening attempts to reconstruct a series of relationships: between captain and crew on board ship, between Europeans and native inhabitants of the Pacific islands, and between the mutineers and the law in England. This task required him to research a wide variety of historical sources, including plans of the Bounty, ships' logs, notebooks and correspondence of Bligh and the mutineers, papers of eighteenth-century 'explorers' of Tahiti, and British naval and legal records. 'I have never recovered', Dening has subsequently written, 'from the historian's first excited discovery that most of history comes from unpublished sources – from letters, diaries, logs – imprinted as much with tears, sweat, blood and the dirt of the time as by ink and pencil . . . I have always felt as well that because so much of living is lost in the writing of it down, the historian's obligation is to saturate her- or himself in all there is' (Dening 2004, 36). The focal issue of the study is why the mutiny occurred and the extent of Bligh's own responsibility for it, a standard subject in historical accounts as well as popular treatments of the topic. And in scholarly fashion, Dening uses the voyage and the events that surrounded it to broach a series of larger historical themes: the social history of seafaring, the logistics of colonialism and the impact of European exploration on native populations (Dening 1992).

So far, so historical: in these ways Dening's study appears to conform to most of the conventions of research in the subject. At another level, however, *Mr Bligh's Bad Language* is subversive of many of the basic protocols of scholarly research and the writing of history. As the subtitle *Passion, Power and Theatre* hints, historical practice for Dening is understood less as a matter of objective reconstruction than of rhetorical performance. In his own words he is interested in 'the moment of theatricality in any representation . . . the space created by the performance consciousness of the presenter in which the audience – or the reader or the viewer – participates in the creative process of representing' (Dening 1992, 372). The book is thus designed in the format of a play, with prologue, acts and scenes rather than chapters, reminding the reader of the factitious and rhetorical nature of the events being recounted. Although it contains elaborate notes on the sources consulted, no references appear in the text to disrupt the flow of narrative and analysis. Nor is the narrative written chronologically. It moves backwards and forwards in time and place, so that the trial and execution of the mutineers is described early in the book while discussion of versions of the story on stage and in film are mixed with an historical account of the experiences of the mutineers in Tahiti. The text also employs multiple tenses: events in the immediate aftermath of the mutiny are recounted in the present tense, for instance, a dramatic effect generally deemed illegitimate in scholarly history (Dening 1992, 6–7).

Dening's leading argument, if less heretical, remains idiosyncratic. The cause of the mutiny is attributed not to conditions aboard, revolutionary ideas or, still more conventionally, Bligh's abuse of what were in any case harsh standards of naval discipline. Instead, by carefully analysing the social relations of authority enacted on the Bounty, Dening concluded that the catalyst for the revolt of over half the crew in 1789 was Captain Bligh's 'bad language'. This consisted not so much in the violence of Bligh's speech, though there were plenty examples of that, as in his inability to master the language of command in a credible and unambiguous manner. Bligh's language was 'bad', and contributed directly to the mutiny, 'because men could not read it in a right relationship to his authority' (Dening 1992, 61). In accordance with the book's dramatic form, the action which sparked a revolt and had repercussions throughout the British navy is depicted as resulting from an individual's inability to perform convincingly the rites of authority. In order to sustain this argument and rhetorical structure Dening drew eclectically on cultural theory, in ways that I shall indicate shortly.

A very different approach to history is represented by Timothy Mitchell's essay 'Can the mosquito speak?' (2002). As the title jokily intimates, it too is informed by understandings derived from cultural theory, but it bears little resemblance to Greg Dening's work. Mitchell's previous history, *Colonising Egypt* (1991) examined the military and cultural processes by which Egypt under British occupation (1882–1952) became a model of modernisation for other colonised states, using Foucault and Derrida to examine themes of discipline and difference. 'Can the mosquito speak?' is part of a book, *Rule of Experts: Egypt, Techno-Politics, Modernity* (2002), whose title bears witness to continuity with the earlier research, but in which Mitchell concentrates more directly on the economic and governmental dimensions of the modernising project. The essay examines the interaction of a variety of factors, including warfare, agricultural change, hydroelectric power and disease, in the technological modernisation of the Egyptian state and society in the 1940s and 1950s. In particular, it focuses on the spread of malaria through the arrival of the gambiae mosquito from Sudan in 1942, resulting in an epidemic that killed over twice as many people as the battle of Al-Alamein, fought elsewhere in Egypt in the same year between the British and German armies.

In a carefully constructed analysis Mitchell shows how the war, the development of sugar-cane plantations and the building of new dams on the Nile for irrigation all helped to spread the disease. The linking of irrigation channels through dam projects, for instance, enabled the gambiae mosquito to travel between regions, while the increasing monoculture of sugar-cane affected the diet of populations and left them more open to malarial infection (Mitchell 2002, 23–5). In the growth of the epidemic different ecological and technological systems interacted in complex ways beyond the intention of the various institutions and interests involved: government, landowners, the military and others. In the second part of his argument, however, Mitchell shows how the same systems that helped to spread the malaria epidemic also contributed to its cure. After 1942 the building of massive dams such as the Aswan for hydroelectricity was seen as crucial to the success of a public health programme in Egypt, raising the standard of living and enabling populations to develop resistance to the disease. At the same time a successful campaign to eradicate the mosquito by chemical means was initiated in 1943–4 by the American and British military in order to protect Allied troops, based on warfare methods including the use of spray guns and specialist medical 'brigades' (Mitchell 2002, 26). In a further twist to his story, Mitchell argues that it was the development of pesticides, fertilisers and above all, hydroelectricity, of which the Aswan High Dam was to be the most potent symbol, that formed the technological basis for Egyptian nationalism, creating the conditions for independence from Britain in 1952 and the dominance of a new type of techno-politics in Egypt in the 1950s and 1960s.

Such is the substance of Mitchell's essay. Yet as with Dening, there is a set of more profound issues that he seeks to elucidate here and in the book as a whole. Mitchell is concerned first with the interaction of different domains or logics in historical explanation. The task of the historian is thus to illuminate the different logics of what are seen as distinct spheres – economics, governance, the forces of nature – without assuming that they operate in the same way, as implied for instance by the concept of 'capitalist development'. There is according to Mitchell no 'singular logic' at work in the global forces of modernity. Instead the historian has to discern the subtle processes of interconnection and interaction between domains, often not fully understood by the human participants themselves. This, secondly, brings into question conventional understandings of human agency as the object and mainspring of historical explanation. The mosquito is not generally credited with being an historical actor: as part of nature 'it cannot speak' despite the fact that as the bearer of malaria it had a clear and devastating impact on the history of modern Egypt (Mitchell 2002, 50). However, Mitchell's point here is not simply about bringing 'nature' back into the historical picture so much as attempting to decipher the interrelationship between the human and non-human worlds. If the mosquito has its part in any account of Egyptian nation-building, so it is necessary to recognise that the natural world is itself in important degree humanly formed. The river Nile with its dams and irrigation systems is, as Mitchell points out, a technical and social phenomenon as well as a natural one; rivers are hybrid systems (Mitchell 2002, 34). He thus follows cultural theory in seeing binary oppositions such as nature/science, subject/object as a product of modes of nineteenth-century Western thought whose legacy continues to organise thinking in the human sciences, including history. Mitchell pushes this argument further by depicting the very division between 'representation' and the 'real' as an effect of the processes of global modernity whose lineages he seeks to track. One of the consequences of the techno-politics practised in places like mid-twentieth century Egypt was precisely to sharpen the division between objects and ideas, the world and its representations. Mitchell therefore explicitly rejects arguments that would counterpose representation with the real in the manner of much cultural analysis, for to do so in Mitchell's terms is to replicate unwittingly the production of modern techno-power itself. 'Overlooking the mixed ways things happen, indeed producing the effect of neatly separate realms of reason and the real world, ideas and their objects, the human and the nonhuman, was how power was coming to work in Egypt, and in the twentieth century in general' (Mitchell 2002, 52).

In these ways forms of cultural theory are embedded in the work of both Greg Dening and Timothy Mitchell. Theory is integral to their historical analyses, though not in a one-way or uncritical manner; they engage it and engage with it. Each historian draws upon a wide range of theoretical ideas to shape both the way historical problems are defined and the mode by which they are analysed and explained. The work of both Dening and Mitchell is clearly influenced by postcolonial criticism in particular, informing their respective approaches to the politics of knowledge.

Beyond this, however, the two historians give the appearance of inhabiting different intellectual universes. This is partly a function of the different kinds of cultural theory they select to use. In a lengthy coda to *Mr Bligh's Bad Language* Dening provides extensive annotated notes of his theoretical influences as well as his empirical sources (Dening 1992, 375–96). Reflecting his training in cultural anthropology, Dening's study draws heavily on the ideas of Geertz, Douglas and Clifford. It is partly from this tradition, particularly the work of the British anthropologist Victor

Turner, that he derives his interest in the concept of performance, though here the influence of figures such as Erving Goffman is also apparent (see also Burke, 2005; Dening 1996). Equally important in shaping the form of the book is the philosopher of history, Hayden White. Like a number of other historians such as Simon Schama, Dening accepts White's invitation to throw off the mantle of nineteenth-century realism and to experiment with the narrative form of historical writing (White 1990; Schama 1991). No attempt is made to reconstruct the past in Rankean fashion 'as it really was', although a series of literary and historical techniques are used to refigure the Bounty voyage from the divergent points of view of the participants. In hermeneutic fashion, history is presented as an open-ended discourse centred on questions of meaning. 'I am not a historian who replicates the past', Dening has declared. Rather his ambition is 'to fill a certain sort of silence' – the silences variously of the archives, the powerless, the 'inexpressible' and 'everyday ordinariness' – and 'to imagine what the silences mean' (Dening 2004, 32). Dening's approach is therefore strongly marked by the ideas of narrative and cultural interpretation explored in Chapters Two and Three of this book (see also Vann 2000).

By contrast Mitchell's work is informed by the theoretical tradition identified with Foucault which we examined in Chapter Four. It is concerned with how disciplinary knowledges, especially those of experts and policy-makers, shape understanding of the world and their practical effects. The emphasis is thus on agency and effectivity rather than on representation and meaning. By extension, the central theme is the idea of modernity and its multiple historical forms, explored in Chapter Five, embracing questions of technology and reason, science and hybridity. Modernity here is registered through the lens of postcolonialism, a condition forged outside as much as inside the West through the friction of multiple intersecting forms of knowledge and agency, analysed in Chapter Seven. In his rejection of the idea of a 'singular logic' driving historical processes Mitchell echoes in particular the ideas of Dipesh Chakrabarty and Subaltern Studies (Chakrabarty 2000).

Through these two studies, then, we can recognise how different histories are created by drawing on some of the various currents in cultural theory explored in the present book. It might be tempting to see the examples of Dening and Mitchell as standing for two opposed tendencies in contemporary theory, a 'soft' version focused on interpretation, representation and meaning, and a 'hard' one, directed towards knowledge, politics and social effectivity. To do so, however, would be reductive, repeating in another form the old, entrenched division between the humanities and social sciences. It has been part of cultural theory's endeavour, after all, to put these very divisions in question and to reveal their complicities, political or otherwise. Instead, the work of Dening and Mitchell illustrates the diverse kinds of history that are being produced out of the encounter with cultural theory. They share cultural theory's preoccupation with power and its operations, but they analyse power by applying different combinations of theory to their historical objects or questions. The product is histories that are complex, reflexive – and surprising. We may be more convinced by one approach than by the other, but in a real sense there is no need to choose between them since they represent only two of the multiple forms of historical writing that cultural theory opens up to the historian.

After theory?

All this might suggest that a satisfactory marriage between history and cultural theory has already been achieved, that history has become effect-ively 'theorised'. Current evidence, though, indicates otherwise. To begin with, the opening of the twenty-first century has been accompanied by widespread assertions that the moment of cultural theory has passed. According to the literary critic Terry Eagleton, the golden age of high the-ory, associated with figures such as Derrida, Foucault and Lacan, is over; we now inhabit the moment 'after theory' (Eagleton 2004). The high point of theory occurred between 1965 and 1980 when the key works of post-structuralism and postcolonialism first appeared, coinciding with the heyday of the Western left (paradoxically, given that cultural theory is often taken to be politically conservative or a substitute for politics). According to Eagleton, this tradition appears exhausted, lacking a new body of ideas to replenish it. Within historical circles too it has been pro-claimed from various quarters that the cultural turn has passed and with it the epistemological crisis of the discipline. Significantly, these views have come from all sides, from champions and opponents of what continues to be loosely termed 'postmodernism'.

What is involved in such claims? For a critic like Eagleton, the pro-nouncement that we are now in some sense 'after theory' implies not merely the ending of a tradition of 'grand' theorists but also the exhaus-tion of a style of thinking which he associates with postmodernism. The latter he identifies with the predominance of culture as a category (betoken-ing what Marxism lacked), a fetishism of difference and a neglect of the global in favour of the local and particular (Eagleton 2004, 41–73). Eagleton objects in particular to what he sees as a form of gestural politics characteristic of postmodernism, to a viewpoint in which certain intellectual positions are seen as 'radical' and 'disobedient' while leaving both the discipline and the social world intact.

For historians the assertion of the passing of the cultural or linguistic turn has meant a number of different things. For Richard Evans, one of the most vocal critics of post-structuralism in historiography, it signalled a return to normal service. All that appeared to have changed was that, following Hayden White, historians could now 'adopt a strong authorial identity' (Evans 2002b, 14). Others, however, have sought an end not so much to theory as to its cultural dimension. As we saw in Chapter Three, historians like Richard Biernacki are critical of the tendency for culture to serve as the 'new nature', to act as the universal grounding for historical processes in much the same way as the social or the economic did in older forms of historiography (Biernacki 1999). It is argued equally that the emphasis on culture has weakened history's links to the social sciences to the detriment of both. What is required is a return to the study of social processes, informed by the cultural turn as well as by other related developments such as science studies (Bonnell and Hunt, 1999; Joyce 2002). And in yet another variant, Peter Mandler has offered a swingeing critique of the influence of cultural theory on historiography, arguing that it obscures the origin or locus of discourse, confuses the imaginary with the real, and is unable to explain how meaning is constructed and changes over time (Mandler 2004). In its place Mandler urged a return to the virtues of empirical research and a revaluation by historians of the methodologies of social science.

It is important to stress that these positions do not reflect any sort of consensus, even among the critics and historians who have expressed doubts about the continuing influence of cultural theory. Mandler's critique, for example, has led to a series of retorts from historians who might be considered to be sympathetic to some or other of the positions outlined above (Hesse 2004; Jones 2004). Nevertheless, a view has emerged in historical circles and beyond that the cultural turn has done its work and that it is now time to move beyond it. But how far has this work really been accomplished, in history at least? As we observed in Chapter One, historians were slow to respond to the possibilities (or 'threats') of cultural theory. The impact of post-structuralism, in Britain and the United States especially, only began to be felt after the end of Eagleton's 'golden age' of high theory in 1980. Indeed it only came to be a matter of debate outside a few specific areas of research in the last decade of the twentieth century; hence the flurry of publications from the defenders of historical orthodoxy in the later 1990s. Moreover, even where the influence was most keenly felt, among a younger generation of scholars in areas such as social, cultural and international history, its effects have arguably been weak. Writing in 1999, the cultural historian James Vernon noted that concepts drawn from cultural analysis, such as subjectivity, were 'often blandly appropriated to existing methodologies', while many historians sought a position of politic neutrality, 'speaking the language of cultural history while distancing themselves from its critical edges' (Vernon 1999, 4). Even in examining the work of a number of the historians in this book, we have observed a resistance to engaging with some of the fuller implications and diversity of cultural theory.

One way of assessing how deeply the cultural turn has affected the practice of history is to look beyond research and publication and to examine the other aspect of academic practice in which most historians engage, that of teaching. One would expect any significant intellectual change in a discipline to be registered in the subject curriculum at university level, if not at an earlier point in the educational process. After all, this is what occurred in history at earlier periods with the opening up of new branches of the subject, such as social history, and the introduction of new methodologies, such as cliometrics and oral history. Teaching followed research in the institutionalisation of disciplinary innovation. To what extent, then, has cultural theory become embedded in history curricula and training at university level? For Britain, at least, the evidence is equivocal. There have been some signs of theory seeping across into history courses from other subject areas, such as cultural and literary studies, geography and sociology. A study of university history curricula in 2000 by Tim Hitchcock, Robert Shoemaker and John Tosh reached the following conclusion in this regard:

The constant dialogue between the historical profession and the other humanities and social sciences has led to the development of a self-conscious strand of methodological teaching in most history degrees which gives graduates a basic familiarity with a remarkably diverse set of approaches . . . As a result, history graduates are broadly familiar with and competent to use, a range of approaches which transcend disciplinary boundaries. That history students are asked, for example, to draw notions of cultural difference from sociology and of spatial organisation from geography means that, while they are seldom expert in any of these forms of analysis and frequently draw their knowledge second hand from theoretically informed historical writing, they are familiar with the strengths and weaknesses of each (Hitchcock, Shoemaker and Tosh 2000, 49).

Research carried out in 2004, however, reached less sanguine conclusions on the influence of theory in the history curriculum. Less than a quarter of university history departments in England and Wales included a module on historiography, philosophy of history or any form of theory within their undergraduate courses. The equivalent figure for Masters courses – generally considered as laying the groundwork for historical research – was 39 per cent. This meant that almost two-thirds of students undertaking Masters study in history had no explicit opportunity within the curriculum to reflect critically on history as a subject of study, its epistemological foundations or its relationship to theories currently impacting on knowledge across the humanities and social sciences (Gunn and Rawnsley 2006). When combined with programmes of doctoral training that still concentrate overwhelmingly on the identification of archival sources and quantitative methods, the picture emerges of a system of historical education in British universities in which an understanding of theory and an ability to apply it critically are seen as optional rather than integral. There is some evidence that history curricula in other countries are less bounded by convention to the empirical norm and have proved more receptive to theoretical innovation; Australia is one such example (Davison 2000). Yet even in France, where post-structuralist thought might be expected to have had wide intellectual purchase, there have been complaints from historians such as Philippe Minard and Daniel Roche of the neglect of theory and reflexivity in the make-up of the historical profession. Minard, for instance, has commented on 'the weakness of instruction in the history of history in the professional formation of historians, and the weakness of theoretical instruction in general in the apprenticeship for the trade of historian' in contemporary France (Corbin *et al.* 1999, 21, author's translation).

Of all the subjects in the humanities and social sciences, in fact, history is perhaps the discipline where cultural theory has been most fiercely resisted and where its impress has consequently been most superficial. That impress has been greatest at the margins of scholarship, as Vernon suggested, where it may provide a kind of conceptual gloss to what are otherwise straightforwardly empirical studies, and in specific fields, such as the historiography of *ancien regime* France, where theoretical questions have succeeded in setting the research agenda (Jones 2004, 209–11). It would indeed be fruitful to reflect on why theory has permeated some fields of research more fully than others, and what the preconditions for this influence might be. As the evidence of university history teaching indicates, however, its impact on the mainstream of the profession has so far been more modest than heated debate and talk of crisis would suggest.

At the same time, theory as a body of knowledge and mode of understanding will not go away. As Terry Eagleton acknowledges, 'We can never be "after theory", in the sense that there can be no reflective life without it', a point with which Victoria Bonnell and Lynn Hunt concur: 'Historians and sociologists can no longer retreat to a philosophical know-nothingism: any method . . . inevitably poses fundamental philosophical problems' (Eagleton 2004, 221; Bonnell and Hunt 1999, 13–14). The imprint of Foucault and Derrida, Spivak and Bourdieu, to name but a few, continues to infuse the most innovative histories currently being written. And contemporary theorists such as Giorgio Agamben, Zygmunt Bauman and Elizabeth Grosz continue to produce work that occupies the attention of geographers, sociologists and others (Agamben 1998; Bauman 2004; Grosz 2001). In concluding, therefore, it is important to consider those features of cultural theory which remain most salient for historical writing.

Reflexivity, ethics and ambivalence

In the introduction to the English-language edition of *Realms of Memory*, Pierre Nora reflected on shifts in historiography in France since the later nineteenth century. From the mid-1970s, he argued, French historiography had entered a new phase that implied a fundamental break with the traditions of positivism and the *Annales*. 'We have entered', Nora asserted, 'the age of *historiographical* discontinuity', an 'epistemological age'. This age was new because it reflected a 'history that has become critical through and through'; it was 'less interested in causes than effects . . . ; less interested in events themselves than in the construction of events over time, in the disappearance and re-emergence of their significations; less interested in "what actually happened" than in its perpetual reuse and misuse, its influence on successive presents' (Nora 1996, xxii–xxiv). Above all, historiography had been marked by a profound cultural rupture: memory, in the sense of a continuous lived relation to a shared national or communal past, had been replaced by history as the principal vehicle by which that past was communicated to the present (Nora 1996, 1–20). Nora's claim for the growth of a new type of historiography was marked by his specific concern to contextualise the project on commemoration and national identity of which he had been director. But his arguments also acknowledged that wider sets of ideas were recasting the historical discipline as a whole by the late twentieth century. Prominent among these were the ideas broadly defined here as cultural theory.

One consequence of cultural theory identified by Nora is a new attention to the idea of reflexivity. This is not an idea which has conventionally been associated with academic history. Writing of historical education at Oxford and Cambridge in the first half of the twentieth century, Reba Soffer observed that 'teachers rarely reflected on the nature of the study and teaching to which they devoted their lives' because the meaning of history was regarded as 'unequivocal' (Soffer 1994, 33). Reflexivity itself has several different meanings. In Anglo-American educational circles it is often used to refer to a style of pedagogy aimed, in the words of its best-known exponent Donald Schön, to 'give practitioners reason' (Schön 1983). Yet in historiography it has a number of other, interrelated senses. Reflexivity is epistemological: it directs historians towards a consideration of the grounds on which interpretations, including their own, are constructed. It involves a recognition that historical interpretation is not merely a question of 'giving voice' to the sources but that it involves, in Michel de Certeau's terms, a methodological operation which transmutes information from one order of knowledge (that of the archive) to another (that of a scholarly narrative or explanation). Furthermore, the ways in which this operation is carried out, the methods used, are not simply technical or neutral; they actively determine the form of knowledge that is produced. Methods, in short, matter to a far greater extent than historians are usually prepared to admit.

Extending from this understanding, reflexivity encourages a critique of foundations, of those concepts such as social class, the political constitution and economic modernisation around which historiographies have been constructed and histories written. Indeed, as we saw in Chapter Four, a central purpose of a history of modernity is to establish the conditions of possibility of the categories and divisions of modern thought. Reflexivity thus implies an understanding of history as an institution whose own historical formation is inscribed within it, defining both the possibilities and the limits of the knowledge that the discipline is capable of producing. This kind of critical reflexivity is often perceived as hostile and destructive. But it can also be liberating as a means of denaturalising convention and questioning the taken-for-granted. For Pierre Bourdieu historical reflexivity is a vital instrument in the production of knowledge in the human sciences because it is able to counter the 'primary self-evidences' of the social world, what is taken as 'given' or 'natural': 'Only historical critique, the major weapon of reflexiveness, can free thought from the constraints exerted on it when, surrendering to the routines of the automaton, it treats reified historical constructs as things' (Bourdieu 2000, 182). Historical reflexivity for Bourdieu is thus one of the preconditions for producing any effective knowledge of the social world.

If reflexivity is a significant aspect of a theorised history, so too is a heightened ethical awareness. But whereas the former is not something that has traditionally been regarded as part of the historian's armoury, an ethical dimension is deeply inscribed in historical practice. We saw in Chapter Two how the philosopher Paul Ricoeur described history as having an ontology or foundation bound up with the idea of a 'debt to the dead'. For Ricoeur it is the belief that historical representation should do justice to the people of the past that defines history as a form of knowledge and distinguishes it from other species of writing, such as literary fiction. This imperative applies to all types of history, according to Ricoeur, however quantitative or abstract, and to all historians, whether or not they are conscious of it. Examining the autobiographical accounts of their own practice produced by contemporary historians, Michael Dintenfass likewise suggests that historians have in fact become highly sensitised to the ethical dimensions of their subject. Noting their distaste for an over-identification of history with science as well as for the 'self-indulgence' implied by a concern with the self and the aesthetics of writing, Dintenfass describes historians as attaching special value to certain moral qualities: judgement, honesty, objectivity. History in these accounts is depicted as quintessentially a 'moral discipline'. Consequently it was the fear of moral relativism implicit in the linguistic turn rather than its philosophical substance, according to Dintenfass, that commanded so many historians to the intellectual barricades during the 1990s: 'The burden of the epistemological for them has been to secure the ethical' (Dintenfass 1999, 164).

Cultural theory has heightened this ethical sense and brought it into the open. As Chapter One made clear, the origins of post-structuralism in the 1950s and 1960s can themselves be understood as a reaction to the perceived inadequacies of European humanism in the aftermath of the Holocaust and empire. For French intellectuals in particular, the Algerian war of independence brought into sharp focus the contradiction between a French republic founded on the universal ideals of liberty, equality and fraternity, and the violence and torture involved in maintaining French colonial rule in North Africa (Young, R. 2001, 411–26). At the same time, the recognition of the complexity of present reality, engendered in part by cultural theory, augments the sense of responsibility for the representation of the past. The rupture between past and present, memory and history, which Pierre Nora identified as a characteristic feature of the present era requires an enhanced, not a diminished, sensitivity to the politics of historical interpretation. As Greg Dening succinctly puts it in a statement redolent of the ethics of cultural theory, 'There is no escape from the politics of our knowledge, but that politics is not in the past. That politics is in the present' (Dening 1992, 178).

Perhaps the most profound implication of cultural theory for the practice of history, however, lies in the notion of ambivalence, adumbrated in the work of Derrida and Lyotard but elaborated most fully in the postcolonial criticism of Bhaba, Spivak and Subaltern Studies. It is ambivalence that underpins the rejection of positivism, of a history dominated by cause and effect, subject to universal laws and categories, and driven by a single, uniform logic. The concept of ambivalence involves the recognition that there is no one correct way to interpret an historical event or process but also that this does not mean that all interpretations are equal; matters of evidence, coherence and plausibility are still there to be argued over. After cultural theory there can be no return to interpretive absolutism, since it is axiomatic that there are always other ways of seeing and understanding. Ambivalence also represents one of the most consistent aspirations of cultural theory, to expose, destabilise and transcend the dualisms on which so much of Western knowledge appears to rest: the opposition between self and society, representation and the real, even – as in the case of Judith Butler and the queer theory explored in Chapter Seven – that most persistent and 'natural' division, between male and female. Historical analysis has a special part to play in this critical endeavour by enquiring how – that is to say, through what discursive and regulatory mechanisms, under what conditions – oppositions, exclusions and hierarchies came to be constituted as such.

All of this is not to suggest that such dualisms can simply be wished away in an act of what Bourdieu sardonically termed 'performative magic' (Bourdieu 2001, 103; 1992b, 106). Critical analysis alone will not dissolve binary oppositions that are historically inscribed in institutions, discourses and bodies. Yet an attention to ambivalence suggests that it is important to follow Bourdieu, and cultural theory more generally, by seeking to move beyond the dualities of 'objectivism' and 'subjectivism', whatever forms these may take: positivism versus phenomenology, social science versus cultural criticism, and so on (Bourdieu 1992c, 25–9). It requires us at its simplest to accept Bourdieu's 'invitation to hold together the findings of objectification and the equally clear fact of primary experience, which, by definition, excludes objectification' (Bourdieu 2000, 191). Something of the complexity of this demand is evident in Bourdieu's own analysis of the body, understood both as the ultimate repository of the individual and selfhood, and as a fundamentally social entity on and through which a whole series of categories and classifications are imprinted and enacted – sex, gender, status and 'race' among others. 'The body is in the social world', Bourdieu remarked, 'but the social world is in the body' (Bourdieu 2000, 152). Furthermore, it is necessary to accept that human agency is not the only form of historical agency – the natural and material worlds have agency too. As Mitchell's disquisition on the mosquito shows, and other environmental historians have also demonstrated, the human, the natural and the material worlds are involved in complex interaction with each other and history is a product of this interaction, not only, or even mainly, of human wills (e.g. Cronon 1996; Gandy 2002). In short, ambivalence requires that historians rethink a whole series of terms that are conventionally deemed to be antithetical: society/nature, mind/body, subject/object and – not least – true/false.

This brief discussion of reflexivity, ethics and ambivalence suggests only some of the more important ways that cultural theory is impacting on historical practice. But it indicates that the cultural turn is by no means complete; historians are continuing to absorb it and to write in its wake. Cultural theory remains indispensable to history because it is a transdisciplinary and transnational enterprise. It allows historians to escape the confines of their subject and social context and to converse across boundaries of nationality, intellectual tradition and disciplinary belonging. The terms on which this occurs, that of continuing Western dominance of the knowledge economy and of English as increasingly the sole authorised language of scholarly exchange, remain problematic and counter to cultural theory's own centrifugal thrust. Yet for historians, for whom disciplinary isolation seems to have increased rather than diminished in recent years, cultural theory offers the opportunity to engage in debate across disciplinary boundaries and to reconnect history with the wider field of the human sciences. Above all, what cultural theory holds out is the possibility of thinking differently, of rejecting the commonsense historicist view that would see the present and future as no more than the extension of a continuous past. It is a promise that Michel Foucault elegantly expressed as part of a statement read out at his funeral in June 1984: 'There are times in life when the question of knowing if one can think differently than one thinks and perceive differently than one sees is absolutely necessary if one is to go on looking and reflecting at all' (Eribon 1993, 329–30). A theorised history, it seems to me, could have no better expression of its purpose than to bring to light the multifarious different forms of thought and behaviour in the past so as to create the possibility for new ways of thinking and acting in the present.

References

Abrams, Philip (1982) *Historical Sociology*. Shepton Mallet: Open Books

Adorno, Theodor and Horkheimer, Max (1973 [1944]) *Dialectic of Enlightenment*. London: New Left Books

Agamben, Giorgio (1998) *Homo Sacer: Sovereign Power and Bare Life*, trans. D. Heller-Roazen. Stanford: Stanford University Press

Ahearne, Jeremy (1995) *Michel de Certeau: Interpretation and its Other*. Stanford: Stanford University Press

Ahmad, Aijaz (1992) *In Theory: Classes, Nations, Literatures*. London: Verso

Ahmad, Aijaz (1995) 'The politics of literary postcoloniality', *Race and Class*, 36:3, pp. 1–20

Alexander, Sally (1994) *Becoming a Woman and Other Essays in Nineteenth and Twentieth Century Feminist History*. London: Virago

Althusser, Louis (1969 [1959]) *For Marx*, trans. B. Brewster. London: New Left Books

Althusser, Louis (1971) *Lenin and Philosophy*. London: New Left Books

Anderson, Benedict (1991) *Imagined Communities*. London: Verso

Ankersmit, Frank (1983) *Narrative Logic: A Semantic Analysis of Historian's Language*. The Hague: Martin Nijhoff

Ankersmit, Frank (1994) *History and Tropology*. Berkeley: University of California Press

Anon (1999) 'From new historicism to historical epistemology', *Journal of Victorian Culture*, 4:1, spring, pp. 131–9

Appleby, Joyce, Hunt, Lynn and Jacob, Margaret (1994) *Telling the Truth About History*. New York: Norton

Austin, J.L. (1975) *How To Do Things With Words*. Oxford: Clarendon Press

Bachelard, Gaston (2002 [1938]) *The Formation of the Scientific Mind*. Manchester: Clinamen Press

Baker, Keith (1989) *Inventing the French Revolution*. Cambridge: Cambridge University Press

Bakhtin, Mikhail (1968 [1965]) *Rabelais and His World*, trans. H. Iswolsky. Cambridge, Mass.: MIT Press

Bakhtin, Mikhail (1992) *The Dialogic Imagination*, ed. M. Holquist, trans. C. Emerson and M. Holquist. Austin: University of Texas Press

Bakhtin, Mikhail (1994) *The Bakhtin Reader*, ed. P. Morris. London: Edward Arnold

Baldick, Christopher (1987) *The Social Mission of English Criticism, 1848–1932*. Oxford: Oxford University Press

Barnett, Corelli (1984) *The Collapse of British Power*. Gloucester: Allan Sutton

Barry, Andrew, Osborne, Thomas and Rose, Nikolas eds (1996) *Foucault and Political Reason*. London: UCL Press

Barthes, Roland (1977 [1968]) 'The death of the author' in *Image–Music–Text*, trans. S. Heath. London: Fontana

Barthes, Roland (1986a [1967]) 'The discourse of history' in Barthes, *The Rustle of Language*, trans. R. Howard. Oxford: Blackwell

Barthes, Roland (1986b [1972]) 'Michelet, today' in Barthes, *The Rustle of Language*, trans. R. Howard. Oxford: Blackwell

Baudelaire, Charles (1972) *Selected Writings*. London: Penguin

Baudrillard, Jean (1983) *In the Shadow of the Silent Majorities, or, the End of the Social and Other Essays*, trans. P. Foss, J. Johnston and P. Patton. New York: Semiotext(e)

Baudrillard, Jean (1988) *America*. London: Verso

Baudrillard, Jean (1993) 'Hyperreal America', *Economy and Society*, 22:2, pp. 243–52

Bauman, Zygmunt (1987) *Legislators and Interpreters: On Modernity, Postmodernity and the Intellectuals*. Oxford: Polity Press

Bauman, Zygmunt (1992) *Intimations of Postmodernity*. London: Routledge

Bauman, Zygmunt (2004) *Wasted Lives: Modernity and its Outcasts*. Cambridge: Polity Press

Bayly, C.A. (2004) *The Birth of the Modern World 1780–1914: Global Connections and Comparisons*. Oxford: Blackwell

Bell, David (2001) *The Cult of Nation in France: Inventing Nationalism, 1680–1800*. Cambridge, Mass.: Harvard University Press

Benjamin, Walter (1970) 'Theses on the philosophy of history' in Benjamin, *Illuminations*, trans. H. Zohn. London: Jonathan Cape

Benjamin, Walter (1992) *Charles Baudelaire: A Lyric Poet in the Era of High Capitalism*. London: Verso

Benjamin, Walter (1999) *The Arcades Project*, trans. H. Eiland and K. McLaughlin. Cambridge, Mass.: Harvard University Press

Bennett, Tony (1995) *The Birth of the Museum: History, Theory, Politics*. London: Routledge

Bennett, Tony (1998) 'The Foucault effect' in T. Bennett, *Culture: A Reformer's Science*. London: Sage

Bentley, Michael (1999) *Modern Historiography: An Introduction*. London: Routledge

Bentley, Michael (2002) 'Introduction: approaches to modernity' in Bentley ed. *Companion to Historiography*. London: Routledge

Berg, Maxine (1996) *A Woman in History. Eileen Power, 1889–1940*. Cambridge: Cambridge University Press

Berger, Stefan, Feldner, Heiko and Passmore, Kevin eds (2003) *Writing History. Theory and Practice*. London: Hodder Arnold

Berman, Marshall (1982) *All That is Solid Melts into Air: The Experience of Modernity*. London: Verso

Bermingham, Ann and Brewer, John, eds (1995) *The Consumption of Culture 1600–1800: Image, Object, Text*. London: Routledge

Bernal, Martin (1987) *Black Athena*. London: Free Association Books

Bessel, Richard ed. (1996) *Fascist Italy and Nazi Germany: Comparisons and Contrasts*. Cambridge: Cambridge University Press

Beverley, John, Oviedo, José and Aronna, Michael, eds (1995) *The Postmodernism Debate in Latin America*. Durham, North Carolina: Duke University Press

Bhaba, Homi K. (1994) *The Location of Culture*. London: Routledge

Biernacki, Richard (1999) 'Method and metaphor after the new cultural history' in V. Bonnell and L. Hunt eds *Beyond the Cultural Turn*. Berkeley: University of California Press

Biersack, Aletta (1989) 'Local knowledge, local history: Geertz and beyond' in L. Hunt ed. *The New Cultural History*. Berkeley: University of California Press

Bonnell, Victoria and Hunt, Lynn, eds (1999) *Beyond the Cultural Turn: New Directions in the Study of Society and Culture*. Berkeley: University of California Press

Bourdieu, Pierre (1977 [1972]) *Outline of a Theory of Practice*, trans. R. Nice. Cambridge: Cambridge University Press

Bourdieu, Pierre (1990) *In Other Words: Essays Towards a Reflexive Sociology*, trans. R. Nice. Cambridge: Polity Press

Bourdieu, Pierre (1992a [1979]) *Distinction: A Social Critique of the Judgement of Taste*, trans. R. Nice. London: Routledge

Bourdieu, Pierre (1992b) *Language and Symbolic Power*, trans. G. Raymond and M. Adamson. Cambridge: Polity Press

Bourdieu, Pierre (1992c) *The Logic of Practice*, trans. R. Nice. Cambridge: Polity Press

Bourdieu, Pierre (1993) *The Field of Cultural Production*, trans. R. Nice. Cambridge: Polity Press

Bourdieu, Pierre (1996) *The State Nobility*, trans. L. Clough. Stanford: Stanford University Press

Bourdieu, Pierre (2000) *Pascalian Meditations*, trans. R. Nice. Cambridge: Polity Press

Bourdieu, Pierre (2001) *Masculine Domination*, trans. R. Nice. Cambridge: Polity Press

Bourdieu, Pierre *et al.* (2002) *The Weight of the World: Social Suffering in Contemporary Society*, trans. P. Ferguson *et al.* Cambridge: Polity Press

Bourdieu, Pierre (2003 [1984]) *Homo Academicus*, trans. P. Collier. Cambridge: Polity Press

Bourdieu, Pierre, Chartier, Roger and Darnton, Robert (1985) 'Dialogue à propos de l'histoire culturelle', *Actes de la Recherche en Sciences Sociales*, 59, pp. 86–93

Bradbury, Malcolm (1991) *Modernism 1890–1930*. London: Penguin

Braudel, Fernand (1972 [1949]) *The Mediterranean and the Mediterranean World in the Age of Philip II*, trans. S. Reynolds, two vols. London: Collins

Breisach, Ernst (1983) *Historiography*. Chicago: University of Chicago Press

Breuilly, John (1982) *Nationalism and the State*. Manchester: Manchester University Press

Briggs, Asa (1968) *Victorian Cities*. Harmondsworth: Penguin

Brooke, John (1998) 'Reason and passion in the public sphere: Habermas and the cultural historians', *Journal of Interdisciplinary History*, xxix, 1, pp. 43–67

Brown, Callum (2001) *The Death of Christian Britain*. London: Routledge

Brown, Callum (2005) *Postmodernism for Historians*. Harlow: Pearson Education

Bruner, Jerome (1991) 'The narrative construction of reality', *Critical Inquiry*, 18

Burchell, Graham, Gordon, Colin and Miller, Peter (1991) *The Foucault Effect: Studies in Governmentality*. Hemel Hempstead: Harvester

Burke, Peter (1978) *Popular Culture in Early Modern Europe*. London: Temple Smith

Burke, Peter (1986) 'Strengths and weaknesses of the history of mentalités', *Journal of the History of European Ideas*, 7, pp. 439–51

Burke, Peter (1988) 'Bakhtin for historians', *Social History*, 13:1, pp. 85–90

Burke, Peter (1990) *The French Historical Revolution: The Annales School 1929–1989*. Cambridge: Cambridge University Press

Burke, Peter (1999) *History and Social Theory*. Cambridge: Polity Press

Burke, Peter (2004) *What is Cultural History?* Cambridge: Polity Press

Burke, Peter (2005) 'Performing history: the importance of occasions', *Rethinking History*, 9:1, pp. 35–52

Burke, Peter ed. (1991) *New Perspectives on Historical Writing*. Cambridge: Polity Press

Burke, Peter ed. (1992) *Critical Essays on Michel Foucault*. Aldershot: Scolar Press

Burleigh, M. and Wipperman, W. (1991) *The Racial State 1933–1945.* Cambridge: Cambridge University Press

Burton, Antoinette (1998) *At the Heart of the Empire: Indians and the Colonial Encounter in Late Victorian Britain.* Berkeley: University of California Press

Burton, Antoinette (2000) 'Who needs the nation? Interrogating "British" history' in C. Hall ed. *Cultures of Empire.* Manchester: Manchester University Press

Bush, Michael (1992) 'The anatomy of nobility' in Bush, ed. *Social Orders and Social Classes in Europe Since 1500.* Harlow: Longman

Bushman, Richard (1992) *The Refinement of America.* New York: Knopf

Butler, Judith (1990) *Gender Trouble: Feminism and the Subversion of Identity.* London: Routledge

Butler, Judith (1993) *Bodies That Matter.* London: Routledge

Butler, Judith (1999) 'Performativity's social magic' in R. Shusterman ed. *Bourdieu: A Critical Reader.* Oxford: Blackwell

Butler, Judith and Scott, Joan, eds (1992) *Feminists Theorize the Political.* London: Routledge

Bynum, Caroline (1987) *Holy Feast and Holy Fast.* Berkeley: University of California Press

Bynum, Caroline (2001) *Metamorphosis and Identity.* New York: Zone Books

Calhoun, Craig (1993) 'Postmodernism as pseudohistory', *Theory, Culture and Society* 10 (1), pp. 75–96

Canguilhem, Georges (1994) *A Vital Rationalist: Selected Writings from Georges Canguilhem,* F. Delaporte ed., trans. A. Goldhammer. New York: Zone Books

Cannadine, David (2001) *Ornamentalism: How the British Saw Their Empire.* London: Penguin

Carr, David (1986) *Time, Narrative and History.* Bloomington: Indiana University Press

Carroll, Noël (2001) 'Interpretation, history, and narrative' in G. Roberts ed. *The History and Narrative Reader.* London: Routledge

Castle, Terry (1986) *Masquerade and Civilisation.* London: Methuen

Centre for Contemporary Cultural Studies (1982) *The Empire Strikes Back*. London: Hutchinson

Certeau, Michel de (1984) *The Practice of Everyday Life: Vol. 1, The Art of Living*, trans. S. Rendall. Berkeley: University of California Press

Certeau, Michel de (1986) *Heterologies: Discourse on the Other*, trans. B. Massumi. Manchester: Manchester University Press

Certeau, Michel de (1988 [1975]) *The Writing of History*, trans. T. Conley. New York: Columbia University Press

Certeau, Michel de (1990 [1970]) *La Possession de Loudun*. Paris: Gallimard

Certeau, Michel de (1992 [1982]) *The Mystic Fable, Volume One: The Sixteenth and Seventeenth Centuries*, trans. M.B. Smith. Chicago: University of Chicago Press

Certeau, Michel de, Giard, Luce and Mayol, Pierre (1998) *The Practice of Everyday Life: Living and Cooking*, trans. T.J. Tomasik. Minneapolis: University of Minnesota Press

Chakrabarty, Dipesh (1992a) 'Postcoloniality and the artifice of history: who speaks for "Indian" pasts?', *Representations*, 37 (winter), pp. 1–26

Chakrabarty, Dipesh (1992b) 'Trafficking in history and theory: Subaltern Studies' in K.K. Ruthven ed. *Beyond the Disciplines: The New Humanities*. Canberra: Australian National University, pp. 101–8

Chakrabarty, Dipesh (2000) *Provincialising Europe: Postcolonial Thought and Historical Difference*. Princeton: Princeton University Press

Chandavarkar, Rajnaryan (1997) ' "The making of the working class": E.P. Thompson and Indian history', *History Workshop Journal*, 42, pp. 177–96

Charle, Christophe (1994) *La République des Universitaires*. Paris: Seuil

Charle, Christophe (1996) *Les Intellectuels en Europe au XIXème Siècle*. Paris: Seuil

Charle, Christophe (2001) *La Crise des Sociétés Imperiales*. Paris: Seuil

Charle, Christophe and Roche, Daniel (2002) *Capitales Culturelles, Capitales Symboliques: Paris et les Expériences Européenes XVII–XXème Siècles*. Paris: Seuil

Chartier, Roger (1991) *The Cultural Origins of the French Revolution*, trans. L.G. Cochrane. Durham, North Carolina: Duke University Press

Chartier, Roger (1993) *Cultural History: Between Practices and Representations*, trans. L.G. Cochrane. Cambridge: Polity Press

Chartier, Roger (1997) *On the Edge of the Cliff: History, Language and Practices*, trans. L.G. Cochrane. Baltimore: Johns Hopkins Press

Chatterjee, Partha (1993) *The Nation and Its Fragments: Colonial and Postcolonial Histories*. Princeton: Princeton University Press

Chaturvedi, Vinayak ed. (2000) *Mapping Subaltern Studies and the Postcolonial*. London: Verso

Clark, Anna (1995) *The Struggle for the Breeches: Gender and the Making of the British Working Class*. Berkeley: University of California Press

Clark, J.C.D. (1985) *English Society, 1688–1832: Ideology, Social Structure and Political Practice*. Cambridge: Cambridge University Press

Clark, T.J. (1985) *The Painting of Modern Life: Paris in the Art of Manet and His Followers*. London: Thames and Hudson

Clifford, James (1988) *The Predicament of Culture: Twentieth-Century Ethnography, Literature and Art*. Cambridge, Mass.: Harvard University Press

Clifford, James and Marcus, George, eds (1986) *Writing Culture: The Poetics and Politics of Ethnography*. Berkeley: University of California Press

Cohn, Dorrit (2000) *The Distinction of Fiction*. Baltimore: Johns Hopkins University Press

Colley, Linda (1989) *Namier*. London: Weidenfeld and Nicholson

Colley, Linda (1992) *Britons: Forging the Nation 1707–1837*. New Haven: Yale University Press

Conekin, Beckie, Mort, Frank and Waters, Chris (1999) *Moments of Modernity: Reconstructing Britain 1945–1964*. London: Rivers Oram Press

Coole, Diana (1996) 'Is class a difference that makes a difference?' *Radical Philosophy*, May/June, pp. 17–25

Cooper, Frederick and Stoler, Ann (1997) 'Between metropole and colony: rethinking a research agenda' in Cooper and Stoler eds *Tensions of Empire: Colonial Cultures in a Bourgeois World*. Berkeley: University of California Press

Corbin, Alain (1986) *The Foul and the Fragrant: Odour and the French Social Imagination*. Cambridge, Mass.: Harvard University Press

Corbin, Alain *et al.* (1999) 'Les historiens et la sociologie de Pierre Bourdieu', *Supplement à la Revue d'Histoire Moderne et Contemporaine*, 3–4, pp. 4–27

Cronon, William ed. (1996) *Uncommon Ground: Rethinking the Human Place in Nature*. New York: Norton

Crossick, Geoffrey (1991) 'From gentlemen to the residuum: languages of social description in Victorian Britain' in P. Corfield ed. *Language, History and Class*. Oxford: Blackwell

Damousi, Joy, Reynolds, Robert eds. (2003) *History on the Couch: Essays in History and Psychoanalysis*. Melbourne: Melbourne University Publishing

Darnton, Robert (1985) *The Great Cat Massacre and Other Episodes in French Cultural History*. New York: Vintage Books

Daunton, Martin and Halpern, Rick eds (1999) *Empire and Others: British Encounters with Indigeneous Peoples 1600–1850*. London: UCL Press

Daunton, Martin and Rieger, Bernhard eds (2001) *Meanings of Modernity: Britain from the Late Victorian Era to World War II*. Oxford: Berg

Davidoff, Leonore and Hall, Catherine (1987) *Family Fortunes: Men and Women of the English Middle Class 1780–1850*. London: Hutchinson

Davis, Natalie Zemon (1975) *Society and Culture in Early Modern France*. Stanford: Stanford University Press

Davis, Natalie Zemon (1981) 'Anthropology and history in the 1980s', *Journal of Interdisciplinary History*, 11, pp. 267–75

Davis, Natalie Zemon (1983) *The Return of Martin Guerre*. Cambridge, Mass.: Harvard University Press

Davison, Graeme (2000) *The Use and Abuse of Australian History*. London: Allen and Unwin

Dean, Mitchell (1994) *Critical and Effective Histories: Foucault's Methods and Historical Sociology*. London: Routledge

Dean, Mitchell (1999) *Governmentality*. London: Sage

Dening, Greg (1992) *Mr Bligh's Bad Language: Passion, Power and Theatre on the Bounty*. Cambridge: Cambridge University Press

Dening, Greg (1996) *Performances*. Melbourne: Melbourne University Press

Dening, Greg (2004) 'Writing, re-writing the beach' in A. Munslow and R. Rosenstone eds *Experiments in Rethinking History*. London: Routledge

Dentith, Simon (1995) *Bakhtinian Thought: An Introductory Reader*. London: Routledge

Derrida, Jacques (1976) *Of Grammatology*, trans. G.C. Spivak. Baltimore: Johns Hopkins University Press

Derrida, Jacques (1981) *Writing and Difference*. London: Routledge

Derrida, Jacques (1982) 'Différance' in Derrida, *The Margins of Philosophy*, trans. A. Bass. Hemel Hempstead: Harvester

Dintenfass, Michael (1999) 'Crafting historians' lives: autobiographical constructions and disciplinary discourses after the linguistic turn', *Journal of Modern History*, 71 (March), pp. 150–65

Dirks, Nicholas, Eley, Geoff and Ortner, Sherry eds (1994) *Culture/Power/History: A Reader in Contemporary Social Theory*. Princeton: Princeton University Press

Douglas, Mary (1978) *Implicit Meanings: Essays in Anthropology*. London: Routledge Kegan Paul

Douglas, Mary (1994) *Risk and Blame: Essays in Cultural Theory*. London: Routledge

Douglas, Mary (1999 [1966]) *Purity and Danger: An Analysis of the Concepts of Pollution and Taboo*. London: Routledge

Downs, Laura Lee (2004) *Writing Gender History*. London: Hodder Arnold

Driver, Felix and Gilbert, David eds (1999) *Imperial Cities*. Manchester: Manchester University Press

Dworkin, Dennis (1997) *Cultural Marxism in Postwar Britain*. Durham, North Carolina: Duke University Press

Eagleton, Terry (1983) *Literary Theory: An Introduction*. Oxford: Blackwell

Eagleton, Terry (2004) *After Theory*. London: Penguin

Eder, Franz, Hall, Lesley and Hekman, Gert (1999) 'Introduction' in F. Eder, L. Hall and G. Hekman eds *Sexual Cultures in Europe*. Manchester: Manchester University Press

Edgar, Andrew and Sedgwick, Peter eds (2002) *Cultural Theory*. London: Routledge

Eley, Geoff (1992) 'Nations, publics and political cultures: placing Habermas in the nineteenth century' in C. Calhoun ed. (1992) *Habermas and the Public Sphere*. Cambridge, Mass.: MIT Press

Eley, Geoff (1996) 'Is all the world a text? From social history to the history of society two decades later' in T. McDonald ed. *The Historic Turn in the Human Sciences*. Ann Arbor: University of Michigan Press

Eley, Geoff (2003) 'Marxist historiography' in S. Berger, H. Feldner and K. Passmore eds *Writing History*. London: Hodder Arnold

Eley, Geoff and Blackbourn, David (1984) *The Peculiarities of German History*. Oxford: Oxford University Press, 1984

Eley, Geoff and Neild, Keith (1980) 'Why does social history ignore politics?' *Social History*, 5, pp. 249–71

Elton, Geoffrey (1988) 'What is political history?' in Gardiner, Juliet, ed. *What is History Today?* Basingstoke: Macmillan

Engels, Friedrich (1969 [1844]) *The Condition of the Working Class in England in 1844*. London: Granada

Eribon, Didier (1993) *Michel Foucault*. London: Faber

Ermath, Elizabeth Deedes (1992) *Sequel to History*. Princeton: Princeton University Press

Evans, Richard (1997) *In Defence of History*. London: Granta

Evans, Richard (2002a) *Telling Lies About Hitler*. London: Verso

Evans, Richard (2002b) 'What is history – now?' in D. Cannadine ed. *What is History Now?* Basingstoke: Palgrave

Fanon, Frantz (1982 [1952]) *Black Skin, White Masks*, trans. C.L. Markmann. New York: Grove Weidenfeld

Fanon, Frantz (1991 [1961]) *The Wretched of the Earth*, trans. C. Farrington. New York: Grove Weidenfeld

Faucher, Leon (1844) *Manchester in 1844*. London: H. Fournier et cie

Feldman, David (2004) 'The new imperial history', *Journal of Victorian Culture*, 9:2 (autumn), pp. 235–40

Foucault, Michel (1967) *Madness and Civilization*, trans. A. Sheridan. London: Tavistock Publications

Foucault, Michel (1973) *The Birth of the Clinic*, trans. A. Sheridan. London: Tavistock Publications

Foucault, Michel (1977) *Discipline and Punish: The Birth of the Prison*, trans. A. Sheridan. London: Allen Lane

Foucault, Michel (1980) *Power/Knowledge*, ed. C. Gordon. Hemel Hempstead: Harvester Press

Foucault, Michel (1986) 'Of other spaces', *Diacritics*, 16, pp. 22–7

Foucault, Michel (1990) *The History of Sexuality, Volume 3: The Care of the Self*, trans. A. Sheridan. London: Penguin

Foucault, Michel (1991a) 'Questions of method' in G. Burchell, C. Gordon, and P. Miller, *The Foucault Effect*. Hemel Hempstead: Harvester Press

Foucault, Michel (1991b) 'Governmentality' in G. Burchell, C. Gordon and P. Miller, *The Foucault Effect*. Hemel Hempstead: Harvester Press

Foucault, Michel (2002) *Power: Essential Works of Foucault, Vol. 3*, ed. J. Faubion. London: Penguin

Foucault, Michel (2004 [1968]) *The Archaeology of Knowledge*. London: Routledge

Frascina, Francis and Harrison, Charles eds (1988) *Modern Art and Modernism: A Critical Anthology*. London: Paul Chapman

Fraser, Nancy (1989) *Unruly Practices: Power, Discourse and Gender in Contemporary Social Theory*. Minneapolis: University of Minnesota Press

Frisby, David (1985) *Fragments of Modernity*. Cambridge: Polity Press

Frisby, David and Featherstone, Mike eds (1997) *Simmel on Culture*. London: Sage

Fullbrook, Mary (2002) *Historical Theory*. London: Routledge

Gagnier, Regina (1991) *Subjectivities. A History of Self-Representation in Britain, 1832–1920*. Oxford: Oxford University Press

Gagnier, Regina (1999) 'Methodology and the new historicism', *Journal of Victorian Culture*, 4:1, spring, pp. 116–22

Gallie, W.B. (1964) *Philosophy and Historical Understanding*. London: Chatto and Windus

Gandy, Matthew (2002) *Concrete and Clay: Reworking Nature in New York City*. Cambridge, Mass.: MIT Press

Garrard, John (1983) *Leadership and Power in Victorian Industrial Towns*. Manchester: Manchester University Press

Gatrell, V.A.C. (1994) *The Hanging Tree*. Oxford: Oxford University Press

Gay, Peter (1973) *The Enlightenment: An Interpretation, Volume 1: The Rise of Modern Paganism*. London: Wildwood House

Geertz, Clifford (1983) *Local Knowledge: Further Studies in Interpretive Anthropology*. New York: Basic Books

Geertz, Clifford (2000 [1973]) *The Interpretation of Cultures*. London: Fontana

Gellner, Ernest (1983) *Nations and Nationalism*. Ithaca: Cornell University Press

Genovese, Eugene (1975) *Roll, Jordan, Roll: The World the Slaves Made*. London: André Deutsch

Gerth, H.H. and Wright Mills, C. (1974) *From Max Weber: Essays in Sociology*. London: Routledge Kegan Paul

Giddens, Anthony (1996) *Modernity and Self-Identity: Self and Society in the Late Modern Age*. Cambridge: Polity Press

Gilbert, Sandra and Gubar, Susan (1979) *The Madwoman in the Attic*. New Haven: Yale University Press

Gilroy, Paul (1987) *There Ain't No Black in the Union Jack*. London: Hutchinson

Gilroy, Paul (1993) *The Black Atlantic: Modernity and Double Consciousness*. London: Verso

Ginzburg, Carlo (1992) *The Cheese and the Worms. The Cosmos of a Sixteenth-Century Miller*. London: Penguin

Ginzburg, Carlo (1993) 'Microhistory: two or three things that I know about it', *Critical Inquiry*, 20, pp. 10–35

Goffman, Erving (1961) *Asylums*. Harmondsworth: Penguin

Goffman, Erving (1969) *The Presentation of Self in Everyday Life*. Harmondsworth: Penguin

Goffman, Erving (1970) *Stigma*. Harmondsworth: Penguin

Goldberg, David T. and Quayson, Ato (2002) *Relocating Postcolonialism*. Oxford: Blackwell

Goodman, Dena (1992) 'Public sphere and private life: towards a synthesis of current historiographical approaches to the old regime', *History and Theory*, 31, pp. 1–20

Gordon, Colin (1991) 'Governmental rationality: an introduction' in G. Burchell, C. Gordon and P. Miller eds *The Foucault Effect*. Hemel Hempstead: Harvester Press

Gramsci, Antonio (1982) *Selections from Prison Notebooks* eds Q. Hoare and G. Nowell Smith. London: Lawrence and Wishart

Gray, Robert (1983 [1977]) 'Bourgeois hegemony in Victorian England' in T. Bennett, G. Martin, C. Mercer and J. Woollacott, eds *Culture, Ideology and Social Process: A Reader*. London: Open University Press

Gray, Robert (1996) *The Factory Question and Industrial England 1830–1860*. Cambridge: Cambridge University Press

Green, Anna and Troup, Kathleen (1999) *The Houses of History*. Manchester: Manchester University Press

Griffin, Gabriele and Braidotti, Rosi eds (2002) *Thinking Differently: A Reader in European Women's Studies*. London: Zed Books

Grosz, Elizabeth (2001) *Architecture from the Outside: Essays on Virtual and Real Space*. Cambridge, Mass.: MIT Press

Guha, Ranajit (1983a) *Elementary Aspects of Peasant Insurgency in Colonial India*. Delhi: Oxford University Press

Guha, Ranajit (1983b) 'The prose of counter-insurgency' in Guha ed. *Subaltern Studies II*. New Delhi: Oxford University Press

Guha, Ranajit (2000 [1982]) 'On some aspects of the historiography of colonial India' in V. Chaturvedi, ed. *Mapping Subaltern Studies and the Postcolonial*. London: Verso

Guha, Ranajit ed. (1982) *Subaltern Studies I: Writings on South Asian History and Society*. Delhi: Oxford University Press

Guha, Ranajit ed. (1985) *Subaltern Studies IV: Writing on South Asian History and Society*. Delhi: Oxford University Press

Guha, Ranajit and Spivak, Gayatri Chakravorty eds (1988) *Selected Subaltern Studies*. New York: Oxford University Press

Gunn, Simon (2000) *The Public Culture of the Victorian Middle Class*. Manchester: Manchester University Press

Gunn, Simon (2004) 'Urbanisation' in C. Williams ed. *A Companion to Nineteenth-Century Britain*. Oxford: Blackwell

Gunn, Simon (2005) 'Translating Bourdieu: cultural capital and the English middle class in historical perspective', *British Journal of Sociology*, 56:1, pp. 49–64

Gunn, Simon and Rawnsley, Stuart (2006) 'Practising reflexivity: the place of theory in university history', *Rethinking History*, forthcoming

Habermas, Jürgen (1985) 'Modernity: an incomplete project' in H. Foster ed. *Postmodern Culture*. London: Pluto Press

Habermas, Jürgen (1987) *The Philosophical Discourse of Modernity*. Cambridge: Polity Press

Habermas, Jürgen (1992 [1962]) *The Structural Transformation of the Public Sphere: An Inquiry into a Category of Bourgeois Society*, trans. T. Burger. Cambridge: Polity Press

Habermas, Jürgen, (2001 [1981]) 'Modernity versus postmodernity' in M. Waters ed. *Modernity: Critical Concepts. Volume IV*. London: Routledge

Hacking, Ian (1990) *The Taming of Chance*. Cambridge: Cambridge University Press

Hacking, Ian (1991) 'How should we do the history of statistics?' in G. Burchell, C. Gordon and P. Miller, eds *The Foucault Effect*. Hemel Hempstead: Harvester Press

Hall, Catherine (1992) *White, Male and Middle Class: Explorations in Feminism and History*. Cambridge: Polity Press

Hall, Catherine (2002) *Civilising Subjects: Metropole and Colony in the English Imagination 1830–1867*. Cambridge: Polity Press

Hall, Catherine (2004) Review of C.A. Bayly, *The Birth of the Modern World*, http://www.history.ac.uk/reviews/paper/hall.html

Hall, Catherine ed. (2000) *Cultures of Empire*. Manchester: Manchester University Press

Hall, Stuart (1983) 'Cultural studies: two paradigms' in T. Bennett, G. Martin, C. Mercer and J. Woollacott eds *Culture, Ideology and Social Process: A Reader*. London: Batsford

Hall, Stuart (1988) 'New ethnicities' in K. Mercer ed. *Black Film, British Cinema*. BFI/ICA Documents, 7, pp. 23–31

Hall, Stuart (1992) 'Cultural studies and its theoretical legacies' in L. Grossberg ed. *Cultural Studies*. London: Routledge, pp. 277–86

Hall, Stuart (1994) 'The question of cultural identity' in *The Polity Reader in Cultural Theory*. Cambridge: Polity Press

Hall, Stuart (1996) 'Cultural studies and its theoretical legacies' in D. Morley and K.H. Chen eds *Stuart Hall: Critical Dialogues in Cultural Studies*. London: Routledge

Hall, Stuart, Held, David and McGrew, Tony, eds (1992) *Modernity and Its Futures*. Cambridge: Polity Press

Halsey, A.H. (2004) *A History of British Sociology*. Oxford: Clarendon

Halttunen, Karen (1999) 'Cultural history and the challenge of narrativity' in V. Bonnell and L. Hunt eds *Beyond the Cultural Turn*. Berkeley: University of California Press

Hamlin, Christopher (1998) *Public Health and Social Justice in the Age of Chadwick*. Cambridge: Cambridge University Press

Haraway, Donna (1992) *Primate Visions: Gender, Race and Nature in the World of Modern Science*. London: Verso

Harvey, David (1985) *Consciousness and the Urban Experience*. Oxford: Blackwell

Hastings, Adrian (1997) *The Construction of Nationhood: Ethnicity, Religion and Nationalism*. Cambridge: Cambridge University Press

Hegel, G.W.F. (1956 [1821]) *Lectures on the Philosophy of History*. New York: Dover Press

Hesse, Carla (2004) 'The new empiricism', *Social and Cultural History*, 1:2, pp. 201–8

Higgs, Edward (2000) *The Information State in England*. Basingstoke: Macmillan

History Workshop Collective (1980), 'History and language', *History Workshop Journal* editorial, 10, pp. 1–5

Hitchcock, Tim (1997) *English Sexualities*. Basingstoke: Macmillan

Hitchcock, Tim, Shoemaker, Robert and Tosh, John (2000) 'Skills and the structure of the history curriculum' in A. Booth and P. Hyland eds *The Practice of University History Teaching*. Manchester: Manchester University Press

Hobsbawm, Eric (1959) *Primitive Rebels: Studies in Archaic Forms of Social Movement in the Nineteenth and Twentieth Centuries*. Manchester: Manchester University Press

Hobsbawm, Eric (1975) *The Age of Capital*. London: Weidenfeld and Nicholson

Hobsbawm, Eric (1987) *The Age of Empire 1875–1914*. London: Weidenfeld and Nicholson

Hobsbawm, Eric (1995) *Age of Extremes*. London: Abacus

Hobsbawm, Eric and Ranger, Terence, eds (1984) *The Invention of Tradition*. Cambridge: Cambridge University Press

Hoff, Joan (1994) 'Gender as a postmodern category of paralysis', *Women's History Review*, 2, pp. 149–68

Hoggart, Richard (1957) *The Uses of Literacy*. London: Chatto and Windus

Holton, Robert (1996) 'Has class analysis a future?' in D. Lee and B. Turner eds *Conflicts about Class*. Harlow: Longman

Host, John (1998) *Labour History: Experience, Identity and the Politics of Representation*. London: Routledge

Hunt, Alan (1999) *Governing Morals: A Social History of Moral Regulation*. Cambridge: Cambridge University Press

Hunt, Lynn ed. (1989) *The New Cultural History*. Berkeley: University of California Press

Huntington, Samuel (1997) *The Clash of Civilisations and the Remaking of the World Order*. New York: Touchstone

Iggers, Georg (1973) 'Introduction' in Leopold von Ranke, *The Theory and Practice of History*, ed. G. Iggers and K. von Moltke. Indianapolis: Bobbs-Merrill Co.

Iggers, Georg (2005 [1997]) *Historiography in the Twentieth Century*. Middletown: Wesleyan University Press

Jackson, Louise (2000) *Child Sexual Abuse in Victorian England*. London: Routledge

James, C.L.R. (1980 [1938]) *The Black Jacobins: Toussaint L'Ouverture and the San Domingo Revolution*. London: Alison and Busby

Jameson, Frederic (1993) *Postmodernism or, the Cultural Logic of Late Capitalism*. London: Verso

Jenkins, Keith (1991) *Rethinking History*. London: Routledge

Jenkins, Keith (1995) *On 'What is History?': From Carr and Elton to Rorty and White*. London: Routledge

Jenkins, Keith ed. (1997) *The Postmodern History Reader*. London: Routledge

Jenkins, Richard (1992) *Pierre Bourdieu*. London: Routledge

Jenkins, Richard (1996) *Social Identity*. London: Routledge

Johnson, Richard (1978) 'Edward Thompson, Eugene Genovese and socialist-humanist history', *History Workshop Journal*, 6, pp. 79–100

Jones, Colin (2004) 'Peter Mandler's "problem with cultural history", or, is playtime over?', *Social and Cultural History*, 1:2, pp. 209–16

Jordanova, Ludmilla (2000) *History in Practice*. London: Edward Arnold

Joyce, Patrick (1990) *Visions of the People*. Cambridge: Cambridge University Press

Joyce, Patrick (1995a) 'The end of social history?', *Social History*, 20:1, pp. 73–91

Joyce, Patrick (1998) 'The return of history: postmodernism and the politics of history in Britain', *Past and Present*, 158, February, 207–35

Joyce, Patrick (2003) *The Rule of Freedom: Liberalism and the Modern City*. London: Verso

Joyce, Patrick, ed. (1995b) *Class*. Oxford: Oxford University Press

Joyce, Patrick, ed. (2002) *The Social in Question: New Bearings in History and the Social Sciences*. London: Routledge

Kant, Immanuel (1952) *Critique of Judgement*, trans. J.C. Meredith. London: Oxford University Press

Kaye, Harvey (1984a) *The British Marxist Historians*. Cambridge: Polity Press

Kaye, Harvey (1984b) 'Political theory and history: Antonio Gramsci and the British Marxist historians', *Italian Quarterly*, 25 (97–8), pp. 145–66

Kellner, Hans (1980) 'A bedrock of order: Hayden White's linguistic humanism', *History and Theory*, pp. 1–29

Kellner, Hans (1993) ' "As real as it gets": Ricoeur and narrativity' in D. Klemm and W. Schweiker eds *Meanings in Texts and Actions: Questioning Paul Ricoeur*. Charlottesville: University of Virginia Press

Kendall, Gavin and Wickham, Gary (1999) *Using Foucault's Methods*. London: Sage

Kiernan, Victor (1995) 'Antonio Gramsci and other continents' in V. Kiernan and H. Kaye eds *Imperialism and Its Contradictions*. London: Routledge

Kocka, Jurgen and Mitchell, Allan, eds (1993) *Bourgeois Society in Nineteenth-Century Europe*. Oxford: Berg

Kramer, Lloyd S. (1989) 'Literature, criticism and historical imagination: the literary challenge of Hayden White and Dominick LaCapra' in L. Hunt ed. *The New Cultural History*. Berkeley: University of California Press

Lacan, Jacques (1977) *Ecrits*. London: Tavistock

LaCapra, Dominick (1983) *Rethinking Intellectual History: Texts, Contexts, Language*. Ithaca: Cornell University Press

LaCapra, Dominick (1985) *History and Criticism*. Ithaca: Cornell University Press

Ladurie, Emmanuel Le Roy (1978) *Montaillou: Cathars and Catholics in a French Village 1294–1324*. London: Scolar Press

Lambert, Peter (2003) 'The professionalisation and institutionalisation of history' in S. Berger, H. Feldner and K. Passmore eds *Writing History*. London: Hodder Arnold

Landes, Joan (1990) *Women and the Public Sphere in the Age of the French Revolution*. Ithaca: Cornell University Press

Laqueur, Thomas (1989) 'Crowds, carnival and the state in English executions, 1604–1868' in A.L. Beier, D. Cannadine and J.M. Rosenheim eds *The First Modern Society*. Cambridge: Cambridge University Press

Laqueur, Thomas (1990) *Making Sex: Body and Gender from the Greeks to Freud*. Cambridge, Mass.: Harvard University Press

Lash, Scott (1990) *A Sociology of Postmodernism*. London: Routledge

Latour, Bruno (1993) *We Have Never Been Modern*, trans. C. Porter. Hemel Hempstead: Harvester Wheatsheaf

Lee, Nick and Stenner, Paul (1999) 'Who pays? Can we pay them back?' in J. Law and J. Hassard eds *Actor Network Theory and After*. Oxford: Blackwell

Levi, Giovanni (1991) 'On microhistory' in P. Burke ed. *New Perspectives on Historical Writing*. Cambridge: Polity Press

Lévi-Strauss, Claude (1955) *Tristes Tropiques*. Paris: Gallimard

Lévi-Strauss, Claude (1968 [1958]) *Structural Anthropology*, trans. C. Jacobson and B.G. Schoepf. Harmondsworth: Penguin

Lévi-Strauss, Claude (1966 [1962]) *The Savage Mind*, trans. Anon. London: Weidenfeld and Nicholson

Linebaugh, Peter and Rediker, Marcus (2000) *The Many Headed Hydra: The Hidden History of the Revolutionary Atlantic*. London: Verso

Louis, W.R. ed. (1998–9) *The Oxford History of the British Empire*, 5 vols. Oxford: Oxford University Press

Lovell, Terry (2000) 'Thinking feminism with and against Bourdieu', *Feminist Theory*, 1:1, pp. 11–32

Low, Murray (2000) 'Nationalism' in G. Browning, A. Halcli and F. Webster eds *Understanding Contemporary Society: Theories of the Present*. London: Sage

Lowerson, John (1999) 'An outbreak of allodoxia? Operatic amateurs and middle-class musical taste between the wars' in A. Kidd and D. Nicholls eds *Gender, Civic Culture and Consumerism: Middle-Class Identity in Britain 1800–1940*. Manchester: Manchester University Press

Lukes, Steven (1974) *Power: A Radical View*. Basingstoke: Macmillan

Lyotard, Jean-François (1992 [1979]) *The Postmodern Condition: A Report on Knowledge*, trans. G. Bennington and B. Massumi. Manchester: Manchester University Press

Macfarlane, Alan (1977) 'History, anthropology and the study of communities', *Social History*, 5, pp. 631–52

Machiavelli, Niccolo (2005 [1513]) *The Prince*, trans. P. Bondanella. Oxford: Oxford University Press

MacIntyre, Alasdair (1985) *After Virtue: A Study in Moral Theory*. London: Duckworth

MacIntyre, Alasdair (1988) *Whose Justice? What Rationality?* London: Duckworth

Mackenzie, John M. (1995) *Orientalism: History, Theory and the Arts*. Manchester: Manchester University Press

Mandelbaum, Maurice (1977) *The Anatomy of Historical Knowledge*. Baltimore: Johns Hopkins University Press

Mandler, Peter (2004) 'The problem with cultural history', *Cultural and Social History*, 1:1, pp. 94–117

Marcus, Steven (1985) *Engels, Manchester and the Working Class*. New York: Norton

Marshall, P.J. ed. (1996) *The Cambridge Illustrated History of the British Empire*. Cambridge: Cambridge University Press

Marwick, Arthur (2001) *The New Nature of History: Knowledge, Evidence, Language*. Basingstoke: Palgrave

Marx, Karl (1955) *The Poverty of Philosophy*. Moscow: Progress Publishing

Marx, Karl and Engels, Friedrich (1969 [1888]) *The Communist Manifesto*. Harmondsworth: Penguin

Mauss, Marcel (1985 [1938]) 'A category of the human mind; the notion of person; the notion of self' in M. Carrithers, S. Collins and S. Lukes eds *The Category of the Person: Anthropology, Philosophy, History*. Cambridge: Cambridge University Press

Mayne, Alan (1993) *The Imagined Slum: Newspaper Representation in Three Cities, 1870–1914*. Leicester: Leicester University Press

Maza, Sara (1996) 'Stories in history: cultural narratives in recent works in European history', *American Historical Review*, 101, pp. 493–515

McClintock, Anne (1995) *Imperial Leather: Race, Gender and Sexuality in the Colonial Context*. London: Routledge

McCullagh, C.B. (1998) *The Truth of History*. London: Routledge

McCullagh, C.B. (2004) *The Logic of History: Putting Postmodernism in Perspective*. London: Routledge

Mead, George H. (1934) *Mind, Self and Society from the Standpoint of a Social Behaviorist*. Chicago: University of Chicago Press

Melling, Joseph (1999) 'Accommodating madness: new research in the social history of insanity and institutions' in J. Melling and B. Forsythe eds *Insanity, Institutions and Society, 1800–1914*. London: Routledge

Meyers, Norma (1996) *Reconstructing the Black Past: Blacks in Britain 1780–1830*. Oxford: Clarendon Press

Mink, Louis (1970) 'History and fiction as modes of comprehension', *New Literary History*, 1, 514–58

Mink, Louis (1987) *Historical Understanding*. Ithaca: Cornell University Press

Mitchell, Timothy (1991) *Colonising Egypt*. Berkeley: University of California Press

Mitchell, Timothy (2002) 'Can the mosquito speak?' in Mitchell, *Rule of Experts: Egypt, Techno-Politics, Modernity*. Berkeley: University of California Press

Moore, Henrietta (1994) *A Passion for Difference: Essays in Anthropology and Gender*. Cambridge: Polity Press,

Morris, Meaghan (1993) 'Metamorphoses at Sydney Tower' in E. Carter, J. Donald and J. Squires eds *Space and Place: Theories of Identity and Location*. London: Lawrence and Wishart

Morris, R.J. (1979) *Class and Class Consciousness in the Industrial Revolution*. London: Macmillan

Morris, R.J. (1990) *Class, Sect and Party: The Making of the British Middle Class, 1820–50*. Manchester: Manchester University Press

Munslow, Alun (1997) *Deconstructing History*. London: Routledge

Munslow, Alun (2003) *The New History.* Harlow: Pearson Education

Namier, Lewis (1929) *The Structure of Politics at the Accession of George III.* London: Macmillan

Nandy, Ashis (1983) *The Intimate Enemy: Loss and Recovery of Self under Colonialism.* Delhi: Oxford University Press

Nead, Lynda (2000) *Victorian Babylon: People, Streets and Images in Nineteenth-Century London.* New Haven: Yale University Press

Newman, Simon (1997) *Parades and Politics of the Streets: Festive Culture in the Early Republic.* Philadelphia: University of Philadelphia Press

Niethammer, Lutz (1992) *Posthistoire: Has History Come to an End?* London: Verso

Nietzsche, Friedrich (1983 [1874]) 'On the uses and disadvantages of history for life' in Nietzsche, *Untimely Meditations,* trans. R.J. Hollingdale. Cambridge: Cambridge University Press

Nora, Pierre ed. (1996) *Realms of Memory, Vol. 1: Conflicts and Divisions,* trans. A. Goldhammer. New York: Columbia University Press

Nord, Deborah Epstein (1995) *Walking the Victorian Streets: Women, Representation and the City.* Ithaca: Cornell University Press

Novick, Peter (1988) *That Noble Dream: The Objectivity Question and the American Historical Profession.* Cambridge: Cambridge University Press

O'Brien, Patrick and Quinault, Roland (1993) *The Industrial Revolution and British Society.* Cambridge: Cambridge University Press

O'Hanlon, Rosalind (2000 [1988]) 'Recovering the subject: *Subaltern Studies* and histories of resistance in colonial south-east Asia' in V. Chaturvedi ed. *Mapping Subaltern Studies and the Postcolonial.* London: Verso

Ortner, Sherry (1995) 'Theory in anthropology since the sixties' in N. Dirks, G. Eley and S. Ortner eds *Culture/Power/History.* Princeton: Princeton University Press

Otter, Christopher (2002) 'Making liberalism durable: vision and civility in the late Victorian city', *Social History,* 27:1, pp. 1–15

Park, R., Burgess, E.W. and McKenzie, R.D. eds (1967) *The City.* Chicago: University of Chicago Press

Parry, Benita (1987) 'Problems in current theories of colonial discourse'. *Oxford Literary Review* (1 and 2), pp. 27–58

Parry, Benita (2002) 'Directions and dead ends in postcolonial studies' in D.T. Goldberg and A. Quayson eds *Relocating Postcolonialism*. Oxford: Blackwell

Pelling, Henry (1968) *Popular Politics in Late Victorian Britain*. London: Macmillan

Pollock, Griselda (1988) *Vision and Difference: Femininity, Feminism and Histories of Art*. London: Routledge

Poovey, Mary (1995) *Making a Social Body: British Cultural Formation 1830–1864*. Chicago: University of Chicago Press

Porter, Bernard (1975) *The Lion's Share: A Short History of British Imperialism*. London: Longman

Prakash, Gyan (2000a) 'Subaltern Studies as postcolonial criticism' in C. Hall ed. *Cultures of Empire*. Manchester: Manchester University Press

Prakash, Gyan (2000b) 'Writing post-Orientalist histories of the third world: perspectives from Indian historiography' in V. Chaturvedi ed. *Mapping Subaltern Studies and the Postcolonial*. London: Verso

Price, Richard (1972) *An Imperial War and the British Working Class*. London: Routledge and Kegan Paul

Prior, Nick (2002) *Museums and Modernity: Art Galleries and the Making of Modern Culture*. Oxford: Berg

Rabinow, Paul (1995) *French Modern: Norms and Forms of the Social Environment*. Chicago: University of Chicago Press

Rappaport, Erika (2000) *Shopping for Pleasure: Women in the Making of London's West End*. Princeton: Princeton University Press

Rappaport, Erika (2001) 'Travelling in the Lady's Guides London: consumption, modernity and the fin-de-siècle metropolis' in M. Daunton, and B. Rieger eds, *Meanings of Modernity*. Oxford: Berg

Reddy, William (2001) *The Navigation of Feeling: A Framework for the History of Emotions*. Cambridge: Cambridge University Press

Ricoeur, Paul (1965 [1955]) *History and Truth*, trans. C.A. Kelbley. Evanston: Northwestern University Press

Ricoeur, Paul (1984) *Time and Narrative, Volume One*, trans. K. McLaughlin and D. Pellauer. Chicago: University of Chicago Press

Ricoeur, Paul (1988) *Time and Narrative, Volume Three*, trans. K. Blamey and D. Pellauer. Chicago: University of Chicago Press

Riley, Denise (1988) *'Am I That Name?' Feminism and the Category of 'Women' in History*. Basingstoke: Macmillan

Rivière, Joan (1986 [1929]) 'Womanliness as a Masquerade' in V. Burgin, J. Donald and C. Kaplan, eds *Formations of Fantasy*. London: Methuen

Roberts, Geoffrey (2001) *The History and Narrative Reader*. London: Routledge

Rose, Nikolas (1999) *Powers of Freedom: Reframing Political Thought*. Cambridge: Cambridge University Press

Rowbotham, Sheila (1973) *Hidden from History: Three Hundred Years of Women's Oppression*. London: Pluto Press

Ryan, Mary (1997) *Civic Wars: Democracy and Public Life in the American City during the Nineteenth Century*. Berkeley: University of California Press

Said, Edward (1985a [1978]) *Orientalism*. Harmondsworth: Penguin

Said, Edward (1985b) 'Orientalism reconsidered' in F. Barker *et al.* eds *Europe and Its Others*, Vol. 1. Colchester: University of Essex

Said, Edward (1993) *Culture and Imperialism*. London: Chatto and Windus

Said, Edward (2002) 'In conversation with Neeli Bhattacharya, Suvir Kaul, and Ania Loomba' in D. Goldberg and A. Quayson eds *Relocating Postcolonialism*. Oxford: Blackwell

Samuel, Raphael (1998) *Island Stories: Theatres of Memory, Volume II*. London: Verso

Samuel, Raphael ed. (1981) *People's History and Socialist Theory*. London: Routledge and Kegan Paul

Saussure, Ferdinand de (1983) *Course in General Linguistics*, trans. R. Harris. London: Duckworth

Savage, Mike and Warde, Alan (1993) *Urban Sociology, Capitalism and Modernity*. Basingstoke: Macmillan

Schama, Simon (1991) *Dead Certainties (Unwarranted Speculations)*. London: Granta Books

Schiebinger, Lorna (1994) *Nature's Body: Sexual Politics and the Making of Modern Science*. London: Pandora

Schön, Donald (1983) *The Reflective Practitioner*. New York: Basic Books

Schorske, Carl (1980) *Fin-de-Siècle Vienna: Culture and Politics*. London: Weidenfeld and Nicholson

Scott, James C. (1990) *Domination and the Arts of Resistance: Hidden Transcripts*. New Haven: Yale University Press

Scott, Joan (1988) *Gender and the Politics of History*. New York: Columbia University Press

Scott, Joan (1996) *Only Paradoxes to Offer: French Feminists and the Rights of Man*. Cambridge, Mass.: Harvard University Press

Seal, Anil (1968) *The Emergence of Indian Nationalism: Competition and Collaboration in the Later Nineteenth Century*. Cambridge: Cambridge University Press

Seeley, J.R. (1883) *The Expansion of England*. London: Macmillan

Sennett, Richard (1976) *The Fall of Public Man*. New York: Knopf

Sennett, Richard (1994) *Flesh and Stone: The Body and the City in Western Civilisation*. London: Faber and Faber

Sewell, William (1999) 'The concept(s) of culture' in V. Bonnell and L. Hunt eds *Beyond the Cultural Turn*. Berkeley: University of California Press

Shoemaker, Robert (1998) *Gender in English Society 1650–1850. The Emergence of Separate Spheres?* Harlow: Longman

Simmel, Georg (1997 [1903]) 'The metropolis and mental life' in D. Frisby and M. Featherstone eds *Simmel on Culture*. London: Sage

Simms, Karl (2003) *Paul Ricoeur*. London: Routledge

Simons, Jon (1995) *Foucault and the Political*. London: Routledge

Sinha, Mrinalini (1995) *Colonial Masculinity: The 'Manly Englishman' and the 'Effeminate Bengali' in the Late Nineteenth Century*. Manchester: Manchester University Press

Sinha, Mrinalini (1998) 'Britain and the empire: towards a new agenda for imperial history', *Radical History Review*, 72, pp. 163–74

Smith, Anthony (2001) 'Nations and history' in M. Guiberneau and J. Hutchinson, eds *Understanding Nationalism*. Cambridge: Polity Press

Smith, Bonnie (2000) *The Gender of History: Men, Women and Historical Practice*. Cambridge, Mass.: Harvard University Press

Soffer, Reba (1994) *Discipline and Power: The University, History and the Making of an English Elite, 1870–1930*. Stanford: Stanford University Press

Somers, Margaret (1992) 'Narrativity, narrative identity and social action: rethinking English working-class formation', *Social Science History*, 16:4, pp. 591–630

Spiegel, Gabrielle (1997) *The Past as Text: The Theory and Practice of Medieval Historiography*. Baltimore: Johns Hopkins University Press

Spivak, Gayatri Chakravorty (1985) 'The Rani of Sirmur' in F. Barker *et al*. eds *Europe and Its Others*, Vol. 1. Colchester: University of Essex, pp. 128–51

Spivak, Gayatri Chakravorty (1993) 'Can the subaltern speak?' in P. Williams and L. Chisman eds *Colonial Discourse and Postcolonial Theory: A Reader*. Hemel Hempstead: Harvester Wheatsheaf

Spivak, Gayatri Chakravorty (1996 [1985]) 'Subaltern studies: deconstructing historiography' in D. Landry and G. Maclean eds *The Spivak Reader*. London: Routledge

Spivak, Gayatri Chakravorty (1999) *A Critique of Postcolonial Reason: Toward a History of the Vanishing Present*. Harvard: Harvard University Press

Stallybrass, Peter and White, Allon (1986) *The Politics and Poetics of Transgression*. London: Methuen

Stedman Jones, Gareth (1983) *Languages of Class: Studies in English Working-Class History 1832–1982*. Cambridge: Cambridge University Press

Stedman Jones, Gareth (1996) 'The determinist fix: some obstacles to the further development of the linguistic approach to history in the 1990s', *History Workshop Journal*, 42, pp. 19–36

Steedman, Carolyn (1995) *Strange Dislocations: Childhood and the Idea of Human Interiority 1780–1930*. London: Virago

Stern, Fritz (1970) *The Varieties of History: From Voltaire to the Present*. London: Macmillan

Stone, Lawrence (1981 [1979]) 'The revival of narrative' in Stone, *The Past and the Present*. London: Routledge and Kegan Paul

Stone, Lawrence (1991) 'History and postmodernism', *Past and Present*, 131, pp. 217–18

Sturrock, John (1993) *Structuralism*. London: Fontana

Sutcliffe, Anthony (1970) *The Autumn of Central Paris: The Defeat of Town Planning, 1850–1970*. London: Edward Arnold

Swingewood, Alan (1998) *Cultural Theory and the Problem of Modernity*. Basingstoke: Palgrave

Tagg, John (1988) *The Burden of Representation*. London: Macmillan

Taylor, Charles (1989) *Sources of the Self*. Cambridge: Cambridge University Press

Taylor, Miles (1997) 'The beginnings of modern British social history?', *History Workshop Journal*, 43, pp. 155–76

Tester, Keith ed. (1994) *The Flâneur*. London: Routledge

Thompson, E.P. (1966) 'History from below', *Times Literary Supplement*, 7 April, pp. 279–80

Thompson, E.P. (1967) 'Time, work discipline and industrial capitalism', *Past and Present*, 38, pp. 56–97

Thompson, E.P. (1968 [1963]) *The Making of the English Working Class*. Harmondsworth: Penguin

Thompson, E.P. (1978) *The Poverty of Theory*. London: Merlin

Thompson, E.P. (1993) *Customs in Common*. Harmondsworth: Penguin

Tiersten, Lisa (2001) *Marianne in the Market: Envisioning Consumer Society in Fin-de-Siècle France*. Berkeley: University of California Press

Tocqueville, Alexis de (1968 [1835]) *Journeys to England and Ireland*. New York: Anchor Books

Tosh, John (1999a) *A Man's Place: Masculinity and the Middle-Class Home in England*. New Haven: Yale University Press

Tosh, John (1999b) 'The old Adam and the new man: emerging themes in the history of English masculinities, 1750–1850' in T. Hitchcock and M. Cohen eds *English Masculinities 1660–1800*. Harlow: Longman

Tosh, John (2002) *The Pursuit of History*. London: Longman

Toulmin, Stephen (1992) *Cosmopolis: The Hidden Agenda of Modernity*. Chicago: University of Chicago Press

Trumbach, Randolph (1991) 'Sex, gender and sexual identity in modern culture: male sodomy and female prostitution in Enlightenment London', *Journal of the History of Sexuality* II:2, pp. 186–203

Vann, Richard T. (2000) 'Mr Dening's good language', *History and Theory*, 39:1, pp. 77–87

Vernon, James (1993) *Politics and the People: A Study in English Political Culture c.1815–1867*. Cambridge: Cambridge University Press

Vernon, James (1999) 'Thoughts on the present "crisis of history" in Britain', *Projects Archive. Continuous Discourse: History and its Postmodern Critics*, http://www.history.ac.uk/projects/discourse/ vernon.html

Vernon, James ed. (1996) *Re-reading the Constitution: New Narratives in the Political History of England's Long Nineteenth Century*. Cambridge: Cambridge University Press

Veyne, Paul (1984 [1972]) *Writing History*, trans. M. Moore-Rinvolucci. Middletown, Conn.: Wesleyan University Press

Vickery, Amanda (1993) 'Golden age to separate spheres? A review of the categories and chronology of English women's history', *Historical Journal*, 36:2, pp. 383–414

Vincent, Julien (2004) 'Bourdieu and the virtues of social history', *History Workshop Journal*, 58, pp. 129–48

Visram, Rozina (2002) *Asians in Britain*. London: Pluto Press

Wagner, Peter (2001) *Theorizing Modernity*. London: Sage

Wahrman, Dror (1995) *Imagining the Middle Class*. Cambridge: Cambridge University Press

Wahrman, Dror (2004) *The Making of the Modern Self: Identity and Culture in Eighteenth-Century England*. New Haven: Yale University Press

Walcott, Derek (1995) 'The muse of history' in B. Ashcroft, G. Griffith and H. Tiffin eds *The Postcolonial Studies Reader*. London: Routledge

Walkowitz, Daniel (1999) *Working With Class: Social Workers and the Politics of Middle-Class Identity*. Chapel Hill: University of North Carolina Press

Walkowitz, Judith (1992) *City of Dreadful Delight: Narratives of Sexual Danger in Late Victorian London*. London: Virago Press

Ward, Graham ed. (2000) *The Certeau Reader*. Oxford: Blackwell

Warner, Michael (1990) *The Letters of the Republic: Publication and the Public Sphere in Eighteenth-Century America*. Cambridge, Mass.: Harvard University Press

Warren, John (2003) 'The Rankean tradition in British historiography, 1840 to 1950' in S. Berger, H. Feldner and K. Passmore eds *Writing History*. London: Hodder Arnold

Weber, Max (1978) *Economy and Society*, eds Guenther Roth and Claus Wittich. Berkeley: University of California Press

Weeks, Jeffrey (1982) 'Foucault for historians', *History Workshop Journal*, 14, pp. 106–19

Weeks, Jeffrey (2000) *Making Sexual History*. Cambridge: Polity Press

Werbner, Richard and Ranger, Terence (1996) *Postcolonial Identities in Africa*. London: Zed Books

West, David (1997) *An Introduction to Continental Philosophy*. Cambridge: Polity Press

Westfall, R.S. (1993) *Never at Rest: A Biography of Isaac Newton*. Cambridge: Cambridge University Press

White, Hayden (1973) *Metahistory: The Historical Imagination in Nineteenth-Century Europe*. Baltimore: John Hopkins University Press

White, Hayden (1985) *Metahistory: The Historical Imagination in Nineteenth-Century Europe*. Baltimore: Johns Hopkins University Press

White, Hayden (1990 [1978]) *Tropics of Discourse: Essays in Cultural Criticism*. Baltimore: Johns Hopkins University Press

White, Hayden (1990 [1987]) *The Content of the Form: Narrative Discourse and Historical Representation*. Baltimore: Johns Hopkins University Press

White, Hayden (1990) 'The burden of history' in White, *Tropics of Discourse*. Baltimore: Johns Hopkins University Press

White, Hayden (1992) 'Historical emplotment and the problem of truth' in S. Friedlander ed. *Probing the Limits of Representation.* Cambridge, Mass.: Harvard University Press

White, Hayden (1999) 'Afterword' in V. Bonnell and L. Hunt eds *Beyond the Cultural Turn.* Berkeley: University of California Press

White, Hayden (2000) *Figural Realism.* Baltimore: Johns Hopkins University Press

Williams, Raymond (1958) *Culture and Society 1780–1950.* London: Chatto and Windus

Williams, Raymond (1976) *Keywords.* London: Fontana

Williams, Raymond (1977) *Marxism and Literature.* Oxford: Oxford University Press

Wilson, Edmund (1972 [1941]) *To the Finland Station.* London: Macmillan

Wilson, Elizabeth (1991) *The Sphinx in the City: Urban Life, the Control of Disorder, and Women.* Berkeley: University of California Press

Wilson, Kathleen (2003) *The Island Race: Englishness, Empire and Gender in the Eighteenth Century.* London: Routledge

Wilson, Kathleen ed. (2004) *A New Imperial History: Culture, Identity and Modernity in Britain and the Empire 1660–1840.* Cambridge: Cambridge University Press

Wolff, Janet (1990) 'The invisible *flâneuse*: women and the literature of modernity' in *Feminine Sentences: Essays on Women and Culture.* Berkeley: University of California Press

Young, Linda (2003) *Middle-Class Culture in the Nineteenth Century: America, Australia and Britain.* Basingstoke: Palgrave

Young, Robert (1990) *White Mythologies: History Writing and the West.* London: Routledge

Young, Robert (2001) *Postcolonialism: An Historical Introduction.* Oxford: Blackwell

Zedner, Lucia (1991) *Women, Crime and Custody in Victorian England.* Oxford: Oxford University Press

Index